A BOY'S DREAM COME TRUE, A MAN'S WORK MADE REAL, HUMAN LOVE FOR ANIMALS MADE UNFORGETTABLE

This is the story of a boy who saw his pet kitten die, and vowed never again to be so helpless to save an animal he loved.

This is the story of a young man struggling against all the odds to obtain the education he needed to follow his chosen profession.

This is the story of the dedicated veterinarian he became . . . of his world of triumph and tragedy, heartbreak and joy . . . and of the indelibly endearing creatures who share these shining pages with him . . .

"A book for anyone who loves animals . . . you may well wind up writing a letter of appreciation to the author"—*King Features Syndicate*

ANIMAL DOCTOR

Lucas Younker, D.V.M., and John J. Fried

A JOVE/HBJ BOOK

First Jove/HBJ edition published January 1978

Library of Congress Catalog Card Number: 76-15390

Printed in the United States of America
Photographs by John J. Fried

Jove/HBJ books are published by Jove Publications, Inc.
(Harcourt Brace Jovanovich)
757 Third Avenue, New York, N.Y. 10017

For all my friends who have encouraged and helped me, especially my family who made me what I am. For Lucy who saw me through the darkest days, and most of all for Sadie who sustains me.

I would like to thank my colleagues in the California, Southern California, and American Veterinary Medical Associations for their help and guidance throughout my career as a veterinarian.

PART ONE

Chapter One

When I screeched to a halt in front of my office, the Howards were waiting. They had called a few minutes before, scared because they had come home to find their pet basset hound behaving strangely. "We found him when we came home from Midnight Mass," Mr. Howard whispered to me in the silence of the deserted shopping plaza as I grappled with my keys. "I just can't imagine what has gotten into him."

The Howards trailed behind me as I hurriedly snapped on lights and prepared to examine the dog.

"We walked in and he was staggering all over the place," Mrs. Howard said, putting her purse down on the examining table. Like always, she was immaculately dressed, the very image of the proper young Orange County matron. "He was bumping into things, falling over . . ."

"Sounds to me as if he might have eaten something toxic," I said. "Do you keep any poisons around he might have gotten into?"

The Howards looked at each other for a moment, then both shook their heads. "No, nothing like that," Mrs. Howard said.

"Well, any sleeping pills he might have eaten?"

"Gosh, no. We haven't had any since the kids were born."

I examined the dog's eyes and listened to his chest. His breathing came in short, labored puffs. Howard looked at me anxiously. His well-tailored suit, already subjected to an evening in the pew, was beginning to show the stresses of the long night. His tie was open and askew. Weariness lined his face.

"Go on home," I told them. "There is nothing you can do

by hanging around here. I'll call you in the morning. Anyway, it looks to me like you got him here before things got out of hand. If we can figure out what's behind the problem and find the remedy, he should have a good chance. He's wobbly but he can stand and it looks like he recognizes you. It doesn't look all that serious."

They turned to go. "Doc, we'll stay up for a while," Howard said as they reached the front door. "Give us a call as soon as you know something. The kids are pretty worried."

Because the dog had been knocked out by *something* already, I gave him only a mild gas anesthetic and pumped out his stomach. Within a few minutes, the pan on the floor was filled. I looked closely at the contents—in particular at the massive amounts of green bits and pieces that looked like oregano—and reached for the telephone. Howard answered almost immediately.

"Mr. Howard, are you sure you don't have any drugs around?" I asked. "Anything like weed?"

"Weed?"

"Grass. Marijuana."

"Oh no, I'm sure he couldn't have . . ." The voice trailed off. "Hold on a second, will you?"

I winced as the sound of the telephone being dropped reverberated in my ear. The periodic bangs of cabinets being slammed shut reached me through the telephone. I could hear Howard pick up the telephone. "That son-of-a-bitch," he hissed. "He ate our whole stash. Two whole lids of grass."

I had to laugh to myself as I drove back home through the deserted streets. I never cared much about how my appearance—my long hair, beard, bright-colored shirts, and jeans—impressed people in this conservative southern California community. But, if I ever did have even the slightest apprehensions that I might be too "hip" for some of Orange County, those apprehensions were disappearing quickly. The secret hippies, I told myself, looking at the blinking Christmas decorations in the department store windows lining my route home, were being flushed out of their closets by their pets at an impressive rate. This Christmas Eve it had been the Howards. Last month it had been Eleanor Harding.

Eleanor Harding started to bring her cat to me soon

10

after I opened my practice. Unlike many of the other women who come into my office in the ultracasual dress of southern California—the outfit worn to that morning's tennis game, the shorts and halter thrown over the bikini for a quick time out from pool side to take the family dog in for the rabies shot, the loose slacks and blouse worn for puttering around the garden—Eleanor Harding always looked as if she had just come from a tea in the Cincinnati suburb in Kentucky, where I grew up. She was always very reserved when I treated her cat and, despite her several visits, I knew very little about her. Only that she was a legal secretary for a medium-sized law firm nearby.

Late in November, Eleanor had called one day to make an emergency appointment. "He's been acting crazy all morning," she said as she put the large wire cage in which she carried Sam on the examining table. "Just like that, see?" The cat was tearing around the cage, floor to wall, to ceiling, to wall, back to floor. It was like looking into a Bendix front-loading washer. Tom was running so fast around the cage, one could see nothing except a calico blur. Eleanor said nothing as I managed to stop the cat, take him out of the cage, and set him gently on the examining table. For a moment, Tom lay there quietly, staring intently at the wall in front of him. Suddenly, with a venomous hiss, he leaped high into the air, fur standing on end, claws extended. I just managed to get out of the way as the crazed cat propelled himself from the table in a frenzied attack at the wall. Tearing down the crayon paintings some of the children who come into my office have drawn for me, Tom crashed, slid to the floor, picked himself up, and began a frantic chase around the room. He scurried up and down walls, knocking instruments off the counter, overturning bottles once safe on their shelves. Eleanor retreated into one corner of the room, trying to make herself as small as possible. When Tom stopped for one brief moment, I grabbed him by the scruff of the neck and the hind legs, and quickly tossed him back into the cage.

"All right now," I said, trying to catch my breath and watching the cat resume his mad streak around the cage, "do you have any poisons or drugs around the house the cat might have gotten into?"

A puzzled frown crossed Eleanor's face. "Nooo, not that I can think of . . ." She stopped and then her face lit up with a gay smile. "Wait a minute. About two weeks ago we got hold of some 'sunshine.' But we cut the tab in half because it was too strong. Half of it popped off the table and into the carpet and I never did find it in all that shag. I guess the silly cat found it and ate it."

I listened to all this politely. "Sunshine?" I asked, feigning innocence "What the heck is sunshine?"

A blush spread over Eleanor's face and a quizzical look passed momentarily over her eyes as she stared at me. I could see her asking herself if she had misjudged me. "It's a kind of LSD—acid," she answered and looked at me anxiously. "Do you think he'll be all right?"

"I don't know," I said. "I've never seen a cat freaked out on acid before. I think they use Thorazine for people on bad trips and we can try it and see if it will work for him. Anyway, there is also the possibility that if he gets through this episode, he could have problems with hallucinations from time to time."

A week later, after steady doses of the tranquilizer, Tom finally came off his trip. But Eleanor tells me he is just not the same old cat.

When I slipped into the bedroom, I thought Sadie was asleep. "Service called," she mumbled out of the jumble of blond hair on the pillow without stirring a muscle. "Man called about having run over his dog after a Christmas party. He's bringing her into the office." I groaned, turned around, got back in the truck, and, for the third time in less than two hours, sped down Orange Grove Lane. The Christmas lights in the Montgomery Ward display windows blinked a cheerful welcome back through the palm trees to their sole companion during this long night.

I had known it would be like this the moment I had hung up after my conversation with Dave Kaplan a few weeks earlier. "Lucas," he had yelled out cheerfully over the telephone, "you and I have volunteered to work Christmas . . ."

"Wait, wait a minute," I interrupted. "Who volunteered for what? The only thing I've volunteered for is to take Sadie down to Mexico for that long weekend."

"Lucas, listen. You and I are taking emergency calls. Now come on. I've been doing it all by myself the last ten Christmases. I like doing it for our Christian brethren, but

12

now I have another Jewish boy down here and you're going to help me. So, starting at noon Christmas Eve, all calls get referred to us. You cover the northern half of the county, I'll take the southern half. If you have anything you can't handle by yourself just give me a call. I can be up there in twenty minutes. It won't be bad. You'll see."

Yes, it will, I had muttered to myself and now I was being proven right. It's a good thing, I told myself as I pulled back into the parking lot, that this job never seems like work to me.

The man huddled by the office door with a fluffy cream-colored dog cradled in his arms was not one of my own clients. "I, ah, ran over my dog," he told me nervously. "My vet's answering service referred me to you." He and his wife, he went on, had been to a party that had lasted well into the early hours. Although he had not been out-and-out drunk, he had been good and high. He had managed to drive the baby-sitter home. But when he returned, he had driven a bit farther up the driveway than usual. The slight bump he had felt underneath his wheels had been the family dog.

I examined the dog, which was in shock, while the man stood quietly by my side. I quickly gave an injection of Solu-Delta-Cortef and, through an intravenous drip, a blood extract to help her emerge from shock.

"It looks like her hind leg and her pelvis are broken," I said. "I'll have to take X rays to make sure. But the fractures are the least of her problems. Let's just hope there are no internal injuries like a ruptured spleen or a lacerated liver and that she's not bleeding internally."

Although I was upset myself, the look on his face softened me. He was ashen-faced, obviously tormented. He felt guilty enough as it was, I decided and, although I had been tempted, put aside the stern lecture that had been boiling up inside me as I worked on the dog.

"Go on home, Mr. Carlson. A lot of people do the same thing all year round when they are stone cold sober."

By the time I had finished taking and developing the X rays and had satisfied myself that the dog was out of shock and relatively stable, dawn of Christmas Day was beginning to shine through the big plate glass window into the office reception area. With visions, not of sugar plums, but of bacon, eggs, and toast dancing through my head, I made

13

a quick dash to the nearby twenty-four-hour coffee shop. The day's real work, I was sure, was still to come. With one hundred or more veterinarians out of reach while they were opening Christmas presents, trying on new slippers or preparing to take the kids up to Angeles Crest Highway in the mountains to try out their new sleds or over to one of the beaches to try out a new scuba-diving outfit, Kaplan and I were in for a good workout.

I was out in back cleaning out cages and checking on some of the animals that had come in the previous week when one of my own clients, Mrs. Lindstrom, came rushing in. "Oh, thank God, you're here, doctor," she cried. "Someone's shot Greta."

While Mrs. Lindstrom ran out to her car to get Greta, her Burmese cat, I hurriedly prepared the surgery room in case I had to operate. Greta's head was wrapped in a blood-soaked cloth. Only her snout and whiskers hung out. "What happened?" I asked as I gently cut the bandage away.

"I don't know," Mrs. Lindstrom answered. "She'd been gone for almost two days and when I went out this morning to get the paper before breakfast, I found her lying by the bushes, bleeding."

I shaved away some of the fur surrounding the site of the bleeding, and relaxed. "Mrs. Lindstrom, Greta hasn't been shot."

Relief swept across her face, then puzzlement. "But when I cleaned away the blood to put on the bandages I saw a big hole just like a bullet would make. How did she get a hole like that on the side of her face?"

"Fighting, probably," I answered. "When dogs fight, their teeth make slashing wounds and cause lacerations. But cats bite down and they make deep puncture wounds. The skin heals in a day or two, but the long canine teeth have left bacteria deep inside the tissue. An infection builds up at the bottom of the puncture and then after three or four days, as the bacteria multiply, it builds up into an abscess. Often, the skin becomes stretched so tight from the swelling that it actually dies in one small area and lets the pus drain out. Those were cat bites you were looking at, not gunshot wounds."

I drained the abscess, flushed it out with hydrogen peroxide and spread an antibiotic ointment over the area. To make absolutely sure the infection would clear, I gave the cat an injection of antibiotics, and gave Mrs. Lindstrom antibiotic tablets as well as an ointment to take home.

I handed the cat back to her. "Keep Greta inside a few days and out of reach of other cats. She'll live." Somehow, I was relieved that Greta hadn't actually been shot. I didn't want to think that someone out there had chosen Christmas Day to take a potshot at a cat. Not that any other day would have been any better, but after all, Christmas. . . .

My relief, however, was short-lived. Minutes after Mrs. Lindstrom had left, the answering service put through a call from a man in Buena Park. His pet dalmation, the man told me, an edge of hysteria in his voice, was falling over, turning blue, having periodic convulsions that were getting worse and worse. "You better get him in here," I told him. "It sounds as if the dog has eaten some kind of a poison. If you have any poisons around the house, better bring in the labels so I know what to treat him for."

Ten minutes later the dog was on the examining table. I knocked him out with pentobarbital so he wouldn't have any more seizures and then started to pump out his stomach.

"Doc, are you sure the dog's been poisoned?" There was more anger than apprehension in his voice.

"I'm fairly sure of it from the symptoms you described," I told him. "Looks like strychnine poisoning to me."

The man stood silently a moment, gazing down at his unconscious dog. "Well, we don't have any poisons around the house," he finally said. "It must have been that s.o.b. next door. He's been threatening to poison Spots since we got him this summer. He does it on Christmas Day. Can you image that, doc? Christmas Day!"

The day sped by. It had been busy, sometimes harrying, but nothing I could not handle. The clock on the wall said 8:30 and it began to look as if I would get through the day without a major disaster. For the second time that day I was to be proven wrong: A man suddenly stood in front of me with a big mixed-breed hound—Walker and Redbone, it looked like—in his arms. Behind the man stood his wife and three children. There was deep anguish in every face.

"It just started happening, doctor," the man started in without so much as an introduction. "He just started roll-

15

ing around the floor and whining, like he was in real pain. He got all bloated and started dripping saliva . . ." The voice trailed off. I suspected almost immediately what was wrong, but wanted to be sure.

"Did the dog eat Christmas dinner with you?" I asked.

"Yes, he sure did. He's such an old beggar. He likes the turkey and the dressing and just about everything else."

I gently felt the old dog's abdomen. "That probably did it."

"He isn't poisoned, is he, doc?" The man interrupted. "Are we . . ."

"No, it's not poisoning," I told him. "What happens often in these large breeds is that people give them a lot to eat, often at a holiday meal like Thanksgiving or Christmas. The dog then drinks a lot, lies down and starts exercising himself and rolling around. The stomach is so heavy with food that it actually twists around on itself."

I stopped for a moment because I didn't quite know how to tell them the dog would probably die because it had been seven hours since it first showed its symptoms and since it was already clearly in a state of septic shock.

I took the man and his wife aside. At the very least, I didn't want the children to hear me. "Seven hours is a long time to wait in a case like this," I told them. "I really don't think there is very much I can do. There is a very slight chance if we operate and straighten out the stomach. But the surgery is expensive and I couldn't guarantee it would save him."

"How much would it be, doc?"

"It could run between two hundred fifty and five hundred dollars."

The man winced and I could see that he was torn. They weren't my clients, but it was obvious to me that they were not rich people. The money for the operation would cut a deep gap into whatever budget they did have. "Can we go home and think about it?"

"Of course, but don't wait too long because we don't have that much time left."

Barely a half hour later they called and asked me to go ahead. I called Dave Kaplan and asked him to come up and help me do the surgery because I had never done a gastric torsion by myself and I felt I needed his expert help. He arrived before I had finished prepping the dog. The

16

animal was in such a fragile state that we didn't dare expose him to the rigors of a general anesthetic. Hoping that a local would do, we opened him and with some heroic manipulations straightened out his innards. We opened the stomach and emptied the contents—a good two gallons of turkey, dressing, vegetables, goodly amounts of his own dog food, and water.

The dog was in a coma for four days before he woke up. When the whole family came to pick him up and take him home a week later, it was Christmas all over again. There were handshakes from the father, a lot of kissing and hugging from the mother and three kids. Until they moved away from California about a year later, Mrs. Quarry brought a dozen fresh doughnuts to the office every Monday morning. From time to time a messenger would arrive with another present from them, sometimes a bottle of good wine, sometimes a set of fine wine glasses. There was, for the better part of a year, always something to show how grateful they were to have that old dog, a hound they had owned for more than thirteen years, still with them.

It was past eleven o'clock when I got home, close to twenty hours after I had first rushed out of a warm bed to get a dog off his accidental high. Rather than go back in the house right away, I wandered into the yard out in back of the house to check on Sean, our golden retriever, the two owls, the hawk in whom I was trying to implant an artificial elbow to replace the one shot off by hunters, the rabbit, and the half-dozen or so chickens that made their home among the vegetable plants and fruit trees.

The night was cool and moist. A light mist hung in the air. The neighborhood was even quieter than usual. I stopped in front of the aviary a friend and I had built for the hawk and watched the wild bird sit quietly on his perch. I thought back to a time twenty-five years earlier when a group of friends and I had skulked through a Cincinnati park, armed with homemade slingshots (made of dead trees branches and cut-up inner tubes) and bee-bees. Though none of us had ever hit any squirrels or birds with our crude weapons, we repeated the ritual constantly, pretending we were hunters in darkest Africa. But on this one Sunday, I took aim at a little bird sitting on a branch about ten feet away. I released the taut piece of rubber inner tube

17

and, much to my amazement, watched the bird topple to the ground.

I froze and hardly heard all the shouting and congratulating: Lucas, the kid who wasn't good at anything, who always was last or second from last to be picked for a team in the neighborhood's choose-up baseball games, had finally proven to be adept at something. Slowly, I walked over to the bird and picked it up. It was bleeding and, looking closer, I could see that I had hit the little creature right behind the eye. The bee-bee had shattered the skull and had penetrated the brain. I could feel myself shaking, watching the small brown-and-yellow body writhing in convulsions. Quickly, I twisted its neck to put it out of its suffering and bolted from the park. At home, I dug out my Boy Scout hatchet and hacked the slingshot to pieces. I was totally ashamed of what I had done—and now, twenty-five years later, whenever I think of the incident, I still shudder at the thought of what I had done.

I hadn't heard Sadie come out of the house and was startled when I felt her arms around me. "Listen, how about coming into the house now and giving your *shiksa* a break for Christmas?"

I put my arm around her and we walked slowly back to the house.

"Lucas, what were you thinking so seriously about?"

"Nothing much," I said, opening the door into the house. "Just that I am very glad that I am an animal doctor."

After all, I finished the thought to myself, for a long time it looked as if I would never make it.

Chapter Two

It was a clear, crispy Rocky Mountain day, exhilarating and exciting to a kid up from the flatlands of the Midwest. I had just unpacked my bags in the room assigned me for my freshmen year at Western University and, having found no roommate yet to meet, had wandered out to begin my exploration of the campus.

It didn't take me long to decide which way to go. Since childhood, when all my heroes had been radio and television cowboys, my first love had been horses—something, I am sure, my parents never fully understood. They accepted philosophically the continuous stream of stray dogs and cats I brought home to feed, the baby birds and baby squirrels which, rejected by their mothers, I tried to nurture to maturity. My mother even did most of the cleaning up after many of my pets and served as the midwife when puppies or kittens were born to one of my strays. But horses? Like the rest of the Jewish community, they thought that a fascination for horses was, like drinking, one of those inexplicable and peculiar gentile traits one was better off ignoring than trying to understand. Now, in the thin mountain air, the aroma of horses came cutting toward me. I followed the scent to the back of the dormitories and found myself looking at a bunch of cowboys and cowgirls practicing rodeo events. But, since the wooden-bench grandstand was empty, I decided that all the activity in front of me—one cowboy driving a few steers around one half of the corral, another boy practicing roping, a man bouncing on a bucking horse, and, off in the far corner of the corral, a group of cowgirls fooling around with a goat—had to be a rehearsal for the real thing to come.

Delighted, I wandered along the fence to the girls and their goat, which was tied to a fifteen- or twenty-foot rope tied to a stake driven into the ground. One girl leaped on her horse, rode off about twenty yards and then came thundering back at the little animal. In a flash she was off the horse, grabbed the scurrying goat, threw it on its back, and, in a blur of activity, tied three of its four feet together.

Her three companions yelped with delight, congratulating her smooth execution of the difficult trick. One—a slight girl who could not have, weighed more than one hundred pounds and was no more than five feet tall—took her turn to practice throwing and tying the goat. In a cloud of dust she pulled her horse to a sharp halt near the goat, jumped off her horse and grabbed the rope holding the goat. She made her way up the rope and tried to take hold of the goat in order to flank it. But, since she was not much heavier than the goat, she had neither the strength nor the leverage to throw the animal on its side.

The goat, by now caught up in the spirit of things, scurried about, taking advantage of every foot of freedom the long rope tied about its neck gave it, in the process dragging the girl around at will. Thick spurts of dust rose as the goat swiveled and turned, as the girl tried to dig her heels into the ground. The frenzied dance struck me as funny and I laughed uncontrollably. Suddenly, the cowgirl whirled, looked at me angrily and, her pigtails flapping, stalked toward me. With a snap of her arm, she flung her pigging string (the string used to tie the goat's legs) at my face. "If you think you can do better, dude," she snarled, "go ahead and try."

When I was fifteen years old, I had spent the summer on the Prairie Trek Expedition, camping out and working at a ranch in New Mexico. Although I had never participated in a rodeo, I had learned how to flank calves and hold them down while they were being branded. I grinned at her, took the pigging string and, taking hold of the rope, worked my way to the goat, which had stopped its scurring about to follow the new turn of events with some suspicion. When he saw me approach, he tried to bolt, but was a split second too late. When I flanked him, I lifted him into the air, and, in my excitement, flung him to the ground just a little bit too hard, knocking the wind out of him.

"Goddam it," one of the other girls yelled as I started to

20

tie the goat's leg. "Take it easy, that's an animal, you know."

"Darned right," another girl chimed in. "And we paid twenty bucks for it besides."

As I finished tying the goat, I turned to look triumphantly at the girl I had laughed at—but the smile of victory that was forming on my face quickly died: She was on her horse, barely ten feet away, coming at me at a dead run. In my involvement with the goat, I hadn't seen her prepare for her furious charge at me. I had no time to react and in a second the horse's chest hit me full force, sending me sprawling into the dirt. When I took my arms off my face, I saw her wheel her horse, turn back, and come to a stop almost directly over me. "How's that, you goddam little dude?"

Humiliated despite my impressive performance with the goat, I slunk away, laughter ringing in my ears, Sam's (the nickname I heard someone call out to my adversary) glare burning into my aching back. I didn't know how I would be able to show my face around there again.

The concern for my bruised ego soon diminished. As the pace of college life increased, as registration gave way to orientation and orientation finally to a crush of classes, I found myself edging my way back to the corral, searching for some moments of peace and sanity away from the business of getting an education. I hung around the corral so much that after a few weeks some of the cowboys even let me borrow their horses for rides.

Even Sam thawed and forgave me my trespass against her dignity. One day, about two weeks after our confrontation, she intercepted me on my way back to the dormitory after classes. Her long hair, for once, was out of the pigtails she habitually wore and hung loose to her shoulders, framing her cleanly scrubbed face. She was wearing a spotless—and tight—shirt and well-shrunk Levis. "Doin' anything about midnight?" she asked, looking up at me.

My heart began to pound. Barely a month into the adult life of college and my adolescent daydreams were about to materialize. I had nothing, I told her, trying to keep the calm in my voice, planned for that evening. "Good," she laughed, "come on along with us. We're going to exchange the goat."

"Exchange the goat?" I asked, puzzled by this disappointing turn in the conversation. "At midnight?"

"Yeah. That goat's gotten too used to gettin' thrown. Every time anyone even walks by it now, the damned thing flops on its back and sticks its legs up in the air. It's just no good for goat tying any more."

"Well, why don't you just take it back to the farmer where you bought it and ask him to exchange it?"

"We tried, but he wouldn't take it back. Said we'd have to buy a new one. We're not gonna spend another twenty bucks for a goat. We're just going to have to exchange it ourselves."

At a quarter to twelve that night, Sam, Annie, one of the other cowgirls, and one goat were waiting for me in a Ford Ranchero outside the dormitory. I jumped into the back and huddled as best I could against one of the sides. The farm was about ten miles out of town and it was going to be a cold ride in the late autumn air. Fifteen minutes later we rolled off the main highway and into a gravel section road. After a few minutes, Sam, who was also in the back, knocked on the cab's back window. "That's the house over there," she yelled as Annie slowed the Ranchero. "The goats are a bit farther on."

Annie doused the lights and we drove on in almost absolute darkness. Occasionally, Sam would shine a flashlight quickly toward the fields on our right. "Stop. Stop," she finally hissed in a loud whisper. "They're over there."

After the truck had stopped, we grabbed the goat and carefully lifted him over the fence. He took a momentary look around, spotted the herd and headed for his long-lost brothers and sisters. Sam, Annie and I ran to the group of goats, grabbed the first one we saw and dragged the bleating animal back to the Ranchero.

Twenty minutes after the literal kidnapping, we were in an all-night diner, shivering and huddled over hamburgers, coffee, and hot chocolate. For several minutes, as we tried to drive the chill out of our bones no one said a word. Then suddenly Sam began to chuckle, then giggle, and finally laugh. "Oh, God! I'd sure like to be there in the morning to see the look on that old boy's face when he comes out to look at his herd, walks by that critter, and sees it flip itself on its back and stick its legs up in the sky."

I had come to Western University because it was one of the few universities that had both a veterinary school and a college of engineering. I was not quite sure yet what kind of a career I would plan for myself. The childhood years during which I had spent every available moment and every spare ounce of energy on animals had whetted my appetite for veterinary medicine But I felt my father, who was a successful contractor in the Cincinnati area, wanted me to get a degree in engineering and join him in his business.

And, I had reasons of my own for keeping veterinary medicine at arm's length: I simply doubted that I was smart enough to be a veterinarian. To be a doctor—any kind of a doctor—I thought, you had to be perfect, you could never make mistakes. As an MD, you were given custody of people's lives. My grandfather had been a doctor, my uncle had been a doctor. All during my childhood I had heard their praises sung. Someone was always saying what a great physician Grandpa Weinberg had been, what a perceptive doctor Uncle Bert was. I just didn't think I was as smart as any of them.

I figured that if I failed in my efforts to be an engineer, it would prove to everyone that I was not cut out to be a contractor. Then I could take a shot at what I really wanted to be—an animal doctor.

I plunged into the world of slide rules, and courses like Drafting, Physics and Principles of Engineering I. But the struggle to maintain my interest in engineering grew harder and harder. I adopted a little black kitten and, despite regulations forbidding pets in the dormitory, kept her in my room and spent a good deal of time playing with her. I had located the veterinary school the day after I had arrived at the university and I began to hang around the veterinary building when I was not taking time to look in on the rodeo team. At the school's large animal clinics, I noticed that the juniors did not work on the animals themselves, but only helped the senior students by holding the animals brought in for treatment. To blend in better with my surroundings, and to get to participate in the work with the animals, I went out and bought green coveralls like all the juniors were wearing. That way I could be right in at the center of action but not do any damage. Mistaking me for a mere junior, no professor would be likely to ask me to do

23

anything (neither would the seniors—they knew what I was up to and played along). If I had a nine o'clock and an eleven o'clock class at the engineering school, I would spend the hour in between, not discussing logarithms with my fellow engineering students, but peering over the shoulder of a professor who, arm deep into a cow and spattered with a bit of dung, was demonstrating something or other about the animal's interior. Late in the afternoons, my engineering assignments quickly out of the way, I would find an hour or two before dinner to wander over to the veterinary school stalls to help brush down a horse or two.

Late one afternoon I left the veterinary school's large animal clinic where I had spent an exhausting but happy three hours cleaning out the stalls, picked up some kitty litter, and went back to the dormitory. When I opened the door to my room, my stomach lurched: Tiger, my little black cat, was lying on the floor, writhing and meowing weakly. I dropped my books and the grocery bag, picked up the cat, and ran across campus back to the veterinary school, hoping the clinic for animals there would still be open. The writhing and the convulsions intensified even as the senior veterinary student on duty was examining Tiger. She was so weak now she could just barely open her mouth in her attempts to cry. No sounds came out.

"You keep any poisons around your room, kid?" the student asked.

"No, nothing at all, just food for the cat," I answered, my voice quivering. "You think she's been poisoned?"

"Sure looks like it to me," the student answered brusquely. "You might as well leave her here because it won't last much longer anyway."

I left the clinic dazed. I was sad because I had lost a loved companion. Even more, I was plunged into a deep depression: I simply could not understand why anyone would want to poison—and I was convinced she had been poisoned deliberately—a small, harmless creature.

For days I talked to no one because I was afraid the lump in my throat would dissolve into a torrent of embarrassing tears. Since I usually said little or nothing in most of my classes, almost none of my teachers noticed the difference. Except for Dr. Corning, my English teacher, those who did notice my unusual silence did not care. From the beginning of the semester, Dr. Corning and I had carried

24

on a friendly duel and she seldom let a class pass without peppering me with questions or needling me about the "sophomoric" positions I took in class when we discussed the assigned novels or short stories. Somehow, I had learned that she too loved animals and often after class we would spend a few minutes chatting about pets. Now, in the aftermath of the killing, I made no effort to answer or parry back when she addressed me in class. Annoyed at my unresponsiveness, she walked to my chair. "Mr. Younker, if you are not interested in participating in this class," she barked at me, "you may leave." Without a word, I gathered up my books, and stomped out of the room, slamming the door viciously behind me.

After dinner that night, the telephone in my room rang. I answered it. It was Dr. Corning. "Something is wrong, Lucas," she said without ceremony. "Come on over to the house and let's talk about it."

By the time I arrived at her front door, I was shaking. She had barely let me in before I blurted out—for the first time since I had seen my cat writhing on the floor—the whole story. "I'm going to kill the son-of-a-bitch who did that," I sobbed to a finish. "I'm going to kill him."

Dr. Corning looked at me for a few moments in silence. "In the first place, Lucas, you don't know that someone poisoned her on purpose," she finally said, sliding to the edge of the couch and reaching across to me to take my hand. "Maybe the cat wandered into a chemistry major's room and got into a bottle of some chemicals he had there. And, even if someone was cruel enough to poison your cat on purpose, what good would it do to 'kill' him. If you were to hurt someone, you would never be admitted into veterinary school, would you?"

She managed to calm me down and, feeling somewhat better, I went back to the dormitory. Rationally, I knew she was right, that it would accomplish nothing to hurt the person who had poisoned my cat, and that I had best forget the whole matter.

My resolve to stay calm and rational disintegrated within the half hour. I was back at my desk, trying to concentrate on a drafting assignment when Jerry Malamud wandered into my room. Jerry was a sophomore who had come out from New York to study veterinary medicine. "Hey, Lucas, I'm sorry man," he said, walking over to me. "If I had

25

known it would upset you so much, I wouldn't have done it."

I felt myself getting dizzy. "You poisoned my cat?"

"Yeah," he said, trying to look embarrassed. "I didn't think you'd take it like that. I just wanted to joke around with you. But, hey, I'll get you another kitten. I——"

He never had a chance to finish the sentence. With a score of obscenities strung into an almost incomprehensible scream, I hit him in the face. He stumbled over a pair of shoes and fell to the floor, begging me not to hit him any more. I grabbed an old World War II navy frogman knife I kept on my bookshelf above my desk and leaped at the white-faced Malamud. While I waved my knife high above him, I punched him again and again with my free hand. He desperately tried to punch back, reach for the knife, and squeeze out from under me at the same time. I only wanted to scare him but neither he, nor the dormitory counselors who broke the door down in answer to his frenzied screams, could have known that. I felt some hands tear me off Malamud while others showered me with blows. I saw Malamud crawl away. Then everything went black.

As I slowly woke up, drifting in and out of the fog that surrounded me, I looked around. The curtain drawn about my bed, the small panel with a signaling button pinned to my pillowcase all told me that I was in a hospital. Painfully and with a sharp ringing in my ears, I sat up, then lowered myself to the floor. Although I felt groggy from the tranquilizer or sedative I assumed I had been given, I held the back of my hospital gown together and weaved out into the hall.

The hall clock said ten minutes past two. The single night nurse on duty looked up from the records in front of her. "What are you doing up?" she asked not unkindly. "Get back to bed."

I sat on the edge of the bed for a few minutes, waiting for my head to clear completely. When I felt sufficiently sure of myself, I rummaged around until I found my clothes in one of the closets in the room. I didn't need *all* my wits about me to know that I was in deep trouble. I had to get out of there and do some thinking before falling into the clutches of the administration—and perhaps the police.

Although I knew it was a bad ploy, I tried to walk casually past the nurse's station. The room windows were locked and the only other exits were at the other end of the hall. It didn't work. She called out and, when she saw that I had no intention of stopping, reached for the telephone. I bolted. By the time I reached the front entrance of the Student Health Center, I could see two of the campus policemen heading across the quadrangle. I scurried out the door, made it to a nearby tree and shinnied up into its branches. Forty-five minutes later, when they had grown tired of looking for me and I could see them heading back to their office, I shinnied back down, skulked to a phone booth and called Ed McGee

I had met McGee and his wife Janet in a small theater group I had joined. McGee, a graduate English student, was also a political activist. Through him I had come to learn that political thought could go beyond the Republican or Democratic party ideas I had listened to at the dinner table back home. Ed and Janet were part of a group called SIPP—Students for an Intelligent Public Policy. True to the group's acronym, those of us who belonged would gather every Sunday at the McGees' house, sip Ed's homemade beer and philosophize about politics.

In keeping with the campus activism already brewing in the early 1960's, we tried to do more than philosophize. Western University was a land-grant college and, like other similar institutions, maintained a compulsory Reserve Officer Training Corps. Compulsory ROTC, we at SIPP felt, was an unnecessary and undemocratic means of perpetuating the nation's militaristic adventures. Moreover, we felt, it forced students who did not agree with the nation's foreign policy or with its military adventures to join and aid the country's war efforts. Finally, research had shown us, the original land-grant legislation did not require agricultural schools to make ROTC compulsory. The legislation only required schools to make ROTC available. We wanted, therefore, to have ROTC put on a strictly voluntary basis.

In light of what was to come later in the 1960's when the Viet Nam war was in full flower and campuses across the nation were caught up in violent revolt, our campaign against ROTC was downright gentlemanly. We wrote letters to the school paper, pointing out the inconsistencies and injustices of compulsory ROTC. (I wrote one of these

27

letters but, discretion at the time being the better part of my activism, signed it with a pseudonym. I was proud enough of that letter, however, to send it home when it was printed. My father's answer was unexpected. If he were the president of Western University, he thundered, I would be on the next train home to Cincinnati.) In response to our letters, the newspaper invited us to write three guest editorials to outline our opposition to compulsory ROTC. Our editorials were to alernate with three editorials in which the administration would present its point of view.

The debate was more or less a standoff until the last editorial—ours—was printed. In preparing for the "debate" we had written—never really expecting an answer—the Department of Defense, asking if in the Secretary of Defense's opinion compulsory ROTC were necessary for the national security. Much to our surprise, we not only got an answer, but an answer that could be used to support our point of view. "In the opinion of this office," the letter stated, "compulsory ROTC is not necessary to the national security."

With a good deal of glee, we read the administration's last editorial: Essentially Dr. Simpson, the administration's spokesman, wrote that he agreed with many of our points. But unfortunately, he added, the Department of Defense felt compulsory ROTC was necessary if the nation were to stay militarily strong and prepared to defend its security. Were the Defense Department to amend its position, he finished, the administration would do everything within its power to convince the Board of Agriculture (which ran Western) that ROTC be placed on a voluntary basis.

We, of course, were ready for him, and in our third and final editorial published the letter we had received from Washington. We were delighted because we had won the agrument—it was all we had really expected to accomplish. We were stunned when President Simpson actually went before the Board of Agriculture and successfully argued for the abolishment of compulsory ROTC. It was a triumph of reason—perhaps one of the last of its kind on any campus for the rest of the decade.

A few minutes after I had made the phone call, Ed pulled up to the telephone booth in his Anglia delivery truck. I ran out of a darkened doorway where I had taken refuge and leaped head first into the truck. I was glad that I had him to count on. Not only was Ed a loyal friend, but a powerful one: He had been a professional boxer as well as a Ranger in World War II. And, most of all, he looked mean. The hard edge in his eyes was enough to make most people back away from any confrontation with him. He was, in short, a good man to have in my corner.

For the next few days I hid out in a small cabin Ed kept as a retreat in the nearby mountains. Ed, who had stayed up there with me (ostensibly to do some work in quiet on his master's thesis), said little for the first two days. Late in the afternoon of the third day, he joined me on the cabin's back porch where I was fishing the trout-laden stream that ran right past the back door.

"Don't you think it's about time you went down and straightened things out?" he asked, watching me take a trashing foot-long trout off my hook and throw it back in the crystalline water. "As much as you are welcome to stay here as long as you like, you can't hide forever."

"I know," I answered, looking out at the line floating again in the water. "I walked down to the store this morning and called Dr. Corning because I knew she would be worried. She said she would set up a meeting with the dean of students tomorrow. I guess I'll go in. There is not much else I can do."

"I guss not," Ed said. He paused for a moment. "Why are you throwing all those fish back in the water, Lucas?"

I felt a little foolish. "I can't stand the thought of killing them," I admitted. "So, I just throw them back in."

"Well, why don't I kill the next couple you catch? We can have a good trout dinner and then head back to school."

Dr Corning, who had asked to be present at the meeting, smiled weakly at me when Ed and I were escorted into the dean's office. The meeting was short, to say the least, grim, and to the point. The dean did most of the talking. "Your behavior, Mr. Younker," he said, his words falling on my ears like pelting hail, "was inexcusable even in light of Mr. Malamud's deplorable act. Mr. Malamud, you should know, has been asked to withdraw from Western immediately. Dr. Corning has intervened in your behalf, and if you

29

agree, you will see one of our staff psychiatrists every week for the rest of the school year. But it might be better if, come next fall, you were to enroll in another college. Do I make myself clear?"

Chapter Three

In the days and weeks that followed Tiger's death, my attack on Malamud and my confrontation with the Dean of Students, I found myself spending less and less time in the engineering school and more and more time at the large animal clinic at the school of veterinary medicine. I enjoyed spending as much time as possible with the animals the school kept for instruction purposes or the animals the townspeople and local ranchers brought for treatment in the school's outpatient clinic. I couldn't get enough of watching the veterinary students develop and perfect the skills they needed to help animals.

As time went on and I was able to look back on what had happened with some objectivity, it occurred to me that rage at Malamud was not the exclusive reason for my attack on him. To a great extent, I had been beside myself with anger that anyone—particularly a preveterinary student who had already committed himself to a lifetime of work with animals—could purposely poison a small helpless creature. But what had really driven me to strike out at the hapless student had been a deep-seated frustration with my own helplessness, my inability to help an animal that had been dying right before my eyes.

It was not the first time I had suffered this type of frustration. As a child growing up near Cincinnati, I had been the kid on the block to whom all the other children brought orphaned animals—kittens that had wandered away from their mothers, dogs that had gotten lost, baby birds that had fallen out of their nests or which had broken wings in the first attempts to fly, little squirrels, which, for some inexplicable reason, had been pushed out of their nests by their mothers. I spent many sleepless nights with these creatures, trying to nurture them back to health. Knowing nothing about the food requirements of baby animals, I tried to force bits of milk-soaked bread down their small throats (birds, baby squirrels and kittens alike, even though their nutritional requirements varied widely) in the vain hope the food would give them the strength to live through the night. Knowing nothing about broken wings or legs, internal injuries or unseen hemorrhaging, I made ineffective splints for broken bones and clumsy bandages for those wounds that I could see. Largely, my efforts were ineffectual. Slowly, as I and a friend from up the street (a girl who also loved animals) held one funeral after another, the ample backyard behind my house was overrun with the markings of the dozens of small graves I had dug for my unfortunate "patients."

Tiger's death, then, revived all these old frustrations. But I suspect it may also have helped crystallize my desire to be an animal doctor. Others, I told myself, could build their dams and their parking structures. I was going to be an animal doctor and for once have the power to do something to help animals in distress. That fall I enrolled in Midwestern University's agricultural program, the required prerequisite for admission to the school of veterinary medicine.

With fervent zeal—I was now in the mainstream leading to a degree in veterinary medicine, not just a wistful hanger-on—I plunged in among all the boys and girls from midwestern and southern farms to study the ins and outs of animal husbandry, genetics of livestock breeding, endocrinology, dairy husbandry, swine production and other related subjects. Now I was not brushing a steer or a horse to help someone else out or to entertain myself, but to learn something specific about the animal.

The only course to which my love of living things did not extend was a course in bee-keeping. I had always been afraid of insects. However, a teacher I had grown to like and respect taught a course in bee-keeping. What a fine opportunity, I told myself, to learn about bees and perhaps to get over my irrational fear.

The professor's lectures were a delight. But the laboratory sessions, that part of the course I thought would force me to handle bees, thereby freeing me of my antibug feelings, were a disaster. I was terrified every time I had to put on my gloves, my hood and my coat to work in the bee-hives. Unlike the teacher and many of the other students who just matter-of-factly worked with the bees, I would smoke the hell out of the hive to tranquilize the bees before I ventured in among them.

My Waterloo was the final exam. "For the final," Dr. Paine announced toward the end of the semester, "I am going to take a queen out of the hive. The rest of the hive will follow her to the branch where I put her. You will be tested on your ability to recapture the swarm and return it to the hive."

I froze with fear but steeled myself for the ordeal. Two weeks later, on a Friday morning at ten-thirty, I walked into the laboratory for the final. The room, except for the teacher who was puttering with some of the tools we had used during the semester, was empty. "Where is every-body?" I asked. "Are they already outside?" Dr. Paine glanced up at me, a look of pity for my stupidity on his face. "Younker, the final was yesterday, Thursday." I had been so frightened by the prospect of handling a whole swarm of loose bees that I had subconsciously put the exam ahead twenty-four hours. Dr. Paine refused to take a swarm out especially for me so that I could make up the final and gave me an F for the laboratory segment of the course. Luckily, I had an A for the lecture part and aver-aged out my grade to a passing C. I still don't really like insects.

With my academic attention focused entirely on animals, my spare energies were now turning toward the political activism to which I had been introduced at Western. In the state where I was now going to school, the issue of the hour was desegregation.

The home town of Midwestern University is lovely, but along with some of the charm of the old South came some of its vicissitudes, not the least of which was the enduring conviction that segregation—enthusiastically practiced in the town's restaurants and bowling alleys—was here to stay. The Confederate flag flew proudly in the town, pro-claiming haughtily the inviolability of the South's coveted way of life.

In time, as the racism found in some of the spots around town became more and more offensive to me, I gravitated toward the Congress of Racial Equality (CORE). CORE at the time was a loosely knit organization. Each chapter in the national network was allowed to set its own policies and its own methods of fighting segregation. In a way this made sense since racial problems varied from locality to locality. But I was, nevertheless, a bit wary about this method of organization. I felt that if some hotheads in the New York chapter of CORE felt that a good antisegregation ploy was something inane like running through a supermarket to fill scores of shopping carts with groceries and then to leave them standing in the aisles, I did not want to be held responsible for their actions if I told someone I was a member of CORE. Still, I joined the Midwestern University chapter. It had a good reputation for being reasonable in its objectives and methods. Furthermore, it had a faculty adviser who didn't let the chapter go off half-cocked and who kept it from flying off the handle (of course, his activities in CORE later cost him tenure at the university).

Our policy, first and foremost, was to negotiate. Four of us, two blacks and two whites, for example, once called on the owner of a small snack shop near the campus. We spent more than three hours with the man, drinking his coffee, trying to bring him around while he nervously looked out the big store-front window to see if anyone could spot the two blacks in his little place. Cajoling, philosophizing, appealing to his better instincts as a human being had gotten us nowhere. "Look," Bob Andrews, one of the white guys, finally said. "Why don't you just try it for two weeks."

"I can't do that," the man, a short, balding man with the look of someone who had squinted too long through the smoke of a greasy grill, said. "It would hurt my business. I already told you, I ain't got nothing against nigras or anything like that but it's going to hurt my business. My white customers won't stand for it."

"It won't hurt to try," Andrews cut in, sensing a weakening in the opposition. "Just two weeks. Let's look at your books and see what your take was the last two weeks. Then, we'll look in two weeks and if your business has slipped, we'll just forget the whole thing."

The man stared at Andrews as if he were completely out of his mind. "I'm not gonna let you go through my books!"

Andrews had brought off a classical bargaining maneuver. He had made two requests—one for the man to open his place to blacks and for him to open his books to us—hoping the man would respond negatively to just one. Naturally, the man refused to open his books for inspection. But in the process of answering negatively to one request, he made it seem (involuntarily, of course) that at least he would consider the other. Andrews jumped right into the hole he had opened in the man's defenses.

"All right, then," Andrews countered. "We'll take your word for how your business runs during the two weeks you'll serve Negro customers."

The man heaved a sigh and gave in. "All right, all right, I'll try it. But just two weeks, understand? An' if I start losing business, I put the word out that it was all a mistake. I ain't going out of business after fifteen years because of a couple of hungry nigras."

That shot out of the way, we shook hands all around and parted company. The man, of course, had no way of knowing that he could not win the test period. In anticipation of our final argument, we had already recruited, as we had done often before, a platoon of our white friends to patronize the man's place as soon as we announced that we had come to an understanding with him. For the next two weeks, the poor man was worn to a frazzle trying to keep up with the upswing in his business. I don't know whether the truth eventually dawned on him or not, but it didn't really matter. Whatever else he was, he was a man who kept his word and, since his business had obviously not suffered, he kept the snack shop open to blacks. Most of his regular white customers, he learned, didn't give a damn anyway whether there were blacks at the next table or not.

Not all the segregationists were that easy to crack. For months we carried on a running discussion with Giorgio Conti. Conti, a short, fat and swarthy man, had come to the United States from his native Italy about fifteen years earlier and had settled near Midwestern University's campus. In quick order he had opened two movie theaters and two restaurants. He was, in short, an American success story. But, if we thought that the availability of opportunity that he had found in this country would make him sympathetic to the needs of others, we soon found that we were mistaken. Conti would have no part of American blacks on any of his premises (I say American blacks because for some strange reason he would serve black African students if they showed proof they were not Americans!).

"Look-a here," he yelled at us in what turned out to be our last attempt at peaceful negotiations, "when I a-come to this country fifteen years ago, they treat-a me like a shit. They call-a me Dago. They call-a me Wop. I no like-a that. But I can do nothing.

"But now is-a different. I am-a big man. I own-a this theater and one across town. I own-a two restaurants. I own-a the whole thing and if I want to call-a nigger a nigger, I can. Cause I am-a an American!"

I could not believe what I had heard. "You mean you studied to be an American citizen, you passed your citizenship exam and after all that you think that one of the privileges of citizenship is to call someone a nigger and keep them out of your places. That's what being an American means to you?"

Conti tried to set his flabby jaw. "Thass-a-right. This is-a free country. Now get-a the hell out of here and don't-a come back."

We did, of course, come back. En masse. We held several nonviolent sit-ins at his various places. Eventually, when he saw we weren't going to stay away and that the sit-ins were disrupting his businesses more than a handful of black customers ever would, he gave in. Not graciously. But he gave in.

Largely because of my activities in CORE, I was pretty much the loner in agricultural school—not many of the students had much use, as one whispered to me one day, for a "nigger lovin' Jew."

But, until they fell victims to the passions swirling about the movement toward integration, I did have Ed McGee and Jeannie Willis. Ed, my friend from Western, had found a job teaching in a small black college about thirty miles from where I lived. Jeannie and I had met in the very unromantic surroundings of Animal Husbandry I.

Animal Husbandry I was one of those courses that made my preveterinary school education particularly exciting. As an optional part of the course, each student could borrow an animal—a cow, a pig, a steer—from the school. The student could then, for additional credit, groom and prepare the animal for show later in the year. This might have been routine for the farm kids in the class who had already spent most of their lives taking care of animals in this way. For me, it was sheer, unalloyed joy. No matter what happened in the course of the day, I could look forward to an hour or two in the beef barn (where most of the animals were kept) brushing and pampering my black heifer. At the beginning of the semester, I could also look forward to the beef-barn sessions because I could exchange flirting glances with Jeannie. Flirting with her was not all that easy, however. Not that she was not receptive. But Jeannie was a petite girl and the magnificent Hereford steer she was preparing to show was much bigger than she was. When she moved over to work on the other side of the animal, I could just barely manage to see the crown of her blond head peeking over the steer's back. In time, we began to date. Then, Animal Husbandry I became an absolute pleasure because after brushing and currying our animals, we could disappear into the hay loft for an hour or two. Sometimes we would spend part of the time discussing how we could steal Jeannie's steer which, much to her despair, was destined for the slaughterhouse at the end of the semester. (When I had chosen an animal to care for, I had deliberately chosen a heifer because I knew she would not be sent to slaughter.)

When Jeannie and I wanted to get away from school, we would spend time either on a farm belonging to Eddie Smith, one of the men who cared for the agriculture school's animals, or on the old, broken-down farm Ed McGee had bought himself.

To me, the visits to these farms were a special treat because as a city boy I had always tried to spend as much time as possible on farms around Cincinnati.

The summer I had once spent on Lem Hannaby's farm had been particularly memorable because it was the summer I had brought a pig home to keep as a pet. One day Lem and I had been out checking on the sows farrowing out in the woods. Just as we were about to return to the farmhouse for breakfast, we heard one of the sows making an incredible racket. We ran toward the direction of the squeals and grunts and saw the sow chasing a fox that was carrying off one of her babies.

The fox, intimidated by the angry sow, dropped the little

piglet. We ran over and examined the little animal. Its small body was covered with lacerations and both of its front legs were broken. Lem picked up a rock and prepared to smash its skull to put it out of its misery.

"Wait!" I yelled. "Don't kill it!"

Lem put down the rock and squinted at me. "You gonna take care of it?"

I nodded a relieved yes.

"Well, all right. You can feed her with some of the sow milk replacer yonder."

(That conversation took place in July and by then I knew about "yonder." But when I had first arrived at the farm, I spent a lot of time searching all over the farm, trying to figure out which "yonder" he was talking about.)

"Yonder where?" I asked.

"Yonder! Yonder to the barn!"

I took note of the sow milk replacer supply and found some popsickle sticks to use as splints on the piglet's broken legs. For several days, Lem's wife, Bess, and I alternated getting up every two hours at night to feed the pig. (Bess was a nice lady. Once—I don't know how—we got on the subject of her unshaven legs. I asked her why she never shaved them. " 'Cause Lem don't like whiskery legs," she told me. It took me a while to figure that one out as well.)

When I was fairly sure that the piglet would survive, I christened her Amy, after one of my girl friends. I also wrote my parents to tell them about the piglet and the way I had saved her life.

A few weeks later, as the summer was drawing to a close, I called home. After a few minutes of chitchat, I broached the question. "Can I bring Amy home?"

There was a momentary silence on the other end of the phone. "Amy? Who's Amy? What happened this summer? Did you get some girl in trouble?"

"No, ma! Amy is my pig! I wrote you about her."

Mom was so relieved that I was not bringing some barefoot and pregnant country girl home that she, without really thinking, gave me permission to bring Amy home. Thus, when Lem drove me home at summer's end, a look of complete mystification crossed mom's face when I got out of Lem's old truck with Amy.

"A pig! Who said you could bring a pig home?" Mom sputtered.

"You did. Don't you remember when I called?" I protested.

Mother began to say something, but Dad broke in. "Let him keep the pig. We can build a pen for her out by the cottage where we keep the garden tools."

Amy—for a while—enjoyed a good life at our home. Mom found that Amy liked pancakes for breakfast and got in the habit of preparing them for her every morning. Even on rainy days, my mother, still in her nightgown, one hand clutching an umbrella, would make her way to the pen, a plate of steaming pancakes and crispy bacon ready for Amy.

Sometimes, Mom's catering to Amy was inadvertent. Early in the fall my parents had planned a gala party. Mother had ordered chrysanthemums (by the truckload) to decorate the backyard. Without realizing what she was doing, sometime during the afternoon, Mom let Amy out of her pen. While my mother was in the house looking after other matters, Amy made short work of the potted flowers. As if that were not enough, giving lie to the myth that pigs can't swim, she jumped into the lily pond that graced our backyard and ate all the water lily flowers. Amy, now sated, suddenly found herself in trouble. Although she had gotten into the pond, she could not get out. Mom, alerted by her desperate squeals, ran out to rescue her. Only when Amy was out of the pond, dried and safely wrapped in a Saks Fifth Avenue towel, did Mom look around and see what she had done. I still don't know what kept Mom from throwing her back into the water.

I made myself scarce for the rest of the day—not just because of what Amy had done, but because I did not want to go to the party. But when I got home at midnight, I was faced by a surrealistic scene. It was foggy and the garden lights were casting a soft glow through the mist. My mother, in a formal dress, was holding a five-iron and swinging at an imaginary ball. Two golf pros, both of them wavering slightly, were heatedly arguing about a cure for her imaginary slice. Across the yard, Mr. Seidenbaum was sitting cross-legged on the slates lining the edge of the lily pond, a bottle of expensive Scotch in one hand, a champagne glass in the other. There was a platter of small ham

39

sandwiches on Jewish rye at his knees. A very drunk Amy was standing in front of him, alternately munching on a sandwich and taking sips of Scotch from the champagne glass.

Amy's good life in our house came to an end when she got out of the yard and rutted a long furror across a neighbor's lawn. I had to take her back to Lem's and leave her to a very mundane life.

Late in the afternoon one day, I went to visit Jeannie at her dormitory. I was tense and nervous because it had been a difficult day. CORE was beginning to change and the first signs of strain between the black and white members had begun to emerge. Joe Davis, a strident, militant black who also had a penchant for seeing his picture in the paper and his name in print, had recently been elected president of the chapter. His election was a distinct sign of changes to come: He had never tried to hide his animosity toward the white members of CORE.

That afternoon, during an innocent discussion over strategy for an upcoming bargaining session with another restaurant owner, Davis began to bait the whites at the meeting with his "you're-just-doing-this-because-you-feel-guilty" routine.

"Davis, lay off," I finally told him. "What do you care why we do this. It's the right thing to do and that's all that matters. And I don't have anything to feel guilty about. I have never mistreated a black person in my life."

"Maybe you didn't. But your grandpappy did. He ran the slave boats."

I got up to leave because I could feel my temper slipping. "Davis, you are a crock of shit. My grandfather spent most of his life trying to avoid getting killed by the czar's cossacks who didn't like the fact that he was Jewish," I snarled at him, the words now pouring out of me. "Let me tell you something else, you don't goddam impress me with that oppression number either. My people have been oppressed for five thousand years and that's about four thousand, five hundred years longer than your people. If you want to talk about oppression, friend, talk to a Jew!" And with that I left to see Jeannie.

The dormitory lounge, as usual, was crowded. Despite the long walk, I was still upset over my debate with Davis

40

and wanted to be alone with her. "Come on," I told her when she came down the stairs to greet me. "Let's get out of here."

"I can't, Lucas, it's almost time for dinner," she answered. "Besides, the wind's blowing and it will mess my hair."

I gritted my teeth and grabbed her by the wrist. "Come on!" I repeated, pulling her toward the door. "I don't want to stay in here. Never mind your hair. I'll buy you your goddam dinner. Let's go."

About a week later I left my last class at the agriculture school. But instead of making my usual stop at the beef barn to work on my heifer, I hurried over to the office of the Dean of Students. I had grown weary of living in the university's institutional dormitory and wanted his permission to live in a room or in an apartment by myself. (Those were the days in which students were still considered wards of the university and needed special dispensation to live "off campus.") When I announced my name to the dean's secretary, she looked at me coldly and, without a word, ushered me into the man's office.

Dean Walden gave me a withering look. A shiver worked its way down my spine. What, I wondered, was going on here?

"Well," Dean Walden finally said. "You certainly got here fast enough, Mr. Younker. I presume you got my letter. What do you have to say in defense of yourself?"

I was completely puzzled. "Sir? I haven't received a letter from you. I came here to get permission to get my own apartment next semester."

Dean Walden laughed and reached for a file laying on the left side of his desk. "Your own apartment? Mr. Younker, you'll be lucky to still be here next semester, much less have your own apartment."

Walden fished through the file and pulled out a letter. He found a pair of glasses on his desk, adjusted them and began to read. "Dear Mr. Younker," he read. "It has come to our attention that on the afternoon of May 28, you were seen striking one of the women students during an argument, repeatedly striking her in the face and about the arms. Upon receipt of this letter, you will immediately present yourself to the office of the Dean of Students for appropriate disciplinary action. Yours truly, etc., etc." He put down the letter. "What do you have to say for yourself, young man?"

I was completely baffled. I started to stammer something but suddenly remembered the incident with Jeannie at the dormitory the week before. How in the world did that innocent little squabble turn into a reported beating?

I told Dean Walden the story but could see that he did not believe me. "If this person I supposedly beat up so bad would say that nothing of the sort happened, would you believe her?"

Dean Walden smiled at me. "Younker, don't try to bluff your way out of this. Do you seriously think that this young woman would testify in your behalf after what you did to her?"

"You just give me a few minutes," I answered and walked out of the room. I found the nearest phone booth and called Jeannie. I hadn't seen her in almost ten days—since the incident at the dorm—because that same day we decided to stay away from each other until finals were over, so we could study. She had no idea what I was talking about and fifteen minutes later met me at the dean's office.

Dean Walden read her the letter, outlining the alleged brutality with which I had treated her. "Dean Walden," she told him when he had finished. "None of those things happened. We were talking at the dorm. Lucas wanted to go outside. I didn't. He grabbed me by the wrist and sort of pulled me out. But nothing else."

Dean Walden looked intently at Jeannie. "Honey," he said, his voice suddenly soft. "Don't worry. You just tell the truth. We won't let him hurt you."

I almost flew across the room. "Listen, you son-of-a-bitch," I yelled at him, leaning across his paper-laden desk. "You can't talk to her like that. She is not lying."

Jeannie jumped out of her chair and pulled me away from him. Dean Walden, unruffled, opened a desk drawer and pulled out a piece of paper. "All right," he said, handing the paper over to me. "If you will just sign this, we'll call an end to the whole matter."

I read the paper: In it I agreed to seek psychiatric care and to "behave like a gentleman at all times while at the university."

I flung the paper back on the desk and grabbed for the

telephone. The dean caught my hand and made me drop the receiver. "Who the hell do you think you're going to call?"

"First, I am going to call my father. Then I'm calling my friends Joe Jacobson and Tony Hennessey." Dean Walden regarded me carefully for a moment, trying to decide what to do. I might have been bluffing, but then, he couldn't take a chance. Joe Jacobson and Tony Hennessey were both high officials in the state Democratic party—and here the Democratic party controlled both the legislature and the governor's chair, the school's prime sources of money.

"Okay, let's talk about this," he said finally. "Don't sign the paper, but at least agree to go to the mental hygiene clinic once a week."

I was adamant. I would accept no punishment, no matter how trivial. I was not about to admit in any way guilt for something I had not done. Jeannie interceded. "Can I talk to him alone for a minute, dean?"

She pulled me out into the hall. Facing her alone, I could see that she was terrified. "Lucas, just sign that damned thing and let's get out of here."

"I don't see why I should sign anything, Jeannie," I countered. "I didn't do anything."

"Lucas, don't you see what's going on," she implored. "It's some kind of a frame, Lucas. They probably thought I'd testify against you because they thought we had broken up since you hadn't been to the dorm in a while and they thought they could do anything they wanted. This guy is just looking for any excuse to throw you out. If you don't sign that paper or agree to go to the clinic, he will, too. You know his reputation. He's thrown out a lot of people for a lot less than refusing to see a shrink one hour a week."

I was trying to think. "You think it's a frame? Because of CORE?"

"What do you think?" she asked impatiently. "Of course it is. I've been telling you not to get involved in that stuff if you want to get into vet school."

"I'm not signing anything," I insisted. "It's a matter of principle."

"Bullshit." An angry scowl crossed Jeannie's face. "You'll just get them mad at you for something else and the next time around they'll really be able to nail you. Jaywalking. Getting me back to the dorm five minutes past curfew. Anything. You're not all that clean you know."

We went back in, I told him I would go see the counselor at the mental health clinic and walked out.

As I slowly made my way to my dormitory after dropping Jeannie off at hers, I could see that she had been right. Most of us active in campus affairs were convinced that the administration had a list of activists—particularly the integrationists—and that the school's officials were always on the lookout for an excuse, valid or not, to throw one of us out. Every once in a while they succeeded. One of the early CORE members, Norman Montgomery, was one of the first black guys to get into the law school. Despite the strain his studies and his position in the law school imposed on him, he stayed active in the chapter. In his last year of law school, the police raided his white girlfriend's apartment. There they "found" a pound of marijuana hidden behind some books. Although he protested bitterly that it was not his grass—we all believed him because Montgomery, in all the years we had known him, had never smoked dope—the girl maintained that it was. He was summarily dismissed from the school and was not allowed to take his final examination. At the subsequent trial, the girl—who had obviously been coerced to testify against him or go to jail herself—repeated her story to the jury. The jury did not believe her and acquitted Norman. But despite his vindication, he was not allowed to return to law school.

I had never expected the same thing to happen to me. I was just a foot soldier in the movement, not a leader whose removal would hamper the cause's progress. Nevertheless, it was reasonable to assume that someone familiar with the administration's policy—in all probability the dormitory house mother—had seen the confrontation between Jeannie and me and, with some embellishment, had reported it to the Dean of Students. They all assumed, of course, that Jeannie was still mad at me and that she would simply refuse to testify in my behalf. They even thought that with some luck she might actually back up the charges trumped up against me. I could not believe the way in which they had planned their scenario down to the minutest detail: Even if they could not make the charges stick (if, for example, Jeannie did refuse to take their side or in case I could dredge up another witness to the scene), they would still be able to get to me. They probably believed I was a radical because I was just a mixed up kid looking for a niche in the world. A little counseling would help me find my place in the establishment. I had acceded to their scheme in the same spirit. If they think that I am in CORE because I'm crazy, I said to myself, and if this will get them off my back, fine, I'll go to see their damned counselor. Even that part of their little plan, however, did not work out. My counselor turned out to be a Palestinian Arab with whom I got along very well and who didn't try to talk me out of my commitment to desegregation.

While acceding to the request to see the therapist did relieve me of further administration pressure, Jeannie did not fare well in the aftermath of the affair. Her loyalty to me was even more offensive to the administration than my own activities. In a way, they could understand me. I was just one of those "outside" agitators, an urban guerrilla who really didn't understand the social structure of the more rural South. But Jeannie was a daughter of the Confederacy, a girl who should have known and been true to all of its traditions. At the end of the school year she received word that she had not "received a satisfactory grade in physical education." She would not be allowed to repeat the course, she was told, and despite her otherwise fine academic record, was flunked out of school.

Chapter Four

Although it was ten in the morning, the day was already hot. The day's morning workouts had already been held and now two water trucks, one slightly behind and to the right of the other one, were lazily working their way around the track, gamely trying to settle the thick dust the horses had kicked up. A few jockeys, stable hands, and trainers stood in the alleyways formed by the long eaves slanting from the roofs of the old green and white barns. But, except for the occasional word or phrase that floated away from the small groups, all was quiet and would stay quiet until the evening's competition began.

It was a racetrack, just across the state line and the Ohio River. I barely listened as the trainer who had hired me to groom and walk horses showed me around. Grooms normally don't hot-walk horses (walk with them after their races to cool them down), but I was hired to do both jobs because the track was shorthanded. For the moment I knew all I wanted to know: For the better part of the summer I would be away from school, CORE, integration. There would be just me and the horses.

A fly buzzed into my hair and I raised my arm to flick it away. My hand never reached my head. A powerful set of teeth clamped down around my wrist. As the dull pain spread quickly through me, I felt myself lifted off my feet, dangled in the air for a second or two and then dropped roughly back to the ground. "You just met Uncle Horace, a son of Count Fleet," the trainer managed to tell me between whoops of laughter as I picked myself up. "That's a helluva racehorse, but crazy. Real crazy. Loves to try and hurt people whenever he can."

I turned around slowly and came face to face with Uncle

Horace, a magnificent, sleek, black six-year-old with a distinctly mischievous glint in his eyes. "It's good you two have been introduced," the trainer said. "Uncle Horace is going to be one of your string."

The days flew by, a swirl of rubbing horses, mucking stalls or sometimes hot-walking horses. During the brief spells of free time I was able to squeeze out, I learned to gallop horses. My teachers were Quincy, a short exercise boy who was too big (and much too black) to be a jockey but who could gallop a horse around the track without spilling a drop from the brimful shot glass of whiskey he would carry in one hand, and Buckwheat, another black exercise boy who was about six three and who weighed ninety pounds after a big lunch. When we had a moment, they would scare up three horses, mount me on one and, taking positions to either side of me, guide me out onto the track. At a signal we'd be off, tearing down the track: The ebony versions of Mutt and Jeff at my sides, I desperately trying to maintain my half-standing position on a thundering horse trained to do nothing but run like hell.

Soon, I even came to an understanding with Uncle Horace. As long as I kept my eyes on him, he would not try to bite me, kick me, or press me up against the sides of the stall with his one-thousand-plus bulk until I could no longer breathe. But, if I ever took my eyes off him, even for a split second, I was considered fair game for all his nasty tricks. I learned to clean and work in every nook, cranny, corner, and crevice of his stall almost by feel. I never, never, from the moment I threw the bolt on the door to enter the stall, lost eye contact with Uncle Horace.

As hard as I tried, however, I couldn't stay out of trouble with my fellow human beings. A few weeks after I had begun work at the track, another hot-walker, a black who had never talked to me, bumped into me as I was hot-walking Uncle Horace in the alleyway that ran around the barn. He did not bother to excuse himself, but I dismissed the incident and went about my business. But the next day, and for the next four or five days, the same thing happened. It could not have been accidental because there was plenty of room in which to walk around the barn without bumping into anyone. Moreover, the black hot-walker never bumped into me when he had a horse in hand, when it might have been his horse pushing him into me. It only happened after he had put his horse away and I was still walking mine.

He was obviously looking for a confrontation for some reason, and I decided to oblige him, if only to get him off my back. The next day when I had to hot-walk Uncle Horace after his workout, I took along a shank that had an eighteen-inch brass chain on it. I doubled the chain over on itself and wrapped the leather part of the shank around my hand. I laid the chain over my right shoulder and went on my walk. A few minutes later, the black put away his horse and came sauntering up the alleyway. Just as he was veering toward me, I lashed out with my chain. I was hoping that at the very least I would knock him off his feet. But the blow was badly aimed and it only skirted his shoulder and neck. Instantly he was on me, showering me with blows. Uncle Horace bolted and I found myself in a hell of a fight. Yells of "loose horse, loose horse," rang in my ears as I tried hard to ward off my opponent's blows and land some of my own. Much to my relief, someone jumped in and separated us. One of the other hot-walkers caught Uncle Horace and brought him back to me. I took the lead shank and, with the black's obscenities and threats bouncing off my back, went on to try to complete my walk around the barn.

I was still breathing hard by the time I reached the other side of the long barn (Uncle Horace must have been wondering if he would have to hot-walk me for a while). I slowed my pace and took deep breaths to control the shaking in my legs and to slow down my heart before it pounded its way out of my chest. I had almost managed to calm myself down when I noticed the spread black boots planted in front of me. I slowly looked up to see who was blocking my route down the alleyway. Before me stood a black man who was all of six feet eight inches tall. He probably weighed three hundred pounds and not one ounce of that bulk was fat. He wore tight Levis and a tight T-shirt and every fiber in both pieces of clothing was hard-pressed not to break into a thousand shreds under the power of the rippling muscles beneath them. One of his hands rested on his hips. The other held (and dwarfed) a large pitchfork. His face was set in a hard glare.

The look on his face told me that he had heard about the fight on the other side of the barn. I'm dead, I whispered to myself. This guy is probably the friend or (even worse) the brother of the hot-walker I tried to hit with the chain.

"Where you stay at, boy?" he rumbled at me. I was so sure that I was about to have hell beaten out of me that I let the question fly by me. I was only interested in figuring out how I could position Uncle Horace between us and how I could get the horse to deliver himself of one of his justifiably famous kicks should the giant make any kind of a move toward me.

"Ah said, where you stay at, boy? Kentucky?"

"Yes," I stammered."

"Ah figgered that," he said, now shaking his head. "You real brave messing with a Muslim, boy."

"A Muslim?" I echoed.

"Thass right, boy. Let me tell you, you in big trouble." I looked at him. Was he one of them, I asked.

"Sheeet, no" he answered, disgust spreading over his face. "Them mothers is crazy. Ah ain't no motherfuckin' Muslim." He stopped for a moment, pity evident in his eyes. "But, boy, you sure in trouble."

Now, of course, I was really worried. If the hot-walker were indeed a Black Muslim, I was a marked man. In those days, the group had a vicious reputation. The "white-eyed" devil was their enemy and they were sworn to his destruction. "If he is a Black Muslim," I asked suspiciously, "how come he's working for a white man?"

"'Cause he only an apprentice, or something like that," he answered. "But that ain't gonna help you. His friends still going to be lookin' for you. Ah tell you what, boy. When you get off work, if they waitin' for you, you just come get Youngblood. Ah'll see if I can help you out."

It was late—close to midnight—when I finally finished up my work. I cleaned up, double-checked the doors on the stalls and, passing the security guard at the gate, strolled slowly toward my car. Luckily, I was only five or ten feet from the gate when I saw them: Three young black men sitting on the hood of the car. In the style of the Black Muslims, they were dressed in white shirts, thin ties and trim three-button suits. I suddenly remembered Youngblood's warning and did a sharp about-face as if I had forgotten something inside. I scurried around the darkened barns looking for Youngblood, desperately hoping he had not gone home. I found him in one of the tack rooms (where the saddles and bridles are stored) cleaning himself up. "I better go talk to them boys," he said when I told him of the group waiting for me.

I trailed after Youngblood, but only as far as the gate. Even his bulk wouldn't be enough if they had guns. Because of my position, I couldn't hear what was being said. But I could see a lot of arms waving, fingers pointing, and heads bobbing. From time to time one of the Muslims would angrily kick the ground or slam a fist down on the hood of my car. After a few minutes, it came to an abrupt end. Youngblood turned and walked back. The Muslims looked at his receding back for a moment, then walked away, obviously in a huff.

Youngblood found me next to the guard (who had early on assumed the studied look of a man who didn't want any part of something he did not understand).

"Them boys won't bother you no more," Youngblood said. "But Ah don't trust them motherfuckers. Tell you what, boy. Tonight Ah'll follow you to the bridge. For a while, Ah'll meet you there in the morning and then follow you back at night until them boys cool down some." I nodded. At that point, I would have left the country if he had suggested it.

We walked in silence to our cars. Before we got in for our ride to the bridge, I screwed up the courage to ask him what had transpired in the heated parking lot conversation. "Ah told them they best leave you alone," he said. "They say they gonna kill you for messin' with one of the brothers. Ah told them if they mess *with you*, they likely to get their own selves killed too."

I looked at Youngblood, my eyes filled (I hoped) with gratitude. "You told them you'd kill them yourself if they hurt me?"

"No, man, Ah didn't say that," he answered, scorn dripping from every word. "Ah told them that your momma was ——'s girl friend." He mentioned the name of an infamous Cincinnati gangster. "Ah told them if they messed with you, —— would put out a contract for 'em. Even the Muslims scared of —— and his boys."

I tried to speak but no words would come out of my mouth. I swallowed. "Youngblood," I finally sputtered. "Are you crazy, man? What happens if they check."

"Don't be dumb, boy. They won't check. Who gonna be

51

dumb enough to go up to—— and ask, 'hey, man, is it true so-and-so's momma is your girlfriend?' Everybody know he a crazy son-of-a-bitch. He likely to have someone hit jest for askin'. Don't worry yourself about it. Nobody be fool enough to ask."

As we headed toward the bridge, I spent more time staring into the rear view mirror to make sure Youngblood was behind me than on the dark road ahead of me. If not exactly overjoyed at the predicament I found myself in, I was at least happy that, once again, I had managed to stumble upon a guardian angel to protect me in my hour of need.

Somehow, it had always been like that. When I and all my friends were ready to start junior high school, we were all slated to attend a school notorious for the hoods who bided their time there until they were old enough to legally drop out of school. As a result, most of my friends and acquaintances were packed off to private school. Not me. When I begged my father to enroll me in a nice private school, he would have none of it. "There are all sorts of people in the world, Lucas," he lectured me. "You had better get used to getting along with all of them. You are not going to be able to do that going to a private school with a bunch of kids who are just like you."

On the first day of school, a greaser spotted me playing on the bleachers in the school playground. He walked toward me, pushed a pencil in my face and growled that I had better "push the pencil around the track with your big Jew nose." I refused. He proceeded to push me down from the bleachers and punch me until he tired of his sport.

There were many days when I returned home with dirty and torn clothes and a faceful of bumps, lumps, and cuts. At first, when my parents asked me about my appearance, I mumbled that I had gotten hurt at football. I was too proud to tell them what had happened. But, when it became obvious to me that I would probably not survive the school year, I broke down and told them the truth. I hoped my father would see the light and finally enroll me in a private school. Instead, he made a few phone calls to friends of his in the police department and managed to enroll me in the police academy's judo class.

Judo, I was to find out, is just fine if you are expert enough at it to finish off your opponent in a few quick strokes or if you are faster than he is so you can run like hell after you have thrown him at the beginning of the attack. When one of the school bullies pounced on me, however, I was only able to throw him to the ground once, maybe twice, before I tired. Not only was I basically weak but I was also slow on my feet. The upshot of the whole thing was that after I had done my little judo tricks, my opponent would get up, run after me, catch me, and, goaded on by hurt pride, beat me to a pulp.

One day one bully—he weighed about two hundred pounds—pounced on me and started to work me over. He got me down on the paved part of the playground and methodically began to beat my head against a sewer cover. I was vainly trying to struggle back when another hood, one I knew to be a member of one of the local gangs, came over, pulled him off me, and mercilessly beat *him* bloody.

My savior's name was Harold. Everybody in school knew him, by reputation if not by sight. He was eighteen at the time and still in the eighth grade. He was determined, even though he could never pass math, to be the first in his family to graduate from junior high school. Harold pulled me to my feet. "Kid," he said, wiping his ham-sized hands on his Levis and then taking a pack of Camels out from under one sleeve of the white T-shirt he was wearing. "We seen you fightin'. We like you on account you fight back. But don't worry about these punks no more. We're gonna take care of you. From now on you meet me after school at the flagpole if you want a ride home. Me and my friends, we'll take care of you."

And they sure did. Every day Harold and his buddies (some of whom were still in school, some of whom merely hung around there looking for a little action from the thirteen- or fourteen-year-old girls) would be waiting by the flagpole of the school, straddling their rumbling motorcycles. I would stroll out (I didn't have to dash out of the school and run home like a scared rabbit any more), jump on the seat behind Harold, and we'd be off in a roar. I spent the rest of the year unharmed.

In the days that followed my fight with the Black Muslim, the tension within me slowly ebbed. The hostile hotwalker cast me suspicious looks from time to time, but otherwise stayed out of my way. Youngblood, true to his word, gave me escort service to and from the bridge until he thought it safe for me to resume my commuting by myself.

Curiously, my relations with the blacks at the track seemed to be more relaxed after my confrontation with the Black Muslim. I had gotten along with Quincy and Buckwheat and some of the others, but I think that they nevertheless regarded me a bit suspiciously. They might have thought my espousal of civil rights to be more studied than natural. The fact that I had not hesitated to take on and fight someone who was black must have convinced them that I was not a phony liberal who went out of his way to be nice to people just because they were black.

Not that my efforts in behalf of civil rights at the track had been strenuous. Quite the opposite. Because I was still tired from the struggles at school, I didn't talk very much to anyone—black or white—about segregation, integration or anything touching on black-white relationships. My one and only involvement in a civil rights question at the track was indirect, certainly inadvertent.

Almost everything involving employees at the track was segregated. Not by law, but by custom. The cafeteria, for example, was divided into two sections by a long rail. The larger section, with its greater selection of small and individual tables, was reserved for the whites. The smaller section was left to the blacks. Since there were many blacks working at the track, the black section was always crowded.

When I came into the cafeteria on that particular day, Quincy, Buckwheat, and Youngblood were eating at one table. I took my tray, picked up some food and walked over to join them. They all looked at me a little bit quizzically. "Say, man," Quincy said. "You ain't supposed to be over here. You gonna start some trouble."

"I'm not starting anything," I answered. "I can sit wherever I want. This isn't Mississippi." And with that, sat down. Nothing more was said about where I should or should not eat and we spent the rest of our lunch hour talking shop.

The next day the cafeteria was in an uproar when I walked in to have lunch. There were blacks sitting all over the place—not just in the Jim Crow section, but at different tables in the white section as well. A few whites were standing around with their trays, not quite sure of what they should do. Some whites had gathered at tables off in one corner of their old section. Others, through with lunch, were standing at the railing, glaring. A whispering hubbub permeated the room and tension hung heavy in the air. Immediately I realized that Youngblood, Quincy, and Buckwheat had taken to heart my casual remark about Mississippi and had organized this impromptu desegregation of the cafeteria.

Youngblood, his tray buried under the customary tonnage of food he ate for lunch, was just coming to the end of the cafeteria line when I walked in. The cafeteria manager, a diminutive man, was waiting for him, assuming that Youngblood was the leader of this rebellion. "Now look-a here," the little man, an ex-jockey, said, trying to maintain some authority in his voice while craning his neck to talk to the big black man. "You colored folk have to sit over there. This here part is just for the whites."

Youngblood slammed his tray down on the rail, sending food flying in every direction. The cafeteria manager took a step back as Youngblood stooped a bit to talk to him. "Listen, motherfucker," he said in a cold and slow tone of voice, "this here ain't Mississippi. Ah'll sit where Ah want to sit."

The manager glared at Youngblood and scurried back to his office. He must have telephoned the Highway Patrol because within two or three minutes two patrol cars came screaming up to the cafeteria door. Four officers, billy clubs and guns at the ready, came rushing in, obviously expecting a full-blown interracial war. "That's the man," the manager yelled, pointing at Youngblood and running up to the officers who had come to a standstill. "That's the man who started this here riot."

The officer in charge looked around at the "riot," a bunch of men standing and sitting around just glaring at each other, and approached Youngblood.

"What's going on here?" he asked.

"This manager says Ah have to sit over there cause of Ah'm colored," Youngblood answered, "Ah told him this here ain't Mississippi and segregation is against the law anyhow."

The trooper turned to look at the manager. "He's right, you know," he said, snapping shut the safety strap on the revolver he had replaced in his holster. "They can sit any-where they want to and you can't do a thing about it."

"But——" the manager started to protest.

The trooper stared hard at him. "It's a federal law, fella. Forget about it."

No one ever said anything to me about the incident, which, as far as I was concerned, was just as well. Not that the confrontation in the cafeteria proved to be a landmark stride toward desegregation: Within a few weeks every-thing was back to normal. The whites were back on their side of the railing. The blacks sat again on theirs.

For the better part of a month it looked as if I could put the Black Muslims completely out of my mind. But then, one night toward the end of the summer, they once again loomed large on my horizons.

It was almost one o'clock in the morning and George, a black groom at the track who often rode back across the river with me, and I were deep in the Cincinnati ghetto heading for a Chinese restaurant. Half a block from the restaurant, my car began to overheat. I pulled over, and looked under the hood. The fan belt had snapped. "Well, let's worry about this later," I told George. "Let's go eat first."

Mrs. Chin—a black woman who had married a Chinese man and had kept the restaurant open after he had been murdered in a robbery attempt—showed us to a table in the back near the kitchen. Half an hour later just as Mrs. Chin was bringing us our chop suey, I looked up and my heart came to a stop. Four black Muslims were walking into the restaurant. Mrs. Chin and George, aware of my sudden silence, looked up too. "Shit," said George, Mrs. Chin, and I in unison.

"C'mon," she whispered. "I'll let you out through the kitchen door."

George and I crouched down and tiptoed out of the din-ing room. We ran through the kitchen and dashed to the car. We were almost in the car when we remembered the fan belt.

"Hey, man," George finally said after a long period of panic-stricken silence. "You got an air conditioner on this car. Let's take one of the belts off and try to use it for a fan belt."

As I started to work on the air-conditioner belt, the

Muslims walked out of the restaurant. "George," I said, nudging him in the ribs. "They spotted us."

George and I slowly backed toward the trunk of the car. I took out the tire iron and gave it to George. I found two tire chains and grabbed one. "Ah, sheeet," George said, "this ain't gonna work, man. There're two of us and four of them and every one of them's probably got a piece. Stay here; I'll go talk to them."

George strode over, trying very hard to be cool. Once again there were pointing fingers, gesticulating hands, and bobbing, angry heads. But five minutes later, the Muslims and George shook hands and the group split up. George, beads of sweat glistening on his face, came back to the car. "It's all right, man," he whispered, letting a slight tremor punctuate his voice. "Let's fix the car and get outa here."

Since we both had to be back at the track in less than four hours, we decided to return there rather than go home. "Let's sleep in an empty stall," I told George. "I have my mother's laundry in the car. We can wrap some sheets around us and just sack out on the straw."

The sunlight filtering into the stall and the smell of fresh coffee brought me out of my exhausted sleep. I wound myself out of the sheet and staggered out into the warm early morning sunlight. I said a cheery hello to the other grooms but received no answer. George came stumbling out of the stall. A finer instinct for these things must have told him something was amiss.

"What's happening, man?" he asked.

"Damned if I know. I'm getting the silent treatment."

George went off to do his work. I was about to go on my way when a hand fastened itself around my upper arm. I turned around to see the track's emeritus groom, old Harry, glaring at me through beady little eyes. "I just can't believe you, boy," he said. "I just can't believe you. Ain't it bad enough you eat with them and I told you about drivin' them around in your automobile. But goddam it, boy, when you start sleeping with niggers, that's it. We're done with you, boy."

"That's a fifteen-foot stall," I protested. "There was room in there for two people. Where was he going to sleep if I took the stall? Where would I sleep, if he took it. It was the only place left."

"If'n that was the only place left, you shoulda gotten it,

boy. You're white." Harry's voice dripped contempt. "You know somethin', boy? You are about the most ignorant goddam white person I ever did meet. Maybe you are a nigger, like everyone says you are."

Later I ran into George. "Hey, by the way, what did you tell those Muslims last night?"

"I told them they shouldn't mess you," he answered, a wide grin on his face.

"Jesus, George. You didn't tell them my mother was ——'s girl-friend like Youngblood did, did you?"

George quickened his pace and pulled away from the spot where I had momentarily stopped. "No, man, I didn't tell them nothin' like that," he called back. "I told them to leave you alone 'cause you was all right. You so dark skinned from the sun, I told them you only looked white, 'cause you had processed hair. I figured you could pass."

Chapter Five

The bald man—the one sitting between the other two interviewers—tried to smile encouragingly at me as I settled into the deep lounge chair provided for those of us who had come to be interviewed for admission to the veterinary school.

"Well, now, Mr. Younker," he said, the smile never leaving his face. "The first person we interviewed tonight was a girl. The second was a nigra. And now we are talking to you, a Jew. If you were on this committee, what would you think of that?"

I was baffled. I couldn't quite see where his question was meant to take us. "The girl I didn't see," I answered, sensing anger well up in me but unable to repress it. "I wouldn't have noticed Johnson was black unless someone mentioned it to me. And, as far as me being a Jew, what makes you think I am?"

The smile evaporated. "Well, now," he said, glancing down at the copy of my application in front of him. "From your name. Younker is a Jewish name, isn't it?"

"As a matter of fact," I told him, shifting uneasily in the depths of my chair, "the name happens to be German. My mother is Jewish and because of that I am Jewish. But my father is not." (He actually is, but I wanted to make them squirm.)

The smile crept back, first to the corner of his mouth, then over his face. "Well, now, Mr. Younker, I hope you were not offended. I don't have anything against girls, nigras or Jews, of course. It was just that I wanted to give you an example of how far we had progressed."

There was a momentary silence. The committee member to the smiler's left cleared his throat. He was the man who

59

had come out into the hall to get me. "Mr. Younker, I noticed that when I came out you were reading a book."

Thank God, I said to myself, now we are off on the right track. He noticed that even in what could have been an idle moment I had taken care to make good use of my time. "Yes sir," I answered strongly, "I was reading *An Essay on Morals* by Philip Wylie."

"And just what do you think of Mr. Wylie?"

Without so much as a deep breath I launched into a ten-minute discourse singing Wylie's praises as a writer and social philosopher. I smiled at the end, proud of my incisive analysis.

My questioner leaned forward on the table, putting his weight on his arms, which were folded in front of him. "I'll tell you one thing, Mr. Younker," he said. "I wouldn't read anything that dumb son-of-a-bitch wrote."

I didn't know if I was expected to press the conversation. I did. "If you don't mind my asking, sir," I said, trying to be friendly. "What don't you like about him?"

The man stared at me for a moment or two, then leaned back in his chair. "You know what canals are, Mr. Younker? Kids drown in canals. When I lived in Florida, we had a big campaign in our neighborhood to fence in some canals. That dumb son-of-a-bitch told someone that if kids don't learn how to swim, they ought to drown. Anyone who advocates drowning kids is a dumb son-of-a-bitch in my book!"

From then on the interview went downhill. I was asked three or four more perfunctory questions and was dismissed. I slunk back to the student union to meet Elizabeth, a girl I was dating, and to drown my sorrows in a cup of coffee.

Elizabeth listened to my tale of woe in silence. To her, it was an old story. "Maybe you still have a shot," she said sardonically. "At least you weren't a black Jewish girl trying to get in."

I groaned. "I hate to make this night a total washout for you," she added, "but I might as well tell you now. We can't go to the dance together Saturday night. I suggested it to the guys and they hit the roof."

I shrugged. I wasn't really surprised. "I can't say I blame them. Why should the black queen of a black fraternity bring a honkie to her coronation ball?"

Jim Stevenson, on the prowl looking for me to find out about my interview, came over for a quick cup of coffee. It cheered me up a great deal to see Jim walk over so casually. Jim, a farm boy from a small hamlet near the Missouri-Arkansas border, had, disdaining the wrath of our fellow "aggies," befriended me early in the school year. Why he would choose me as his closest friend was not quite clear to me at the time, especially when, in light of my activities in CORE, he had once proudly told me that "no nigger ever spent the night in my county except one and he did it hanging from a tree." When I first had begun dating Elizabeth, Jim went to great pains to avoid us when we were together.

His feelings about blacks were so deeply ingrained that he would not sit down with us for a hand of bridge or a cup of coffee in the union. But Jim, though I never said one word to him about it, came to realize that his feelings about blacks made absolutely no sense. Through sheer exercise of intelligence and will power, he forced himself to join us, to engage in small talk, even to smile at Elizabeth. Soon, she became just another one of my girlfriends to him.

Although Jim was sure he had overcome his feelings about blacks, he was convinced that he could never convert his wife, that she was too much of a Southern girl to ever be close friends with a black. For some time he was adamant about not letting me bring Elizabeth along when he invited me home for dinner.

One day, shortly after he had made peace with Elizabeth, his wife, Joan, came into the student union. Jim was not around and Joan, without so much as a second's hesitation, came over to our table and sat down. I never got to say very much because she and Elizabeth hit it off immediately. When Joan had finished her coffee, she got up, casually invited us for dinner that night, and turned to leave.

"Hey, wait," I said, sensing an opportunity for a bit of fun. "Don't tell Jim we're coming. Just make sure he answers the door. And, don't tell him anything about having met Elizabeth."

At six-thirty we rang the doorbell. Jim answered and paled. He looked at Elizabeth, glanced quickly over his shoulder to see if Joan had spotted her, and then turned back to me with a look that said he'd gladly like to kill me. When he heard Joan come up behind him, he almost went to pieces. His mouth opened and closed as he unsuccessfully tried to say something. He feebly moved the door back and forth as if he were trying to fan down an excessively hot closet.

Joan peered over his shoulder. "Hi, Elizabeth," she called out cheerfully. "Hi, Lucas. Come on in. Dinner is almost ready."

With straight faces, Elizabeth and I walked past Jim, who was still standing there tightly clutching the door handle. After a moment, he shuffled into the small living room area, sat down and stared as Joan and Elizabeth, talking animatedly, went into the kitchen. He turned to me with a silent plea to please explain the situation. Sadistically, I only smiled at him.

". . . it didn't go too well, eh?" I heard Jim saying.

I snapped to. "Terrible," I answered and again launched into the story of my interview.

"I wouldn't worry about it," Jim said when I was through. "You knew anyway it would be tough to get in after just three years of undergraduate school." He stopped for a moment. "Don't worry about it, Lucas. You'll make it next year."

If Jim was optimistic, I was not. That weekend, still full of despair, I went home to talk the situation over with my parents. My father was more than sympathetic. "We have good friends in the capital," he suggested. "Why don't you let me see what I can do for you there?"

As much as I wanted to get into veterinary school, I didn't want to do it that way. "No," I answered. "I want to do it fair and square. I want to get in like everybody else."

"It doesn't look to me like you'll get in fair and square. Obviously they don't think you are, as you say, 'like everybody else.'"

I knew that he was right. But still . . .

Dad pressed on. "How many Jews have been admitted to the school in the fifteen years it has been open. Do you know?"

I knew. "Three."

"Out of what—four hundred or five hundred admissions. And you don't think they are antisemitic? Even after that interview?"

"I don't know, dad. I think that in their minds they

weren't being antisemitic. I think they really thought it was neat that they had talked to a girl, a black, and a Jew."

"I think you're being silly. Guys will get in that have worse grades than you do and have never gone out of their way like you have to be with animals. But, its your life. . . ."

Nothing more was said. I went back to Midwestern for another year of agricultural school and then reapplied for admission to the veterinary college. Much to my surprise—and relief—I was admitted. But it was to be another four years before I found out that my father, unwilling to see me lose my life's ambition because of someone's bigotry, had taken it on himself to help me along.

On the day I graduated from veterinary school, I was walking the halls for one last look around. Although it had been a hard, and sometimes unpleasant, four years, I was, on that day, full of happiness. A yell of "Hey, Younker" stopped me as I was about to walk out the front door. It was one of the professors, hurrying to catch up to me.

"I want to ask you something I've put off four years asking," he said, taking me by the arm and guiding me into an empty classroom. "Just where did you get the influence to get into this school?"

"What do you mean influence," I protested. "I worked my ass off that last year in ag school and got good grades so they wouldn't have an excuse to turn me down again."

"Yeah, yeah," he waved aside my explanation. "I know all that. But I also know that I was on the admissions committee. In the ten years before you got in, we had maybe one or two Jews in a few of the freshman classes. But there were *three* in your class alone."

"Did——" I tried to interrupt.

"All I know is that someone got to the governor's office," he continued. "They called the chancellor's office, the chancellor's office called the dean of the veterinary school and the dean called the chairman of the admissions committee. The message all the way down the line was that your freshman class better be ten percent Jewish and that one of those Jews better be called Younker or else the veterinary school would run out of money very quickly.

"Now: How did you get to the governor?"

"I don't know," I said. "Before I went to college I spent some time as a construction worker. The union I was a member of is pretty powerful in this state. Maybe some of my buddies put in a good word for me. They knew how disappointed I was when I didn't get in the first time I applied."

I don't know if he believed me or not, but since I was not really sure of what had happened four years earlier, there was not much more I could tell him. Maybe my Uncle Harry (not really an uncle but my parents' best friend) who had many "connections" had put in a good word for me. It didn't much matter. I had made it into school and had managed to bring in two other Jews with me. And now, I had graduated and was on my way to being a full-fledged animal doctor.

Chapter Six

For six weeks now I had kept a hungry eye on that patch of weeds growing out in the pasture just east of the veterinary school clinic. When I had first spotted it, I couldn't believe it was just growing there wild and unattended. Since I had been in the veterinary school less than two months, I did not want to go near it. Maybe one of the professors was growing it for an experiment with animals. But, when it became obvious that no one else was remotely interested in the bounty of that field, I found myself a shopping bag and, one Sunday morning in late October, scurried out to do some harvesting.

I was so busy picking that for a moment I did not see the huge shadow that had materialized next to me. I looked up to see Dr. Stack standing next to me. He was a huge man with a big, barrel chest. A big shock of white hair and a white handlebar moustache graced a kindly, almost impish (and very red) face. The look in his eyes said he was interested in my activities. I smiled up at him weakly.

"Picking a little Cannabis Sativa, variety *indicus*, eh, Younker?"

So. Somebody did know about the marijuana growing out there. How was I going to get out of this situation? "Well, sir," I stammered, hoping the explanation would not sound too ridiculous. "I'm working on my poisonous plant collection."

Dr. Stack struggled to suppress a laugh. "That certainly shows a lot of foresight, Younker, seeing that you don't have that course for another three years."

He shook his head and resumed his walk across the field. A few feet away he stopped and turned around. "I'll tell you what, Younker," he called out, pointing at a patch of weeds at his feet. "If you want to get a real buzz, smoke some of this here wild lettuce. It has opium in it."

Dr. Stack was a man of wide interests and deep knowledge. He was well known in the field of toxicology and was eagerly sought out as an expert when there were difficult poisoning cases to be solved. But, because he was so brilliant a man, he had difficulty teaching: He simply wanted to impart too much to his students.

He would earnestly start lectures with the intended subject—a discussion of one particular plant hazardous to cows, let's say. But if that plant happened to be the source of a dye, he would soon be telling us about the local Indians who used that dye to decorate their teepees. Before the hour would have ended, we would have learned a great deal about painting as a form of expression in the Maya, Aztec, and Inca civilizations as well. A lecture about the deadly nightshade, a poisonous plant, would lead to a side remark that a patch of the weed could be found next to the old railroad trestle outside of town—and that in turn would lead to a twenty-five-minute lecture on wheel formulas in old locomotives.

As much as I liked and admired Dr. Stack, I wanted to have the opportunity—just once—to see if I could catch the old guy. Just once I wanted to see whether or not that font of knowledge was real or whether it was a consummate bullshitting act.

One day I ran into Stack in the hall. "Ah, Lucas," he greeted me. "I saw you at the concert last night. What piece did you like best?"

I was somewhat at a loss. Classical music had never been of great interest to me. I had been at the concert only because I was dating a music major at the time and she had prevailed on me to go to the concert. With Dr. Stack standing there in front of me now, I was desperately trying to think of what composers had been on the program. The only one I could think of—and whose name I could pronounce—was Samuel Barber.

"Yes," Dr. Stack said pensively. "It wasn't my favorite, but it certainly was an interesting piece. Did you notice the similarity between that piece and the music from ancient China?"

I stared at Stack. "Well, sir, actually I didn't."

"Very interesting, you know. They used the split sixteenth note very similarly. Very interesting, yes."

That, I thought to myself, is too much. The guy has to be giving me a line. I went to a phone and called Donna, the music major. "Did you notice that Barber used the split sixteenth note the same way that they did in ancient China?"

"To tell you the truth, I hadn't. But now that you mention it, yes, it's true, there is a similarity. But wait. You didn't think of that. Who told you that?"

"Stack," I said. "Who else?"

Eventually, Dr. Stack, his family (his wife and children were no less brilliant than he) and I gravitated toward each other because we liked and admired each other and because we had many interests in common. I was especially comfortable with them.

No one else in the school quite understood why I would not put perfectly healthy animals to sleep. During one laboratory session in an immunology class, each two students were given a guinea pig. We were told to inject the animal with a substance that would trigger a severe immunologic reaction and a fatal case of resultant anaphalactic shock. I told the instructor that I refused to kill my guinea pig.

"There are fourteen other guinea pigs in here I can watch die," I told him. "I won't kill mine. You could sacrifice just one animal if you have to show us this way what anaphalactic shock is like. And, in fact, you don't have to kill that one either. Why not just induce the shock and then give it cortisone to save it?"

The instructor listened patiently. "Are you going to kill your animal or do you want a failing mark in the laboratory part of this course?" he asked when I had finished.

"You can fail me for the whole course," I told him with some heat. "But I'm not going to kill the guinea pig."

The rudest awakening for me was that some of the other people studying to be animal doctors, as well as those charged with teaching them, could be so cavalier about taking life. Since then, I have come to terms with the knowledge that perhaps I go out of my way not to kill animals, but back then, to someone full of ideals about the sanctity of life, it was disappointing to find that others in my chosen profession had no qualms about killing animals for the slightest of reasons. Someone once brought a litter

67

of kittens to the clinic and asked that they be killed. The teacher took the bag, gave it to me, and told me to. "dispose of them."

"There is nothing wrong with these cats, except that the guy doesn't want them," I protested. "Why kill them? They don't need to die."

The teacher shrugged. "The guy doesn't want them because they are a mixed breed. There is nothing I can do."

I looked inside the bag at the little all-white balls of fur huddled inside. "What breed are these supposed to be?" I asked.

"He was looking to get pure-bred Siamese."

I was dumbfounded. "But these are Siamese! Didn't anybody tell that guy that Siamese are born all white?"

"I guess not. Anyway, it's too late."

I handed back the bag. "If you can kill these, go ahead. I'm not going to do it."

He took the bag and walked to the back room of the clinic. It was the last I saw of the kittens.

Whenever I could, I tried to save healthy animals from the system. My specialty was stealing dogs from the physiology department. Every semester, the department bought twenty or thirty dogs from the pound for physiology experiments. At the end of the experiments, the dogs were killed. I knew that I could not save all of them but I did help some. I spent many nights around the school because I had a part-time job with one of the professors. Whenever a new batch of dogs arrived at the school, I would examine them. If one or two seemed especially healthy and alert or if it seemed obvious that they had once been someone's pet and were well trained, I would spirit them out of the laboratory and give them to my friends.

In my junior year I even stole my own surgery dog. In surgery class, two or three students were assigned to a dog on which they practiced different surgical techniques during the semester. I would have preferred to operate on animals that legitimately needed surgery to survive. The school, of course, operated a small clinic to which animals belonging to townspeople and farmers were brought. But, before the school was willing to turn us loose on the clients' animals, we had to learn to do the surgical procedures on animals owned by the school. Thus, for the surgery course, the school bought animals that otherwise would have been put to sleep by local pounds. Every effort was made to make sure the animals did not suffer unnecessarily. It may have been more humane to do just one surgical procedure on each dog and then euthanize it before it woke up, but I guess the school didn't have enough money to buy all the dogs such a system would have required. Instead, each two or three students had to do many different procedures on the same dog.

I managed to force myself through most of the surgeries. Although I tried hard to find an excuse to avoid it, I even managed to make my way through the second from the last surgical technique we had to perform—the removal of one eye. Only one operation remained before we would have to put the dog to sleep: the removal of one limb.

Here I drew the line. Two weeks before that final operation, I had been assigned to the take care of the school's surgery kennels. The night before the scheduled amputation, I finished my work around the kennel, put on my raincoat, put the dog underneath it, and walked out of the building.

The next morning, feeling quite good, I went to class. Most of the students were already busy at work, taking one leg off their dogs. But my two surgical partners were standing at our operating table looking very glum and talking to the teacher. "Our dog disappeared," one of my partners said as I walked up. "I went down to the kennel to get it and it was gone."

I hoped that my voice would stay casual as I made my way through the explanation I had concocted. "I was going to call you guys but it was too late at night," I said. "I came down to check on how the dog was doing after the eye operation and she had died. I took her down to the post-mortem lab and it was just when the truck was leaving for the rendering plant. I threw her in with the other animals."

I'm not sure they believed me because by now my penchant for saving animals was getting to be well known. But I didn't much care. The dog had contributed enough to my education. Now it was getting a well-deserved rest at a friend's house in the country.

I didn't always have to resort to absolute subterfuge to get an otherwise doomed animal out alive. Sometimes I even had what could be called the tacit approval of the teacher who had supervision of the animal.

Every year the anatomy department bought a horse, a broken-down old nag ready for the slaughterhouse, to use as a "palpator." Those of us in anatomy class had to dissect a dead horse in the laboratory; then, theoretically, we were supposed to go to the school's barn and find the anatomical landmarks we had uncovered with the knife on a live horse by touching, or palpating, it. Of course, not many of the students bothered to take advantage of the palpator. Few wanted to bother walking all the way over to the barn where the horse was kept. Traditionally, at the end of the semester, the palpator was put to sleep, embalmed and then placed in the cooler to serve as the dissecting specimen for next year's anatomy class.

When I took anatomy, the palpator was a black Morgan mare. She had been starved for quite a while—or at least fed no more than a subsistence diet—and she was all skin and bones. Her mane and tail were full of burrs and she was covered with mud. Since I liked grooming horses, I started to take care of her. The anatomy department provided only hay for its palpator, so I borrowed a little grain from the clinic where privately owned animals were kept while they were being treated. I got all the burrs off her, trimmed her fetlocks. By the end of the semester, she was a pretty, slick-looking horse. I was determined she would not wind up in the cooler, awaiting next year's knives.

While it had been easy to sneak dogs out of the physiology kennel by simply walking them out on a leash one at a time, spiriting away a full-grown horse would be quite another matter. I decided I would take the direct approach: I would just ask Dr. Neery, the anatomy teacher (and the head of that department), if I could keep the Morgan and get him another horse—one that would have to be put to sleep anyway—to use instead of the Morgan as the dissecting specimen for the following year.

Neery regarded me for a moment. "Absolutely not, Younker," he said, "that would set a bad precedent."

I couldn't quite imagine what the bad precedent would be, but I decided to let it pass. "Sir," I countered. "It sure would be too bad if someone stole your horse one night and left you without a dissecting specimen for next semester."

Neery, who had begun shuffling some papers on his desk as a signal that I was dismissed, glanced up. "Are you telling me you would steal that horse, Younker?"

"Not me, sir. I wouldn't steal anything. The night that horse disappears I'm sure I'll be having dinner with someone. Dr. Stack, probably."

From the look that was now spreading over his face, I saw that it had suddenly dawned on Neery that he had a good opportunity to make life a little difficult for me. He knew that I had put in a lot of extra time and effort to fix up the Morgan and that I had built up an emotional attachment to her. "I'll tell you one thing, Younker," he said after a moment's thought. "If that horse were to disappear, I would have to have two to replace it."

If I wanted my horse, then I would have to pay dearly for her. It would be a struggle, he thought, for me to find the money to buy him two horses, even two broken-down old horses.

Luckily, I had come to be good friends with the professor who had supervision of the veterinary school's outpatient clinic. Farmers who brought animals in for treatment but who were told that the horse or cow could not be helped would just leave their animals there to be put to sleep. Dr. Lawrence would keep two such horses for me to turn over to Neery.

A day or two after we had struck our bargain, a farmer brought in an old mare that had broken her leg. The break could not be repaired properly and, rather than kill the animal immediately, Dr. Lawrence gave her to me to make my first payment to Neery. I was glad to have her, but I still wanted something special to round out the deal. I couldn't let Neery get away with his little scheme so easily.

A week later, I was hanging around the clinic waiting for another horse. Dr. Lawrence, another student, and I were on the platform that served as the clinic's receiving dock for large animals, enjoying a cup of coffee during a temporary lull in the afternoon's activities.

Just as we were about to go back into the clinic, a dark green pickup—well waxed and bearing handsome gold lettering on the door—pulled up. Cal Lundberg, the herdsman from one of the richer local farms, shut off the engine and climbed out of the cab. The sideboards of the truck shook violently with a fearsome banging. "Howdy, boys,"

Cal called out. "Got one of Mr. Roberts' mules here. It's one of them he imported from South America to pull his daughter's buggy. He's a mean bastard but you should be able to handle him. He's feeling not too good."

As he removed the tailgate we saw a well-groomed miniature mule, about the size of a Welsh pony. "He's been bellyachin' the last few days, doc," he told Lawrence. "Ain't real bad though, ain't been doin' no rollin', just pawin' the ground. I dosed him with some salts but he ain't passed no manure to speak of."

The three of us stood there, waiting for Cal to get the mule out of the truck. Cal looked up from where he was standing. "You boys ain't afraid of a little old mule, are you?"

The mule was staring suspiciously at us, both ears laid back. Finally, I moved toward the lowered tailgate. The mule swung his head toward the cab and let out a fearsome kick in my direction.

"Lucky he ain't feelin' too good," Cal drawled. "He'd be feelin' better, he'd a knocked your head into Kansas. Never knowed that mule to miss."

Dr. Lawrence pushed me aside. "Younker, get out of the way. You're not even in clinics yet." Dr. Lawrence took a rope, climbed on top of the cab and managed to get a loop around the mule's neck. By leaning over the side rails, he was able to fashion the loop into a war bridle and lead the mule peacefully from the truck.

We led the mule to a set of stocks where it could be restrained while Dr. Lawrence gave it a rectal examination. "Cal, there are masses in there. I think it's cancer, but the only way we would know for sure if he can be saved is to open him up and do an exploratory."

Cal nodded his approval. "Mr. Roberts is mighty partial to that team of mules. You better open him up and see what you can do."

Dr. Lawrence gave him a local anesthetic and a heavy tranquilizer and opened the mule. The animal had tumors in its intestines, the mesentery tissue binding the various organs, the liver, the spleen and at least one of the kidneys. Dr. Lawrence told Cal there was no way to save the animal.

"Better put him down, doc," Cal said. "Mr. Roberts is over in France lookin' at some cattle. But I know he wouldn't want the critter to suffer."

After Cal left, Dr. Lawrence handed me the lead shank. "Here is your other horse, Younker. Better get him over to one of Neery's stalls in the basic sciences building before the tranquilizer wears off."

I laughed as I pictured Neery trying to handle that mean mule when he went in to euthanize it to use as the dissecting specimen. But I would have given a good deal to see the expression on his face when his freshmen students the following year opened the abdomen to get their first view of the organs of an animal and found instead a belly full of tumors. Poor Neery would have to buy still another animal for his students to use.

By that time, of course, I would be well out of his reach. But for the moment, the struggle I had been engaged in with him almost all of my freshman year would continue. Neery had been stalking me since the beginning of the semester. Sometimes I thought it was because I was "different," because I had come to the veterinary school with a reputation as an activist, a "troublemaker."

More often, I was sure that it was my religious background that rankled Neery. Hardly a class went by (and there were many since Neery taught the bulk of the freshman classes) when he did not find an occasion to make a remark about my religion. And, when he could not find a ready-made opening, he would settle for snide remarks he considered subtle. His favorite ploy was to pretend that he could not get my name right. "Tell us, Mr. Younkerman . . ." or, "Looking at this specimen, Mr. Younkberg . . ."

I tried to discuss the problem with one of my other teachers, Dr. Connolly, a large, rotund Irishman who taught large animal medicine and surgery. Connolly would have none of it. "You're paranoid," he told me. "And you are going to let your paranoia destroy you. It's not the Jews he doesn't like. He just doesn't like *anybody*. You shouldn't let things like that bother you. When I first came here, the head of the anatomy department didn't like Irish Catholics. He didn't speak to me at all for the first two years I was here."

But that was precisely the problem. Any student—or teacher, for that matter—who was not of white Anglo-Saxon stock was suspect or ostracized completely. Jews were just barely tolerated. For most of the school's history, blacks didn't have to be tolerated at all because they simply were not admitted. The first black to attend the school was an African who came to Midwestern during my third year. He was a government official who had enrolled as a graduate student in pathology because he wanted to learn about effective techniques to increase farm-animal production back home. But even his standing as a foreign dignitary did not protect him from petty harassment.

In time, however, Omar, the African, was able to bring the razzing to a dramatic halt. He was a big man, tall and stout, who was even more ominous for the three parallel tribal scars that cut across each cheek. He had already earned his doctorate in Europe and was always willing to share his knowledge with those students who would ask him for help.

Several of us, including one professor who delighted in pretending that Omar was little more than an ignorant bushman, were in the school's post-mortem laboratory going about our various chores one afternoon. The post-mortem lab had several uses. I was in there because I was learning how to do cataract operations. Like other students learning surgery and learning to perform this particular procedure, I was practicing on dead animals. I had to do the operation one hundred times on dead animals before I would be allowed to work on a live one.

Omar, the professor and the other students were in the post-mortem lab working on turkeys. The school is in the midst of a rich turkey-farming area. Many of the farms grow as many as one hundred thousand turkeys a year. Because the economic stakes are so high, every two weeks turkey farmers would pick twenty or thirty turkeys out of the hundreds of pens on their farms and bring them to the school to be killed and autopsied. Thus, any incipient disease could be spotted and treated before it spread to the entire turkey crop.

On that particular day, the lab was full of gobbling turkeys and chattering students. Every once in a while the professor would look up, give Omar an idiotic grin and call out to me a variation of "Hey, Younker, now make sure Omar doesn't cut himself with that knife." Omar, intent in his work, said nothing.

Late in the afternoon, a truck bearing a new supply of turkeys pulled up to the large double doors that opened into the post-mortem laboratory. As the farmer was unloading his birds, one, knowing full well the fate in store for him, thrashed out of the man's hands and took off into the field adjacent to the lab, moving just as fast as his legs and flapping wings allowed.

All of us started running after the bird, but Omar stopped us with an imperative shout of "No! Leave this to me!" We stopped dead in our tracks and turned to face Omar. He picked up a post-mortem knife, ran out about six steps into the driveway, and, with a fluid sidearmed motion, flung the knife far out into the field. Hypnotized, we watched that old, clumsy knife with an eight-inch blade and a cumbersome handle sail gracefully through the air. After what seemed to be an interminable time, the knife, looping sideways handle over blade, caught up with the turkey, neatly severing its neck. The head flew off, the bird, carried by reflex action, ran about twenty more feet and then dropped dead. There was deep silence all around.

"Jesus," I finally muttered. "You sure are good with that knife, Omar."

"No. No. Actually I am a much better marksman with a spear," he said, speaking in that refined, precise king's English he had learned in Europe. "Sometimes I do miss with the blade. I have never missed with a spear."

After that, no one ever had an untoward word for Omar again.

Although Omar had settled (perhaps inadvertently, since there never was any indication that he had meant his demonstration to be an overt warning to anyone) his problems with the professor harassing him, I could find no way to ease Neery's pressure on me. In fact, as the semester progressed, matters worsened. They came to a head the day Neery simply stole my lecture notes to all my classes.

Neery had an unwritten rule that the coat rack that graced the hall outside his gross antomy class could be used only to hang coats and hats. Everything else was forbidden. Since the class involved dissecting animals—a process that made a mess of everything and everybody in the room—we all ignored the rule and left anything we were carrying, including books and class notes, on the rack. Two weeks before finals I came out of the gross anatomy class to find that the spot where I had left my lecture notebooks was empty. The notes had vanish.

"Dr. Neery, have you seen my notes?" I asked.

"No, I haven't seen your notes. Where did you leave them?"

"On the coat rack."

I thought I saw a glint of triumph steal its way into his eyes. "Younker, you know, don't you, that there is a rule against leaving anything on that rack except hats and coats," he lectured me. "If you had learned to follow rules, you wouldn't have lost your books."

Shaking with anger, I left the building. I had just finished outlining the entire neuroanatomy book, making charts and diagrams of all the tracts in the nervous system. All the outlines—representing eight hours of work a night for the last two weeks—were in those notebooks. I didn't know what to do. Since the middle of the semester, when fear of Neery had begun to take hold of me and had begun to put me in a deep depression, I had been keeping Smith, Kline and French in business by swallowing a good deal of Dexamil every day. I was a nervous wreck because on amphetamine, your head keeps going but your body is falling apart. For weeks I had been coming home from class at six in the afternoon and had been studying until two or three in the morning without stirring from the chair.

I was so involved with my thoughts I did not hear Jim Stevenson pull up beside me. "What's the matter with you?" I suddenly heard him say. "You look god-awful."

"That son-of-a-bitch Neery is out to get my ass," I answered. "I left my notes to the lectures out on the hall coat rack and the son-of-a-bitch stole them and won't give them back to me."

"I wouldn't worry about it too much," Jim answered with sympathy in his voice. "Hell, you can borrow mine. They'll get you through."

He stopped when he saw that he wasn't helping me. "Look," he finally went on. "Why don't you come with me. I'm going to palpate some cows this afternoon. I'll teach you how to do it."

Jim had been taking a course in animal fertility. As part of the course, he had to learn to test cows for pregnancy by palpating them, by sticking his arm up their rectums and searching for and feeling the cows' reproductive organs. By feeling the uteruses and the surrounding areas, it could be determined whether or not the cows were pregnant. To practice the procedure, he periodically had to go to the local slaughterhouse to palpate cows before they were killed.

I didn't want any part of palpating cows that afternoon. "That's not going to take my mind off anything," I snapped.

"Come on, stop feeling sorry for yourself," Jim answered, a bit disgusted with my sullen behavior. "If you learn how to do it, you can help me in my business."

I stared at Jim with wonder. What kind of business was he in now? When he had come to Midwestern to start undergraduate school, he had arrived with a wife, a child, a twenty-eight-foot house trailer and a set of equipment for making concrete bricks that looked like building stones. For twenty dollars a month, he had rented a little factory that had no heat or plumbing and had, in his spare time, made bricks and then sold them door to door. As he accumulated a little money, he bought a bigger, better trailer. But instead of selling his old one, he rented it to another student. With money he accumulated from the rental, he bought himself still another trailer and in time was carrying on a nice little business buying and selling trailers. He ended up with eight or ten ten-thousand-dollar trailers.

Just recently, he had taken up real estate, buying and selling farms. In fact, he had just been to visit his family in Arkansas and had, accidentally, come across a one-thousand-acre farm on the market for one hundred thousand dollars. He called his banker and simply said, "I've got a farm I want to buy. How's my credit?" The banker did nothing more than tell him to write a check for it and "we'll cover it." Jim bought the farm, held it for a few weeks and resold it for one hundred and twenty-five thousand dollars. By the time we graduated from veterinary school Jim owned three farms of several hundred acres.

I had an understanding for the brick business and the real estate. But how would you turn a profit by sticking your arm up a cow's ass to see if it was pregnant? How could you make a profit from cows that were "cutters and canners," cows so old, so broken down they were sold to the slaughterhouses for a mere fourteen cents a pound because their meat could be nothing but filler products in other foodstuffs?

Jim laughed. "Well, it occurred to me that a lot of these farmers were bringing in cows that were pregnant—that's how I got to practice palpating, right? But just because the

77

cows were in bad shape didn't mean that you had to waste the calves they were carrying. So, I got to be good friends with the owner of the slaughterhouse and after a while he let me come down on my own to palpate cows and buy back from him any pregnant cows I could find.

"I wait for the calf to be born and then I have me a nice heifer or bull calf I can fatten up for market. I feed the mother pretty good too while she is pregnant so that by the time she calves she is pretty fat herself and I can sell her back to the slaughterhouse for more than I paid for her. How's that?"

It was, I admitted, pretty good.

After two hours of palpating cows, we washed up to go for dinner. Jim had been right. I did feel better and more relaxed.

"Listen, I had an idea in there," Jim said as we were walking home. "You're pretty good friends with Virginia, Neery's secretary, aren't you? Why don't you ask her if she knows anything about the notes?"

The next day after classes I went in to see Virginia. "Can you find out what Neery did with those notes?" I asked her after telling her my tale.

"I don't have to find out. I already know. I heard him telling someone that he has them hidden in the bacteriology lab. In one of the cabinets."

With barely a thank you, I ran out of the office and to the bacteriology lab. The laboratory had almost one hundred cabinets in it and in a frenzy I ran around the room tearing open and slamming shut cabinet after cabinet door. Finally, tucked away in the back of one little cubbyhole, I found my notebooks. I took them out, examined them to make sure all my notes were there, and tore a blank page out of a notebook. "You creep," I scribbled on the page. "Someday you'll get yours." I put the paper in the cabinet and left.

With my notes back in hand, I was temporarily out of the woods. But I knew that Neery was a determined man and would not be defeated so easily. When it came to vendettas, I had learned, Neery had no equal.

Neery's next attempt for my hide came after the first final exam—the one in histology—had been given. I knew that I had done badly in the test because, trying to prepare myself for Neery's examination, I had neglected my other courses badly. But I knew that I had not flunked histology. Dr. Göller, the course's teacher, was a friend of mine. Moreover, Göller had not flunked anyone on that final because he had set his curve for passing at fifty percent. I had gotten a fifty-four, barely squeaking through.

Two days after the histology exam, I walked by the school's main bulletin board. Since I had a minute, I stopped to look at the posted grades to see how others had done in histology. When I came to my name down at the bottom of the alphabetical list, my heart stopped: My mark in histology was an F. I had flunked! Because the school did not allow repeats of courses, I had flunked out of veterinary school as well.

"What the hell is going on?" I yelled as I rushed into Göller's office, enraged at the betrayal. "Why did you flunk me? You didn't flunk Windstrom and he got fifty-one percent on the test."

"What the devil are you talking about, Lucas?" Göller asked in his soft German accent. "I passed you."

We went back into the hall and I showed Göller the posted grades. He grabbed me by the arm and we charged into Neery's office. (Rather, he charged. I was dragged along.) Neery readily admitted that he had changed my grade. "You should not have passed Mr. Younker," he told Göller.

Göller was beside himself with fury. He was so mad that his accent thickened perceptibly. "Iv I am not allowed to giff ze grades I belief my student should half," Göller told him through gritted teeth, "zen you may be assured zat I will leaf this school. My grant money vill go vith me and zo does the electron microscope!"

It was a potent threat. The microscope alone was worth more than one hundred and twenty-five thousand dollars and was considered to be a prime piece of equipment. Göller, moreover, had been one of Neery's recruiting coups because Göller was an internationally known figure in his field. And, unlike others in the department, Göller could count on annual grant money from prestigious organizations like the National Institute of Health. Neery, deciding that he would not be wise to lose someone like Göller because of someone as insignificant as me, backed down. I kept my barely passing grade in histology.

"Hans, you know he still has one more shot at me," I

said to Göller as we walked back to his office. "I still have to go to his oral exam. No matter what I do in there, he can simply say that I flunked because there won't be anything in writing and it would just be his word against mine. Would you sit in on my oral exam?"

Without hesitation, Göller assured me he would, and on the designated day we both walked into the examination room. Neery's face fell.

"Do you think for a moment I would not be fair to you, Younker?" Neery asked, obviously aware of why Göller was there.

I laughed. "After all that has happened, this is your last chance to flunk me out, Dr. Neery. I didn't want to take the chance."

Göller stayed. And, since I had crammed night and day for the orals, I passed with flying colors.

Neery's untoward behavior toward me had at least one unexpected bonus. The following semester I was to have the one other teacher who, according to the previous Jewish students, was a virulent antisemite. However, that entire following semester, Dr. Downey almost tied himself up in knots trying to be nice to me. Later, I found out that the one thing Downey disliked more than Jews was Neery. Apparently, stories of Neery's harassing tactics against me had reached Downey. If Neery had been nasty to me, why then, he was going to be nice to me—just to spite Neery. Personally, I was glad he had chosen to take my side. Downey, I thought, was far smarter than Neery. If Downey had been determined to flunk me out, he might have succeeded.

Eventually, Neery was relieved of his duties as head of the anatomy department and fell so much out of favor that he wound up as the only full professor serving as nothing more than a laboratory instructor. But not before Hans Göller and I had a chance to have a little fun at his expense.

One day, three years after Neery had spirited my notes off the coat rack, I was stopped by a fellow student on the way to class. "Younker," he asked, "did you steal Neery's galoshes?"

I couldn't imagine what he was talking about. But before I had a chance to ask him what he meant, another classmate wandered up to us. "Hey, Lucas," he called out as he approached. "Where did you hide Neery's galoshes? In the bacteriology lab?"

Finally, I got the story: Neery's galoshes were missing and he told several people that I had taken them. I hadn't, of course, but several possibilities came to mind. One was Göller, who was not above a good prank once in a while.

"Hans, do you know anything about Neery's galoshes?" I asked when I found him in one of the laboratories.

Göller grinned and motioned conspiratorially for me to come closer. "On ze coat rack that is exclusively reserved only for ze hats and ze coats," he intoned, deliberately thickening his accent, "I haf found a few days ago, a pair of galoshes. It was my dooty as a good citizen to take zem avay."

"Hans, that's all very funny," I protested. "But I'm taking the heat for it."

"Ach, don't worry. He has already found them. I left a note that said, 'Only coats and hats are allowed on this rack by the chairman of the department. And we know someone with cold feet.' He is smarter than we thought he is because he figured out after only one day what the note meant. Yesterday I saw him go to the anatomy lab, open the cooler, wheel out the horse in storage there and remove the galoshes from the feet where I had wired them."

"Then why is he still making a fuss?" I asked when I could stop laughing.

"He probably wants to make you feel guilty and think someone has really stolen them."

I thought things over for a minute. "That is terrible," I said, feigning indignation. "I think he should be punished for that, don't you?"

Göller grinned. "You think we should steal them again?"

"Definitely," I said.

Chapter Seven

The insistent banging on the front door penetrated the two pillows under which I had buried my head. Debbie, fast asleep beside me, did not stir. If she were faking her deep sleep, I couldn't much blame her. It was barely seven-fifteen on a Saturday morning and we had been in bed only a few hours. We had been up most of the night, partying and smoking dope with friends who had dropped by Friday evening. I groaned and tried to push my head deeper into the pillows.

The banging persisted. Painfully, I lifted myself off the bed, struggled into my tangled bathrobe and stumbled to the front door. The well-dressed young man on the other side reached inside his coat pocket, took out a wallet, flipped it open, and stuck the shiny badge in front of my eyes. "John Smith," he barked. "Federal Bureau of Investigation."

Reflex action took over and I slammed the door in his face. I ran back to the bedroom and grabbed Debbie. She bolted up, terror on her face. "It's the FBI at the door, Debbie," I yelled, shaking her. "Is there anything else around here besides what we were smoking last night?"

Debbie leaped out of bed and into her slippers and housecoat. "I have some hash in my purse. God, where did I put it?" In her excitement Debbie had forgotten to put on her glasses. Virtually blind without them, she dropped to her knees and started groping around, hoping to find her purse by touch.

The banging on the door started up again and I joined the hunt for her purse. I found it just as she located her glasses under the night table.

"Okay," I said. "Go to the door and see what they want.

I'll get rid of this stuff with the joints we have by the toilet." (In those days, the deadly fear of a marijuana bust meant that you always kept your stash by the toilet, ready to flush it away at a moment's notice.)

"Not a chance," Debbie protested. "You go!"

"Debbie!" I whispered hoarsely.

Reluctantly—and with a searing backward glance at me—she headed for the door.

"John Smith, Federal Bureau of Investigation," the voice barked out once more.

"Is this one of Stevenson's stupid jokes?" Debbie asked, apparently maneuvering for position. "Are you a friend of his or something?"

"No, ma'am. We just want to ask your husband a few questions."

Debbie, now wanting to come clean, told him we were not married. "Anyway," she needled him, having regained her composure. "Do you always make your investigations at the crack of dawn?"

Having flushed everything down the toilet, and having taken one last look around, I wandered out into the living room. If he wasn't one of Stevenson's jokes, what could it be? What had I done? Was the federal government now leaning on CORE too?

"Oh nothing like that, Mr. Younker," he said with an attempt at an ingratiating smile. "I just want to ask you about Jean Rene DuVaul. He has applied for the Peace Corps and we want to check into his background."

Jean had been my roommate at Western.

"Did he go out with girls? Did he like boys? Did he . . ."

I told the man everything he wanted to know. Jean was a confirmed heterosexual. His politics were middle of the road. Not that my information helped. Jean wrote me later to tell me that he had not made the final cut because the last psychiatrist to interview him had labeled him a "latent hothead," probably because during the hour-long interview he had not been able to goad Jean into losing his temper.

Although I was relieved that the FBI man had not come because we were in CORE, living in sin, and occasionally smoking a joint, I had too much adrenalin running through my body now to go back to bed. Instead, I decided to go to the clinic. Dr. Highland was seeing patients there this morning and I could give him a hand.

I had a curious relationship with Highland. I had met him at the clinic. I enjoyed listening to him talk about veterinary medicine. But by mutual, unspoken agreement, we talked only about veterinary medicine. Politics was out of the question. He knew that I was a "radical" and I knew that he was a conservative. Just *how* conservative he was I did not find out until we happened to be standing next to each other at a pair of urinals.

The Minutemen—a fanatical group of right-wingers who held midnight drills in local cornfields to practice tactics they would use to defend the nation against communists, Russian and otherwise—were very active in the area. That day, as we were relieving ourselves, I saw that there were Minutemen stickers glued on the wall in front of us.

"Look at that, will you?" I said with disgust. "Why do they deface property like that?" I was just making conversation, never suspecting I might hit a raw nerve.

Highland stared straight ahead. His voice, when he finally spoke, was matter-of-fact but carried a chilling undertone. "I'm a Minuteman." And with that zipped up forcefully and walked out of the lavatory.

Even though it was still early in the morning when I arrived at the clinic building after the meeting with the FBI man, the place was already buzzing with activity. Saturday mornings were traditionally hectic: People who were too busy to come in during the week, took advantage of the Saturday morning session to bring in their ailing animals.

Highland and I were continuously busy seeing a stream of people whose animals were having problems with reproduction or with their reproductive organs. At noon, just as we were about to finish up and go home, a young man of about sixteen or seventeen rode up to the clinic building on his horse. "Could you take a look at her, doc?" he asked Highland. "I don't rightly know what's the matter, but she is impossible to get into foal."

Dr. Highland led the mare to the examining stock and began an inspection of her hindquarters. He saw the problem almost immediately.

"Look here," he said to Larry, another student, and me. "The way some mares are built, their vulvas do not close properly and they suck air into the vagina, causing a chronic vaginitis. These horses usually have a fairly flat croup, a high tail head, a sunken anus and underdeveloped vulvar lips. See how her vulva is tilted? The upper part of it is horizontal rather than vertical. When she trots or even just walks along, air is alternately pulled into the vagina and forced back out again. You know what the condition is called, Younker?"

"Yes, sir, she's a wind-sucker."

Highland gave me a dirty look.

"Pneumovagina," Larry chimed in, happy to be of service.

"Okay. Let's suture up the vulva and see if we can help her."

While Larry went to search for the surgical instruments, I wrapped up her tail and started scrubbing her for surgery.

Dr. Highland blocked the nerves on the edge of the vulva with a local anesthetic. But apparently there was a small area which had not been blocked well because as he began to trim the edge of the mucous membrane with his scissors, the mare kicked over the stock gate. Highland saw it coming and instinctively leaned back to get out of its way. Instead, he managed to lean back just far enough to catch the full brunt of the hooves squarely on his upper chest.

(The closer one is to a horse, the better the chance of escaping serious injury. The closer one is, the less chance the kick has to build up power and snap. Of course, the best way to avoid injury is to walk in front of the horse. If one has to walk in back, one should closely hug the horse's hindquarters and walk around it, keeping a gentle hand on the animal's rump.) The blow sent him sprawling. We stood frozen, afraid that he had been killed. Just as we recovered sufficiently to go to his aid, he staggered to his feet. His face was gray and his eyes were a bit glazed, but otherwise he was unharmed. He dusted himself off, rubbed his chest and reached for the vial of anesthetic. Still breathing a bit hard, he filled the syringe with a whooping dose of anesthetic. After that second injection the mare didn't feel a thing for the duration of the operation—and probably nothing for a full week thereafter.

The FBI man's visit was the only jarring note in an otherwise peaceful and good spring semester. I was out of Neery's clutches, I was living with Debbie who, among other things, made good fresh bagels from scratch every Saturday morning. And, it looked as if I would finish the year with a good academic record. Just a few days before the term ended and we were about to start summer vacation, the year came to a glorious end.

"I found out this morning that there are not enough upperclassmen to fill the internships in the clinic this summer," Dr. Lawrence told me when I ran into him in the hall one day. "Would you be interested? There are two places left."

Did I want it? Could there be any question? Most of the school year had been spent dissecting dead animals or experimenting with live ones. But for a few hours here and there, I had had little chance to do anything medically helpful for animals. But now I could have three full months in which to involve myself with the delivery of medical care to animals that needed it.

Chapter Eight

I had only been at the clinic a week when one of the professors, Dr. Charles, called me over to an operating table where an anesthetized young bitch lay strapped down. "Younker," he said, "you are going to scrub in and assist me on some spays this week. Hopefully, you can be doing some yourself by next week."

The thought that I would be performing spays myself within a week was pretty scary. Neutering a female animal is a major operation because it involves opening the abdomen and taking out the ovaries and the uterus.

Sure enough, a week later, after assisting Dr. Charles on an endless number of spays, he told me that I was about to perform my first spay and that he would assist me. I perspired more than usual but managed to get through the surgery. After assisting me on two more spays, Dr. Charles told me that I could do the surgery by myself from then on—as long as there was a professor somewhere in the clinic. I was very proud of myself and threw myself with vigor into every single case. I even wrote out detailed reports for the charts of the animals I operated upon. Most of the doctors and senior students made a few scribbled notes in the animal's chart. I wrote out a whole page, describing in tortuous detail just how I had made the incision, how I had retracted the abdominal muscles, what blood vessels I had tied off, how I had located the left horn of the uterus. . . .

But at times even I had trouble believing myself the Ben Casey of the animal world.

By tradition, the clinic was staffed by junior and senior students (that year I was one of two exceptions to the rule) who served as assistants to the doctors who actually attended the animals. As part of their duties, juniors were required to carry a thermometer, a hemostat (a small instrument used to cut off or slow bleeding), and a pair of scissors. It was suggested that I do the same. Unfortunately, more often than not, I left these instruments on the dresser at home, right beside my keys or my lunch money.

My forgetfulness caught up to me on a day two seniors, a junior, Dr. Connolly, and I were off to make morning rounds at some of the neighborhood farms. Our first stop was to see a cow which, according to the farmer who had called us, had "been actin' kinda sickly last couple a days."

Businesslike, we strode over the early summer grass to the corner of the field where the cow was standing quietly. Dr. Connolly and I got there first.

"Give me you thermometer, please, Younker," Connolly said.

I reached into my pocket and instantly knew I was in trouble. "I'm afraid I left it at home, sir," I mumbled.

Luckily, Dr. Connolly had a sense of humor—and wanted to spare me the embarrassment of having to ask one of the other students for his thermometer. Even if Connolly did not have to take the temperature right away, he had to make a show of doing so because it was expected. "All right then," he whispered to me so that neither the farmer nor the other students who had stopped a bit away could hear him. "Give me your ball-point pen."

"I haven't got a ball-point pen," I said, desperation in my voice.

I thought he would kill me. Connolly reached into his pocket, pulled out his ball-point pen, placed it in his hand so that no one could see what it really was, and stepped up closer to the cow.

"Well, now let's see what we have here," he said, flashing the farmer a reassuring smile. With a quick flick of his hands, Connolly lifted the cow's tail, pushed the ball-point pen into its rectum and waited a minute or two, casually calling back idle remarks to the farmer. After an appropriate wait for the temperature to register, he withdrew the pen and made a show of "reading" the temperature. "Well, now, as near as I can tell . . ."

Toward the end of the examination, he asked the junior for his thermometer, "just to make sure." Later, as we were

90

walking back to the truck, Connolly bent over to whisper in my ear. "Next time, Younker, bring your thermometer, will you?"

On general principle, Connolly, I felt, was a good teacher. On ambulatory calls, most professors would do the work by themselves. They would diagnose the problem and would prescribe the treatment. The students were expected to learn by watching. Not Connolly. Often, for better and sometimes for worse, he placed many cases directly in the hands of the students.

We had been called to a hog farm because one of the animals out there had been sick for a day or two. "Got her at a sale 'bout three days ago, doc," the farmer told him. "She ain't been right since. The other ones I bought there, they seem all right."

Connolly waved me forward and I got down on the sawdust and wood shavings to examine the sick pig. She was lethargic. Her temperature (taken with the themometer that was now never out of my pocket) was over 105°. "She won't eat neither," the farmer said. "And she ain't been movin' round at all."

Connolly had been standing by silently. "What would you say it is, Younker?"

"Looks like hog cholera to me, except that there hasn't been any around this area for years. It could be erysepelas."

"All right then, how do you want to treat her?"

I suggested penicillin and told the farmer we would be back to see her the next day to check on her. When we returned the following afternoon, the animal was still down. In fact, she looked a bit worse. "Well, Younker?" Connolly asked. "What do you think? What about that loose stool she's developed?"

"That could be from the penicillin. Let's go ahead with the treatment."

The next day matters were even worse. I was beginning to get scared. "Her temperature is still up," I told Connolly. "She's still not eating. Her respiration is rapid and she's got a very bad case of diarrhea. It looks to me like's she's dying, Dr. Connolly." I was in agony.

Connolly hunched down to get a closer look at the animal. Then he turned to me. "Want to reconsider the diagnosis?"

"You mean I was wrong?" I couldn't believe he had allowed me to make a near fatal mistake.

"I didn't say you were wrong, Younker, I just asked if you want to reconsider your diagnosis," Connolly said.

"Well, sir," I replied, "I think it is beginning to look more like a salmonella infection than erysepelas."

"I'd have to agree with that," Connolly said softly. "You know if I'd told you that three days ago you'd make the same mistake again. I don't think you'll have trouble diagnosing your next case of salmonella."

The nice thing about Dr. Connolly was that he gave you the opportunity to be right. With many of the other professors, you could never be anything but wrong—even if, once in a while, you had judged a situation correctly.

We were called out to Lone Oak Farm to see a mare that had retained her afterbirth after foaling. The membranes that surround the foal in the uterus before birth are usually passed out after the foal has been delivered. But this mare had foaled five hours earlier and she still had not completely passed her afterbirth. Some of the membranes were hanging from her vulva. But the majority were still in the uterus.

Because I had spent Christmas and Easter vacation (as well as other free stretches of time) at a Lexington horse farm, and because it was well known in school that horses were my first love, Dr. Jorgensen, the teacher on duty at the clinic that day, turned to me. "You're the horseman in the group. What do you think we should do?"

I opted for a conservative approach. "The mare only foaled five hours ago, Dr. Jorgensen. I would just give her some oxytocin and see if she will pass the membranes."

"You don't think we should remove the placenta right now by peeling it out?"

"Dr. Wilkinson at the farm in Lexington doesn't worry too much about a placenta until twelve hours go by. He just gives her the oxytocin and waits. He says you can leave it for as long as twenty-four hours if you give the horse antibiotics and anthihistamines."

"I don't happen to agree with your Dr. Wilkinson," Jorgensen replied coldly. "I think the placenta should be removed if it is retained longer than three or four hours. Go ahead and give her some oxytocin and if she doesn't pass the placenta in half an hour, we'll have to remove it."

Fortunately, nature interceded in the confrontation. Twenty-five minutes later, the mare passed the entire placenta.

As far as I was concerned, he was lucky that nothing serious had happened. A few years later I had the satisfaction of knowing that the ideas that I had picked up on my visits to modern breeding farms had come to be generally accepted among practitioners in the field.

I loved ambulatory clinic not only because it gave me the opportunity to treat animals, but because seldom a day went by that did not provide a surprise or a good laugh.

Of the many farmers we called upon on a regular basis, our steadiest customers were the Strummonds. Old man Strummond was eighty-six years old. His son, who worked the farm with him, was sixty-five. They were both widowers. Perhaps because they were old and didn't have much energy, perhaps because they really didn't care very much any more, the farm was in a state of advanced decay. The fields were overgrown with weeds, the fences were down, most of the buildings were badly in need of repair and paint. There was so much junk lying all over the place that their cows were continually tearing up their teats on rusted machinery. Most of the calls we made to the Strummond farm was to sew up one cow or another.

The two men were deeply religious Baptists. Whenever we called on them, we would, invariably, get long lectures from the two somber farmers about the evils of smoking or drinking. (We brought these lectures on ourselves. One of us always had a cigarette in hand. Once in a while there was a six-pack in the truck.)

One Saturday morning, however, we called to find the two Strummonds awaiting us with foolish grins on their faces. The most innocuous remark or question elicited a gale of laughter. Every time one of them whooped, he would whip off his hat (they both wore small-billed hats that looked like shortened baseball caps) and would slap the other one on the rear end or back.

Caught up in the spirit of things, I started giving them their own fire and brimstone sermon, warning them that they were going to "burn in the eternal flames of Satan" if they went on this way, hitting the bottle so early on a Saturday morning.

Old man Strummond, who had been laughing when I

started my talk, stopped short. "We ain't been drinkin', young feller," he said with indignation. "Y'all know we don't drink!"

"Well, you guys sure are acting funny today, I'll say that."

"That may be, young feller, but it is cause we ain't feelin' too good," the son chimed in.

"That's right," the father said. "We spent the whole mornin' burnin' that pasture out yonder. I guess we musta took in too much smoke and it made us feel kinda light-headed."

I wandered over to the edge of the field and looked around. Small wonder they were acting funny. They had burned off a pasture full of marijuana and had been standing downwind while the flames did their job. I picked up a sample that had not been burned and walked back to the Strummonds, who were still trying to put their dignity back together.

"You guys know what this is?"

"Sure do, young feller," the old man answered. "Why my pappy had this whole farm in hemp when he was young. Why, during the War between the States this county grew more hemp than any county in the confederacy." He stopped short, a look of nostalgia and regret mixed in his face. "They don't make rope out of it no more. That stuff is just an old weed now, ain't got no value. You can't get rid of it though, just seeds itself back every year. Every two or three years ya plum got to burn off the pasture to get rid of it."

I casually pocketed the sample of weed I had picked. I could dry it out for use later on. "Well," I said, trying hard to keep a straight face, thinking of the hundreds of thousands of dollar's worth of marijuana they were burning off. "Next time don't stand downwind of the fire. Hemp smoke will make you do funny things."

Full-time work among the farmers of the region brought one revelation after another. Most of the men and women working the land were conscientious, intelligent, and knowledgeable people. I had always suspected that to be a farmer, you had to be possessed of a special, even above average, intellect and ability. But as a city dweller, I ultimately learned, I had been too well propagandized into believing that the American farmer, *without exception*, was the most advanced, most sophisticated farmer in the world.

As a result, I was often not prepared for the days when we would suddenly be faced with a run of plainly crazy people, days when I had a hard time understanding how the country managed to feed itself.

A cloudy, muggy July morning, six weeks after I had started clinic, proved to be such a day.

We had been called to a farm where a horse had developed a strange ailment—a severe skin condition on just one side of its body.

After the farmer had led us to the corral where the horse was standing, Dr. Smith, who was the professor on call that day, asked me to examine the horse.

"What do you think it is, Younker?"

I was faced by a puzzling sight. The horse had little bumps—each about half an inch high—on just the left side. I ran my hand lightly over the animal, hoping touch would give me a clue because I was completely stumped. "I don't know," I finally said. "It could be an allergic reaction to something. Maybe she brushed up against a poisonous shrub or something."

But as I talked and as I looked closer, something struck me as peculiar. One of the bumps was giving off puss, certainly not the hallmark of an allergic reaction. I gently squeezed the bump, draining off the yellowish fluid until only red blood came out. On the last squeeze, a piece of buckshot popped into my hand.

A bit startled, I turned to the farmer who had been standing off to one side, watching the proceedings with an air of indifference. "Do you own a shotgun by any chance?"

"Course I own a shotgun."

I didn't want to ask the next question because on its face it was stupid. "Did you shoot this horse?"

The man shrugged. "Sure did. I needed her to do some work few days ago and I kept running after her 'cause the bitch wouldn't come when I called her or nothin'. So I went and got me the shotgun. I just wanted to teach her a lesson. Hell, I didn't figger I'd hurt her none. I couldn't get close enough. Just figgered I'd sting her good."

We spent the next forty-five minutes in grim silence, cleaning out the buckshot pellets. "When that man gets his bill next week," Smith said as we drove off, "he's going to have a lesson *he'll* never forget!"

As we drove on, the mood inside the truck almost matched the gathering darkness outside. And, if our mood had been soured by the idiotic farmer who had shot his horse because it had refused to listen to him, it was not helped by what we found on our call to the Hollowell place.

By the time we reached the small, one-hundred-fifty-acre farm, the clouds had made good their morning-long threats and were letting loose a torrential rainstorm. We had been scheduled to look at a cow that was having trouble calving. Dr. Smith drove into the farm, stopped the truck, and looked at the corral where a solitary cow was lying in the mud. "I bet that's her," Dr. Smith said, looking glumly at the quagmire that was the muddy pasture. "I'll bet we won't be able to get her to move any place that's dry."

We were about to get out of the truck when we noticed Hollowell walking slowly toward us. Hollowell was one of the county's marginal farmers. In fact, he had to sell insurance to make ends meet. The man, who was never very cheery anyway, looked especially distraught as he walked up to the truck's cab.

"How's she doing?" Dr. Smith asked, a trace of wistfulness in his voice.

A pained expression crossed Hollowell's face. "I guess I might as well tell you," he said, the rain washing down his face. "I guess I made a mess of things."

A look of what-has-this-guy-done-now crossed Dr. Smith's face. He didn't know how bad it would be.

When no words of comfort were forthcoming from Smith, Hollowell screwed up his courage and continued. "When I came out about six this mornin', there was this little leg stickin' out. I figgered it wouldn't be too long."

He stopped and looked back at the cow. "I can't get her to move," Hollowell offered as an explanation. "Anyway. About nine or so this mornin' the leg was still stickin' out. I tried to reach in there to help out, but couldn't do anything."

Smith groaned. Some farmers were always doing this sort of thing. Sticking dirty hands and arms inside animals to help them deliver. On the other hand, he probably thought, if this is the worst of it. . . .

Hollowell took a deep breath. "I had an idea. If the calf was stuck, maybe if I pulled it out with something else. . . ."

A grim look was spreading across Dr. Smith's face. I could feel myself growing queasy. "I tied a rope to the leg and the rope to the tractor. . . ." Hollowell said, looking down at the ground. He didn't finish the sentence.

We grabbed our bags, threw open the doors and slugged to the cow. While Dr. Smith washed his hands and arms we scrubbed the cow. Dr. Smith reached inside the animal. "What a mess. He pulled one leg right off. The calf is dead. I'm afraid we'll have to cut the rest of the calf out ourselves." Dr. Smith did his work quickly and gave the cow some medicine. We looked around for Hollowell but he was nowhere in sight. We cleaned up and left in a hurry.

As foolish as Hollowell had been, he had at least been honest about what he had done. Other farmers who had done foolish, though not as deadly, things would often not admit they had tampered at all with the birth process.

Several weeks earlier, a farmer had brought his cow right to the clinic because she had been having trouble calving. "Have you stuck your hand in her?" the doctor on duty asked, wanting to know if he should take added precautions against a possible infection of the uterus.

"No sir, not at all," the farmer answered. "Just brought her in here when I saw she was havin' all that trouble."

When examination made it obvious we would not be able to deliver the calf normally either, we went on to do a cesarean section. As we pulled the calf out of the uterus, all the afterbirth followed. Right in the middle of the placenta we found a gold ring with the man's initials on them. The attending doctor carefully examined the ring in front of the red-faced man. "Since you didn't stick your hand in, this couldn't be your ring. I guess I can keep it." The man confessed that maybe he had put his hand in "jest a little bit."

On our next call we were scheduled to castrate some pigs on the Carson farm, just down the road from Hollowell's place. With little enthusiasm left for the rest of the day, we drove over. The rain stopped as we pulled in the driveway. "Big deal," Smith mumbled, refusing to accept the weather's cease-fire. "You boys are still going to have to catch those pigs and drag them to dry ground where we can cut them."

Hollis Carson, who had been tending to his cows in one of the barns, came running over to us, a raincoat still perched on his shoulders. "I'm afraid you're wastin' your time, boys," he called out, simultaneously reaching into the cab to shake hands all around.

Smith peered out the windshield. "It's all right, Mr. Carson. It looks like it's stopped for a while. We can get the job done before it starts in again."

Carson shook his head. "No, that ain't what I mean. You just cain't do the pigs today. The moon ain't in the right phase."

"What do you mean the moon isn't in the right phase, what kind of nonsense is that?" the senior who was with us asked.

Carson looked offended. "Ain't nonsense at all, son. I checked the almanac and it says the moon ain't in the right place for castratin' pigs, is all. It'll be right in about ten days' time. Come on out and do it then. But thanks for comin' today anyway."

Smith did not look surprised as he listened to all this. "You've had the appointment for three weeks, Mr. Carson. The least you could have done is call us and cancel."

"Doc, I would have if'n I'd a realized. I just plum' mis-figgered the moon."

"Well, okay. But we're going to have to charge you for the mileage for coming out here, you know."

Carson was not to be dissuaded. "That's all right, professor," he answered, wiping his face. "Rather do it that way than take a chance that somethin'll go wrong 'cause we ain't doin' it at the right time."

"What an asshole!" the senior said as we pulled out of the gate and back onto the highway. "The moon is not in the right phase for castrating pigs. Jesus!"

"Hey, George," I said. "How do you know he isn't right. I've noticed a difference in clotting time on the spays I've done. They're shorter or longer, depending on the time of the month."

"Okay, Younker. So you're as full of shit as he is."

I shrugged. "I'm not saying he is right. But maybe pigs do bleed more at certain times during the lunar cycle. And people have said that more pigs bleed to death if castrations are done at certain times of the month."

Smith had been listening to all this in silence. "When I first got out of school," he said after a moment, "I went over to Europe and worked for a practitioner in the south of France for a while. The farmers there believed in witch-

98

craft and very often wouldn't let you treat an animal unless you gave them a little hocus-pocus along with the real medicine.

"So the first day I went out with the practitioner, he told me that he would have to tell his clients that I was an expert on witchcraft from Paris and that I had come to help him out. The very first call we made was to a farmer who had some pretty sick pigs. I don't remember what they had, but I do know that it was something relatively simple like an iron deficiency. We cleared it up with one injection. But after we had given all the animals all the injections, the practitioner told the farmer that I advised that he should burn a candle every night in the northwest corner of the barn for a week. Of course, the pigs all made a 'miraculous recovery.'

"I went back to that area for a vacation about ten years after that. The farmers still remembered me as the great witchcraft expert from Paris! Unfortunately, that kind of thing is universal. You can't get away from it."

By the time we arrived at the Warren farm, the rain had started up again. Warren, who had called us late the previous day, took us into an old, broken-down barn. There were cracks in the sides about an inch wide. The roof was leaking and the ground was as muddy inside the barn as it was outside.

Warren had bought some cattle a few weeks earlier. A dozen of his newly purchased Herefords were lying about and even at first glance looked like very sick animals. They all had diarrhea and several looked dehydrated. Their breathing was very labored, as if they were suffering from pneumonia.

Smith was grimly silent as he examined the cows, talking only when he had to give one of us an order or only when Warren addressed him directly. And when Smith talked it was only in the shortest of sentences. "It looks to me like shipping fever," Smith finally said. "Let's get them on some antibiotics."

We finished up, hosed down our muddy boots and drove off. Smith was still saying little or nothing.

"Damn," George finally said. "Can you imagine letting things slide that far? Those cows must have been sick from the day they were unloaded. He'll be lucky if half of them pull out of it."

Smith finally spoke up. "Like I told you. That foolishness is universal."

"What foolishness?" I asked. "He didn't mention any superstitions."

"Didn't you see that each cow had a horn with the tip cut off?" Smith asked. I had thought it strange that each cow seemed to have one mutilated horn. "That old fart was treating those cows for hollow horn disease."

"Hollow horn disease?"

"That's it. A lot of these guys classify every ailment their cows get as hollow horn disease. They think that the cow gets sick because the horn has lost its insides. What they don't realize, even after working a lifetime with cows, is that all horns are empty to begin with.

"When a cow gets sick, they chop off the top of the horn and then pour vinegar into what's left. That's supposed to help matters. In the case where the disease is self-limiting, the problem goes away and they think they've cured the animal. Sometimes the animal just dies. Luckily this guy was smart enough to see he wasn't doing very well and called us to bail him out."

We rode on in silence, digesting that novel piece of information. Dr. Smith chuckled to himself. "Of course," he said, "you have to realize that hollow horn disease isn't nearly as serious as worm-in-the-tail disease."

"I'm almost afraid to ask," George said.

Smith cleared his throat and launched into a mock lecture. "Cows and dogs," he said, "are very prone to worm-in-the-tail disease. Little teensy worms supposedly make their way into the tails of these animals and cause all sorts of diseases. The way to cure the problem is to bite the end of the tail off the dog or chop it off the cow and then pull out all the little worms."

We were nonplussed. "You mean they really believe that?"

"Sure. Because they think that what they see when they bite off or chop off the tail are worms. They are not, of course. What they are looking at are tendons inside the tail. They just look like worms to them."

"Well what the hell," George said. "Let's call it a day. Maybe things will get better tomorrow."

Chapter Nine

The tall, good-looking woman who had just stepped into the room looked on as the laboratory technician sitting with me ran through some of the procedures used in the laboratory.

A second or two later she strolled over, hands in her laboratory coat pockets. "Who. the hell is this?" she demanded, nodding toward me.

"This is our new technician, Mrs. Brown," my instructor answered, deference noticeable in her voice. "He was hired last week while you were on vacation."

Traditionally, junior and senior year veterinary students were hired to work as technicians in the university's human medical center blood bank. Because school had settled into a comfortable routine by my third year and because I was something of a work-o-holic, I had applied for one of the blood bank jobs when it had become available.

I felt a bit uncomfortable. Mrs. Brown (who, as it turned out, was the head of the laboratory) was scrutinizing me intently with flashing eyes. "All right," she said after what seemed to be an interminable amount of time. "You go back to your other work. I'll take over."

Mrs. Brown sat down next to me, her legs pressed close to mine. She picked up the blood bank manual that was lying on the table in front of us and began leafing through it. The pressure against my thigh did not diminish, even as she began to ask me questions to see if I had studied the manual before I had reported for work. I had, of course, and knew the answer to every question she asked. She put down the book, turned to me and, for the second time, fixed her fiery eyes on me. "You are obviously good at this, Mr. Younker. Are you good at anything else?"

I felt heat surging up in me. Maybe the veterinary school could provide all the animal drama I needed. But unless I was very wrong about Mrs. Brown (I wasn't, it turned out), it looked as if the medical center would provide me with a little human excitement.

In fact, every day it became clearer that nothing I had ever heard about the goings-on at a medical center had been exaggerated. Shortly after I had started work, I received my first middle-of-the-night emergency call. There had been a car wreck, someone had been seriously injured and, as the technician on call that night, I had to go to the hospital and do the blood typing and cross-matching for the emergency surgery that had been scheduled.

I rushed over to the laboratory and managed to do the necessary analysis of the car wreck victim's blood. To get the cross-matched blood to the operating room quickly, I ran to the elevators, caught one and pressed the "Express" button to get up there without having to make intermediate stops. As in many modern buildings, there were two sets of elevators on both sides of the same corridor. On the surgical floor, operating room A, where the emergency surgery was taking place, was to the right if you stepped off one bank of elevators, to the left, if you stepped off the other bank. Because I had been in a hurry (and because I was still half-asleep), I hadn't noticed which bank of elevators I had chosen. Thus, when I got off my elevator, I stumbled down the corridor to my left, thinking I was approaching room A.

I could not understand why that particular corridor was so dark if they were doing surgery. I slammed through the double doors leading into the operating room and ground to a halt. On the operating table, a nurse and intern (judging from the clothes they still had on) were getting it on.

"Is this surgery room A?" I asked idiotically.

They never missed a beat. "No," the young man replied hoarsely as he glanced over to me. "It's on the other side of the hall, shmuck."

Even the patients tried to get into the act from time to time.

The university medical center handled private patients as well as public charity patients. And, it also dispensed medical care to the inmates of a nearby women's prison. A week or so after Christmas, two women prisoners were brought

102

in while I was on duty. One had broken her leg when she tried to escape from prison by jumping out of a third-floor window. The other had been brought in for a gall-bladder operation. For a few hours, they shared the same room. But they were so happy to be out from behind bars that they were raising all sorts of hell and had to be separated. The woman with the gall-bladder problem was moved into a room with a sweet, twenty-three-year-old Baptist whom I had never seen without a Bible in hand.

Most of the patients who had been in the hospital for a while knew me and simply stuck out their arms when I walked into the room. Suzanne was new and so I had to explain the procedure to her. "Let me get the sample now," I said as I finished, expecting her to put out her arm.

Instead, she whipped the sheet away from her body and pointed at the very upper reaches of her inner thigh. "That's the only vein you are going to get from me, buddy," she announced.

I glanced quickly at the Baptist, wondering if she had seen. The pinkish color on her cheeks told me that her concentration on the Passion According to St. Matthew indeed had been disturbed. "Only doctors are allowed to take blood from that vein, m'am," I said. (I wasn't being funny. Doctors really were the only ones allowed to work with the femoral vein.) "I really will have to have one of your arms. Are the veins there really that bad?"

Yes, she nodded, never taking her eyes off me.

I was determined, however, to stay away from her thigh. "Well then just give me your best arm."

Obviously scoffing at my medical and sexual cowardice, she offered me her right arm. I turned it over. It was covered with scar tissue from bicep down to her forearm. She must have been shooting dope for fifteen years.

Without much hope, I began to palpate her arm, trying to find traces of a vein. When I thought I had spotted one, I poked with my needle. Nothing came into the syringe. I poked again and again. I couldn't get a drop of blood out of the arm.

"Look," I said in desperation. "Let me see the other arm. Maybe that one isn't as bad as you think."

She shrugged and gave me her left arm. There was hardly a needle mark on it. Obviously she was left-handed and had been shooting dope mainly into her right arm. But

I was hopping mad. "Why did you give me that business about your arms being in such bad shape. This one isn't great, but it's better."

"Listen, buddy," she shot back. "If you had been locked up for the last three years and some young guy came into your room, you'd try to make him see something other than your arms too!" She stopped and gave the Baptist a quick glance. "I'll tell you one thing. If we were here alone, I'd make you feel like one cat in a whole bagful of tricks!"

The little Baptist turned a final shade of red.

If working at the human medical center gave my life a little extra spice, it also provided me with an accidental glimpse of the way my life might have turned out if, as a youngster, I hadn't been so determined to work with animals.

On a Wednesday evening while I was on duty, a lady who was to have major heart surgery within the next few days was brought into the hospital. Because the operation would be long and difficult and because she was to be placed on a heart-lung machine, the hospital wanted to have at least twenty-five pints of her type of blood on hand. Unfortunately, the woman had a very rare blood type, one found in less than one percent of the population.

Desperately, we began to cast about for blood, even calling state blood banks as far away as California. We also went to the state penitentiary (as we often did when we needed blood donations), hoping that among its large population of inmates we might find a donor who would have the blood type and cross-match with the patient. Since we were pressed for time and since there were hundreds of prisoners to be screened, we worked fast and furiously. None of us bothered to look at the faces of the men who had volunteered to give blood. All we saw were arms and bulging veins.

Suddenly, a hand grabbed hard at my shoulder. "Hey, doc," a man said. "I know you, don't I?"

I couldn't imagine how a convicted felon might know me, but I picked up the medical information card he had made out and looked at his name. I couldn't believe it! It was Harold! "Hey, man," I shouted, "I'm Younker."

With a whoop, Harold threw his arms around me, practically lifting me off the ground in a massive bear hug.

Three guards came running. "It's all right, it's all right." I waved them off. "We're friends."

"What's the story, man?" I asked.

Harold shrugged. "I got ten to life for armed robbery. My third time in the joint." I wasn't sure, but I thought I detected a small measure of pride in his answer.

"Hey man," Harold said, a happy lilt in his voice. "D'you ever learn to ride a hog?"

I laughed because I remember why Harold was asking. Shortly after I had come under his protecting wing in junior high and had joined his gang, Harold had tried to teach me to ride his gigantic Harley. Not only was the machine big and cumbersome, but at the time motorcycles had the shift lever on the side of the gas tank. If you wanted to change gears you had to take one hand off the handlebars. I managed to shift all right—even to downshift as I approached a red light. But at the light, waiting for it to turn green, I leaned over and put my left foot on the ground, trying to look as "cool" as possible. But I had leaned over too far and was suddenly having trouble keeping the motorcycle in a vertical position. Just as the light turned green, I gave up the struggle to keep the Harley in an upright position and laid it down in front of honking cars on every side of me. Harold, who had been a block and a half away, came running to bail me out. It was the last time he let me solo.

Harold was laughing as we talked about the incident. "If I hadn't been laughin' then too," Harold said, "I'd have killed you."

I wondered what had happened to our colleagues. "Whatever happened to Sam the safecracker?" I asked.

Sam had been one of my early boyhood friends who also had liked animals a great deal. Sam had joined the Birdwatchers Club which I had helped organize in grade school. And he had invented a method of filling bird-feeders that freed us of the necessity of having to climb up and down trees to make food available to the birds.

Sam and I joined Harold's gang about the same time. I stayed more or less in the background. Primarily because I was small, I was used as bait to start fights. I would be sent out to walk casually past the movie house where a rival gang hung out. The other gang, thinking they had found an easy victim, would start pushing me around. Then my gang would come roaring up on their motorcycles and, swinging chains and brandishing knives, would come to my "defense."

Sam, however, used his considerable intelligence to actively pursue a life of crime. He found a library book describing safe-cracking techniques, learned them, and promptly began burglarizing neighborhood stores. When he came across some safes he couldn't crack, he took up the challenge. He went out and learned how to blow up safes with nitroglycerin by studying some chemistry at one of the local university's libraries. He stole the necessary chemicals from the high school lab and went out to tackle the hard-to-crack safes. The first "job" went just fine. But on his next attempt, he blew out the side brick wall of one building. Because it was winter, people thought a boiler had blown up and called the fire department. Firemen, combing through the debris, found Sam unconscious under a pile of bricks, his safe-cracking equipment next to him. The safe was untouched. He was packed off to reform school and, subsequently, to his grandmother's farm.

"Sam did all right," Harold said. "Never did come back to the gang, though."

"How about Amelio?"

"Amelio is in jail for grand theft."

"Billie?"

"In Joliette for first-degree murder. Knocked off a gas-station attendant."

I ran through the other names. The stories were all the same. All were in prison. Only Sam and I had escaped.

Chapter Ten

As the end of the school year and the beginning of summer vacation approached, I began to cast about for a job that would once more involve me with animal medical practice. I had been offered the chance to stay with the blood bank laboratory over the summer. But as much as I liked my own personal facsimile of Peyton Place, I wanted to take advantage of the next three months to broaden my experiences with the treatment of animals. With my senior year rushing toward me and private practice looming just beyond, it would not be long before my mobility and my options were limited.

The perfect opportunity for a last fling at the exotic came along in the form of an announcement posted on the school bulletin board. As it did every year, the U.S. Agricultural Research Service was offering a few summer jobs to veterinary students. Because the ARS wanted to encourage veterinary students to start thinking about joining them on a full-time basis after graduation, the jobs offered were well paid. Most, unfortunately, were not very glamorous. Half of the positions were in the field testing cattle for tuberculosis or brucellosis. The other jobs were in slaughterhouses inspecting meat. I wanted a job in the field, but the idea of spending a summer in Nebraska (or some other place like it) did not appeal to me. Only for some lucky student with a fluent knowledge of Spanish was there something more exciting: A job in sunny Puerto Rico. Exaggerating a bit my knowledge of Spanish, I applied for that job. A few months later I was in San Juan, face to face with the man who would supervise my activities for the summer.

His first word to me was in English: "Hi." The rest was a torrent of Puerto Rican Spanish. I could not understand one word the man was saying to me. "¿ *Puede hablar un poco más despacio?*" I asked him.

He began again, this time talking more slowly. I still could not understand what he wanted to tell me. But this time, instead of responding to my second request that he speak more slowly, he opened a drawer of his desk, whipped out a file that had my name on it and leafed through the pages of my application. "You have committed fraud, Mr. Younker," he said in English. "It says right here that you speak and understand Spanish."

I tried to explain that I thought I spoke and understood it well enough, but that obviously I was not used to Puerto Rican Spanish.

He studied me with a dark look on his face, trying to make up his mind what to do with me. "I could send you back to the mainland and have you prosecuted," he finally said, "but I don't think I will. You will go to Mayaguez, which is on the other side of the island. In the city the people are quite fluent in English. But you, Mr. Younker, will be doing most of your work in the countryside. Few of the farmers in Cabo Rojo, Santa Maria or the other small towns speak English. That should teach you Spanish fast!"

I was about to thank him for the reprieve, but he gave me no chance to say anything. Instead, he launched into a ten-minute lecture about fraud, my dubious future as a veterinarian and an outline of ethics and morality. "And, by the way, Younker," he finished up. "Regulations say that you should not drink on the job."

"That's okay, I don't drink anyhow," I answered truthfully.

"Well never mind that regulation," he went on as if he hadn't heard me. "Down here it is an insult to refuse a drink when it is offered. We are trying to develop a good rapport with the farmers, so if a farmer offers you a drink, you drink it."

My very limited knowledge of Spanish landed me in trouble almost before I had left the city limits of San Juan behind me. The day was hot and dripping with humidity. The government-issued three-quarter-ton truck I had been given to use had no air conditioner in it. Hoping that a stray breeze might cool me off as I drove the steaming road to Mayaguez, I wiggled out of my shirt.

Almost immediately, I saw the flashing blue lights of a

Puerto Rican patrol car in my rear view mirror. Since there was no other car on the road, I gathered that he was after me. I pulled to the shoulder and waited while in the laconic fashion of highway patrolmen everywhere, the cop walked over to the truck as slowly as possible.

A torrent of Spanish soon enveloped me, and I listened very carefully, hoping to understand how I had violated the traffic laws. But the only word I could make out was *"camisa."*

That's it, I said to myself. The man is talking about a shirt—the local way of asking for a bribe is probably to say that he needs a new shirt. I showed him my driver's license, but to no avail. The word *"camisa"* came at me again and again.

Determined not to give him a penny, I ran my hand over his shirt. "No, no," I said. "You have a beautiful *camisa. Muy bonita camisa.* You don't need a new one."

Finally, he gave up. He adjusted his hat, went back to his patrol car and, tires screaming and blue lights flashing, streaked away down the road.

The next day, while I was waiting for the veterinarian to whom I had been assigned to come to the small government office in Mayaguez, I proudly started to tell the lone secretary there how I had conned a cop out of a bribe.

"Did you acutally offer the policeman some money?" she asked with a mixture of horror and amusement.

"Nah. I wasn't going to pay him off."

"It's a good thing you did not," she replied. "This is not Mexico, you know. You could be in jail for offering a policeman a bribe."

I was puzzled. "Then what was all that about him needing a shirt?"

I could almost hear her thinking Washington-has-gone-and-sent-us-another-one. "He didn't need a new shirt, Señor Younker. He was trying to tell you that you needed one. In Puerto Rico it is against the law for a driver of a car to drive without a shirt. If you are the passenger, yes. But if you are the driver, no."

Determined that my rudimentary knowledge of Spanish would not get in the way of my work, I dug my dictionary out of the bottom of my suitcase and, that very night, began to brush up on the vocabulary I would need to make myself understood to the farmers who would be my "clients."

A day or so later—after a proper amount of indoctrination by the veterinarian to whom I had been assigned—I was off to make my first call. *"Buenos días,"* I shouted proudly to the first farmer I called on. *"¿ Dónde están sus vacas? . . ."*

His face lit up. *"Ah, un mejicano . . ."*

"No, no," I tried to explain. *"Soy americano."*

"No, no," he insisted. *"¿Mejicano, no?"*

"Americano," I tried once more after he had babbled on for a minute or two. *"Por favor, habla más despacio."*

Suddenly, the man turned on his heels, stalked back into his house and slammed the door behind him.

I stood there, not knowing what to do or what had happened. A man and woman started yelling in the house, but all I could make out was an occasional, *"Mejicano,"* or *"Americano."*

After a few minutes, a young woman carrying a baby came out. "I am Mr. Gomez' daughter," she told me in English. "My father says you are making fun of him."

"Making fun? I didn't say anything except that I am an American."

"You are really from the mainland?"

"Yes, of course."

"Ah, now I understand. You see, some Mexicans look down on us. He thought you were Mexican and that you were making fun of his Spanish by saying that you were an American to imply that his Spanish was so bad that even a Mexican couldn't understand it."

It took me a minute or two to work out the tortured logic. I convinced her that I was from Kentucky and she went back into the house. In a moment, she reappeared, leading the old man. He still had a petulant expression on his face.

The man turned to me and said something in Spanish. "He wants to apologize," his daughter translated. "He says you and he must have a drink together."

My heart sank. First the language misunderstanding. Now, I was faced with having to turn down his liquor. I could see the Puerto Rican independence movement gaining momentum by the second. The young woman must have had an inkling of what I was thinking. "It is the way," she gently insisted.

The three of us returned to the porch where a wide-mouth jug, filled with a pinkish-looking fluid and fermented fruit, awaited us.

"What?" I whispered to the daughter, "is that?"

"That is his homemade rum. We put it in a jar containing half a gallon of peeled canapes which is a sweet fruit from here, seal the jar and bury it when it is first known that a baby is expected. The jar is dug up later when the child is born."

Knowing what would be in store for me if I drank even half of one of the large glasses the daughter had brought out of the house, I strategically seated myself next to a large potted plant. I graciously accepted each offering the man made—only to pour it little by little into the plant whenever he looked away to point something out to me. When his ruffled feathers had been sufficiently smoothed, we went to work on his herd.

The official in San Juan thought he would be punishing me by sending me to a place where few people spoke English. As it turned out, the eastern part of Puerto Rico was full of English-speakers. The city of Mayaguez boasted Puerto Rico's only all-English public-school system. Moreover, far from being an isolated backwater, Mayaguez hosts two major institutions of higher learning and an Atomic Energy Commission-affiliated research center that offers a Master's degree in nuclear engineering. Mayaguez is also an important industrial center where electronic components, foodstuffs, furniture, clothing, tiles, and agricultural tools are manufactured.

It was Mayaguez's status as an advanced urban center that turned out to be my punishment. Back in the 1940's, Mayaguez had been the center of a major cattle-producing area. Now, because conditions had changed, the cattle population had shrunk tremendously. But apparently no one had bothered to inform San Juan, and officials there believed that their man in Mayaguez had thousands and thousands of cattle to test for brucellosis or tuberculosis each year. That's why they sent veterinary students like me out there—to help that poor doctor cope with his (allegedly) heavy work load.

111

In reality, there was little or nothing to do. Every morning I would make a call or two to the farmers in the area who had stayed on the land and were still trying to scratch out a living. By noon I would either be on the deserted beach or, when forced to, in one of the bars my boss frequented, watching him get drunk as he downed straight rum by the quart.

Mayaguez was also punishment for me because the people there were cold to strangers. The farmers by and large had no interest in you as a person. My boss seldom invited me to his home for dinner. It was difficult to strike up a conversation with anyone in any of the local bars.

In desperation, I began to consider seeking out the city's Jews—if there were any. If they had a temple, at least I could go to services. For several days I had noticed a man hanging around the lobby and the hotel's small dining room. Since he seemed to be one of the friendlier types, I asked him if he knew any Jews in town.

"There is one," he said.

One, I thought, was better than none. I asked him if he could introduce me.

"You have already met him," he said, sticking out his hand. "Antonio David Del Pozo Kaufman at your service." And then by way of explanation: "I am Cuban. But my mother was Jewish and I was brought up Jewish."

Del Pozo had been with Castro. "I was from a rich family," he told me later over dinner. "But I wanted to join the revolution. Because I knew how to fly airplanes, they assigned me to the air force. I thought they had great things in mind for me until they assigned me to fly crop dusters. That was not revolution for me so one day I loaded my tanks with insecticide as usual, climbed into the airplane and headed for the coast. When I got over water, I dumped the insecticide and flew to Jamaica. I flew all the way four feet above the water to stay out of the radar. After Jamaica, I came here."

"Marvelous," I said. "What are you doing here?"

He took a sip of the soup and smiled. "Flying a crop duster. I'm going up tomorrow for a practice run at some sugar fields. Want to come along?"

I readily agreed and arranged to meet him after my one morning call.

The next day I hurried to Toro de Oro Ranch where I

112

was to start testing cattle. Although much of the area around Mayaguez had been in a drought for years, the Toro Ranch was even more arid than others I had visited. Dust and sand seemed to be everywhere. Several of the cowboys even wore kerchiefs across their faces to protect themselves against the swirls of dust kicked up by the cattle as they marched into the various corrals where we were working.

The testing scheduled for the morning went fast (the cattle were so starved and thirsty they had little desire to give us trouble). When I had finished, I wandered over to one of the corrals that had a water tank in it. Rather than waste our precious drinking water to cool myself off, I thought, I could just as well splash myself with a bit of the water used by the cattle. Without thinking twice, I climbed over the fence, passed the groups of bulls that were standing around, swishing at flies with their tails, and strolled over to the three-foot-deep watering tank.

I bent over the tank's edge and put my whole head in the water. It wasn't very cold, but it felt delicious after the heat and the dust. Just as I was about to put my shirt on, I felt as if I had been hit in the rear end with a battering ram. I soared into the air and came down, fortunately, in the middle of the water tank. I struggled to the surface, stood up and looked over to where I had been standing. A good-sized bull was standing there now, staring at the intruder who had dared help himself to some of his precious water. Because cattle are by nature curious all the other bulls ambled over slowly to see what was going on. (One of Dr. Stack's interesting cases had been to determine how eight cows had all come down with rabies at the same time. He found that the cows had all been bitten on the nose by a rabid skunk they had all gathered around to examine.) My boss, the ranch foreman, and the cowboys were leaning on the fence, helpless with laughter. Finally one of the men stopped laughing long enough to get on his horse and ride over to rescue me.

By the time I reached the small landing strip where Del Pozo was waiting for me, my jeans had pretty well dried out—in fact, only my boots were still wet and squished noisily as I walked across the field to the crop duster. Del Pozo ushered me to the plane—it was one of those small biplanes with an open cockpit—and strapped me into the front seat. "The passenger sits in the front," he explained as he adjusted the safety belt. "The pilot sits in the back. But do not worry, it will be fun."

The fields Del Pozo was to dust were not only tucked *between* several mountains in the area, but also *on* the sides of some of those mountains. Thus, from my front seat perch—with nothing to hold onto save the edges of my seat—I would see first the sides of a mountain rushing straight at me. At the very last moment, Del Pozo would dive the plane and head straight toward the ground in order to practice spraying insect killer on the mountainside fields. Only moments before the nose of the plane was to meet earth, he'd pull the plane up and we'd be soaring straight into the blue sky, God knows how heavy a gravitational force was pushing me against the back of my seat.

After forty-five minutes of roller-coastering around the mountain fields, Del Pozo headed for a long expanse of fields full of sugar cane. Much to my relief, there wasn't so much as an anthill to be seen. Del Pozo took the plane into a gentle descent and for a few minutes we lazily flew back and forth over the sugar cane, which was no more than twenty-five feet below us.

I had just begun to breathe easily again when the plane suddenly veered and headed toward the farther reaches of the vast plantation. Off in the distance, I could see something glimmering. We flew closer and closer to it and soon what had been only a shimmering speck turned into a five- or six-story building made entirely of corrugated iron. It was the plant where the sugar cane was processed.

At first I thought Del Pozo just wanted to give me a look at the structure. But as it grew bigger and bigger on our horizon, I saw that he had no intention of turning away from it. As the building began to block everything else out of our view, and I started to see each individual rivet on the iron sheets, I slid down into my seat, bracing myself for the impending crash. At the very last moment (again), the plane seemed to rise like an elevator. Del Pozo flew the plane across the peaked roof and, when we reached the other side, dropped the plane until we were no more than ten feet from the ground.

"I hope you were not too frightened at the building back there," Del Pozo said with a grin when we had landed. "But they have sugar growing right up to the sides of the

114

building. That stuff is very important. You have to dust every bit of the crop. That is why I practice before I make a real run."

Although a friendship with Del Pozo held the promise of relief from my boredom, I could not reconcile myself to spending the rest of the summer doing only half a day's work. I had come here to broaden my experience and, so far, had not managed to learn very much. After an arduous campaign consisting of constant telephone calls to San Juan, I managed to get myself transferred out of Mayaguez. I found myself at the San Juan airport, working in the customs area. I was to inspect animal products or animal by-products brought into the country by travelers.

I had not been on duty very long when one of the customs officers called me over. A priest had tried to bring sausages into Puerto Rico and the agent wanted me to confiscate them because they were made of uncooked pork.

I was stymied. Even after six weeks in Puerto Rico, I was still having trouble with Spanish. But the priest was from Portugal. How was I going to confiscate sausages in Portuguese? With a lot of smiling and hand signaling, I had the priest—a kindly, even meek-looking, man—open the briefcase in which he was carrying the sausages.

"Confiscate them," the agent whispered in my ear.

"Hey, look," I tried to protest. "I'm not even Catholic."

"Don't be silly, Younker. Confiscate them."

I reached into the briefcase and took out the sausages. Alarmed, the priest grabbed one and tried to pull it back. I refused to let go and hung on to my end. He pulled. I pulled. The tug of war might have gone on indefinitely, but suddenly the customs agent began to yell at the priest in Spanish. He yelled back in Portuguese. I squeezed in a yell or two in English. Somehow, we got it across to the not-so-kindly-any-more priest that he had to leave his precious sausages behind. "Lots of fun, huh?" the customs man asked as he turned to take the sausages to the impound locker in his office.

(Actually, my hassles with people who tried to bring uncooked sausages into Puerto Rico were not as bad as the hassles the plant inspectors had with travelers who wanted to bring mangoes into the island. Puerto Rico has mangoes. But the citizen of every South American or Central American country is convinced that the mangoes in *his* country

115

are the only ones that are edible. Thus, even at the cost of leaving something important at home, Latins carry a load of mangoes when they leave their countries. The fights the plant inspectors had with incoming travelers over a mango or two bordered on the fierce. A drug dealer trying to sneak twenty-five pounds of pure heroin into Manhattan would not struggle as strongly to protect his contraband as an Ecuadorian woman trying to bring two mangoes, hidden in her bra, into Puerto Rico.)

Although we took our watch for contraband salamis very seriously, one of our most important jobs was to inspect animals going from the island over to the mainland. Our job was to look for ticks, insects that could be bearing equine and bovine diseases, on the export animals. If we found just one tick on just one animal, we could prevent an entire shipment of horses or cows from going over.

On an otherwise slow day—not even one salami confiscated—a local breeder showed up with eighteen Paso Fino horses he wanted to ship to the States.

"Listen, inspector," the man said, talking quickly. "I got a chartered plane ready to take off, waiting for these horses. Can you pass them right through?"

The horses smelled strongly of insecticide. Many of them had patches of hair missing, indicating that a strong solution had been used to try to kill whatever ticks there might have been on them. Nevertheless, I started the examination. I didn't get very far. In the tail of the very first horse I looked at, I found a big, fat tick.

"I'm sorry," I said to the man. "The horses can't go."

"Come on now," the man said. "One tick, eh. What does it matter?"

"I'm sorry," I insisted. "The rule is that if there is evidence of infestation in one animal, the whole lot is kept back."

The man reached for his wallet. "All right. I'll make it worth your while."

"I'm sorry. No."

In an instant the man came unglued. "You *coño*," he screamed at me. "If you don't let these horses go, I'll have your job. You'll be sorry. You better not leave the airport tonight, understand, 'cause you won't get home . . ."

I excused myself, got to a phone and called the veteri-

116

narian in charge. He called the Federal marshalls and within minutes they were escorting him away.

Because I had managed to get myself back into the good graces of the San Juan office with my conscientious work at the airport, I was rewarded with a junket to the Virgin Islands. One of our inspectors, on a routine trip to the islands (the Federal government did not keep a full-time agricultural service employee there) had found that someone had imported fifty-five hundred pounds of frozen pork ribs from Denmark. It is permissible to import boneless pork because it will be thoroughly cooked. But meat with bone attached is not likely to be cooked thoroughly enough to destroy bacteria or viruses in the bone marrow. Two other inspectors and I were dispatched to St. Croix to confiscate the pork.

We were lucky and found forty-five hundred pounds still in the wholesaler's freezer and five hundred pounds in supermarkets he serviced.

With that meat in hand, we had a choice: We could burn it or we could take it out to sea and dump it there. Because a day at sea seemed to hold the promise of more fun than a day in the local garbage dump, we rented a fifty-five-foot fishing vessel and set off to do our duty—and to do a little deep-sea fishing as well. Unfortunately, the sea would not cooperate. After two hours of trying to cut open the cartons containing the meat (we couldn't just throw the cartons overboard because they could have floated to shore) while fighting fifteen-foot waves, I was so sick that I had to ask we go back to shore. When I finally got out of bed two days later, we found three hundred and fifty more pounds of meat. This time we went to the city dump, gathered up some old tires, put the meat on top of them, and had a giant, if inedible, barbeque.

Because we had not found all of the fifty-five hundred pounds of meat, we had to inspect the island's cattle herds to make sure that there had been no infestation of foot-and-mouth diseases as a result of the contraband.

We found no evidence that the meat had caused problems among the cattle of St. Croix. But we did hit pay dirt in another way.

We had just about finished our inspection at one small farm when one of the other inspectors called me over. When I reached him, he opened his hand. In his palm was a huge arachnid, probably an inch and a half in diameter. "You just took parasitology, Younker," he said. "What the hell kind of a tick is this big bugger?"

"Christ! I have never seen anything that big. It sure as hell is no brown dog tick, I can tell you that."

We packed the tick and sent it to San Juan on the next plane, hoping the laboratory there might be able to identify it. But they were stumped as well and in turn had to forward the tick to the ARS station in Maryland. We received an urgent telegram from them, advising us that the creature was an African Bont tick, the carrier of such exotic and dangerous diseases as heartwater disease and tick-bite fever. The tick had never been seen on the islands before and its sudden appearance there was a mystery we did not solve. But as soon as we knew what it was, we got busy and dipped as many cows and steers as we could before we had to return to San Juan. Another massive project to dip all the livestock on the island in insecticide would begin soon.

On the whole, the trip to the Virgin Islands had been fun. But it also filled me with a new respect for the Agricultural Research Service. The sophomoric opinion among young veterinarians held that only quacks, has-beens and doctors who could not make it in private practice joined the ARS. But working with those men—especially on the St. Croix trip—convinced me that they were highly qualified professionals. Were it not for their dedicated work, we would not be eating half as well as we are in this country.

By the middle of August, my tour of duty in Puerto Rico had settled into an unexciting routine. Although the summer had been fun, it really had not been fully satisfying. I had hoped to learn something new. But my medical knowledge had not been deepened by the few tuberculin tests I had administered in Mayaguez or by the several pounds of sausages I had confiscated from hapless travelers. "If you want to see something exciting," one of the other inspectors told me during a long wait between planes one day, "try to see the horse hospital at the track in Caracas. I don't know if you can get in without an introduction, but it would be worth the try."

Two days later, I was on my way. To make the cheapest connection between San Juan and Caracas, I had to take

118

an excursion flight to Curaçao, a small Caribbean island under Dutch rule, and then, two days later, take another excursion flight into Venezuela.

Because I would have time on my hands (the island is largely desert) I thumbed through the Curaçao telephone book to find a veterinarian I could visit. "Yes, of course, come over," the man told me in a lilting Dutch accent when I reached him. "I would be glad to show you my practice."

A procession of dogs and cats marked the morning. "Do you know anything about horses?" Dr. Van Den Groot, a tall, bearded man, asked me while he was cleaning the ears of a small terrier.

"It's my biggest interest," I said, trying to stop the small dog from snapping at Van Den Groot's hands. "But I wouldn't say I'm an expert."

"No matter. Maybe you can still help. My associate who is the large animal doctor is now in Florida studying for three months. Some horses at the riding club have fallen sick, but I cannot understand what is going on. Come along and take a look."

Six of the horses, I found, had laminitis, an inflammation of the sensitive layers inside the hoof. The disease can be caused by trauma or by a faulty diet. Since there was more than one horse involved, I suspected diet to be the villain.

"Have you changed their feed lately?" I asked the woman who was the manager of the club.

"No, not at all. We always obtain the same feed from the same establishment. As a matter of fact, just a few days ago we received a new shipment."

She left and a moment later came back with a bowl full of feed, grains and other food essentials that had been man-ufactured into pellet form. Since I had no idea of knowing what had gone into the pellets, I asked her to get the guar-anteed analysis tag that had to accompany each bag of feed.

"Here's your problem right here," I announced proudly after skimming the description of the food. "They must have made a mistake at the plant because what they have in this bag is not horse food. It's a food supplement for cows. There is too much protein and too many carbohy-drates in it for horses. That's why they foundered."

The woman was relieved and obviously delighted. "Is there anything I can do for you?"

I didn't have to think very long. "I'm going to Caracas. Do you know anyone who could give me an introduction to the track hospital there? I'd love to see it."

Her face lit up. "Oh, that will be no problem. We often go there for horse shows. When you get to Caracas, just call Mr. Newman. He is president of the riding club where we visit and he has connections at the track. He is a good friend of mine."

It was ten in the evening when my plane landed in Caracas. But since I was anxious to make contact, I called Newman as soon as I passed through customs. He insisted on coming to the airport and picking me up. "They are just finishing dinner over at the club anyway," he said. "We can go there now. I will pick you up in forty-five minutes. Look for a black Mercedes."

By the time we arrived at the club, dinner was over. Since the club members were deeply involved in a John Wayne movie showing on an outdoor screen, Newman showed me around the club. Unlike most of the stables I had seen (even those on wealthy breeding farms in the United States), the stables here all had rich cobblestone floors, floors so spotlessly clean they could have been installed that same day. The box stalls were huge, all deeply bedded in fresh straw. The horses were magnificent, each one more beautiful than the next. Newman was very proud of his club. He delighted in every one of my "wows."

By the time we had finished the tour and had a drink with some of the guests who had lingered on after Wayne had ridden off into the sunset, it was well after midnight. Over their nightcaps, the club members held a serious discussion about where I should stay, vetoing every hotel I found in my *Latin America on Five Dollars a Day* book as too shabby, too dangerous or too much out of the way. Finally, they came to an agreement on a pension a member suggested. "Do you want me to come in and make the arrangements?" Newman asked when we pulled up in front of the little hotel.

"No, it's all right. I've just come from Puerto Rico and my Spanish is okay."

"All right then. One of my drivers will pick you up at ten tomorrow morning. He will take you to the track."

I rang the bell on the front desk and when the sleepy owner of the pension stumbled out, I let loose a stream of my newly polished Spanish. The man listened politely, then smiled and held up his hand. "*Un momentito,*" he said. "*Mi esposa puede ayudarle.*"

Why, I wondered as he disappeared, would his wife have to help me. Smiling broadly, the woman talked quickly and animatedly. It took me the better part of a minute to realize that she was speaking Italian to me.

"No. *Soy americano.*"

"Americano?" she asked. "But you were not talking Italian to my husband?"

At ten the next morning, there was a soft knock at my door. "I'm Uriel Rosenfeld," the young man said. "My uncle has asked me to drive you to the track and introduce you to Dr. Martinez. He will show you around the hospital. He has surgery this morning, but he said you could assist him if you wanted to."

If the riding club the night before had been the epitome of leisure-time activity, the hospital proved to be the ultimate in a medical facility. South America had always been one of those places that was fifty years behind the United States as far as I was concerned. But what I saw here made *me* feel like I was the visitor from an underdeveloped country. They had the most modern equipment, the most fully equipped surgical suite I had ever seen. There was even a closed-circuit television system to allow horse owners, sitting in a comfortable lounge elsewhere, to watch the operations being performed on their animals. In 1965 prices, the hospital must have cost well over half a million dollars to set up.

Helping Dr. Martinez operate did nothing to help me feel very much like the sophisticate either. In school, when there was an operation to be performed, it was the teacher and a student or two who worked in the operating room.

When I walked into the surgical suite, the circulating nurse, the anesthesiologist (who was also a doctor of human medicine), and the scrub nurse had already prepared for the morning's surgeries.

Since Dr. Martinez and I were the last ones in, I moved to scrub my hands quickly. But then I realized that there was not just one sink here as we had at school. There were

121

four and anyone who was to enter the operating room had to move from sink to sink, washing again and again to attain as high a degree of sterility as possible. I scrubbed, put an iodine solution on my hands, and came face to face with a nurse holding up a gown. In all the operations I had done at school, I had never, but never, been confronted by a nurse holding up a gown for me. Trying to look as if it were a perfectly natural and expected thing, I off-handedly slipped into the gown and waited for her to tie up the strings in back. My façade, however, crumbled when I tangled with the surgeon's gloves she was now holding up. The people on television (Dr. Gannon et al.) made it seem so very easy. But in all my years of watching television I had never noticed that to get your hands into surgical gloves, you have to sock your hands down into them with a good deal of force. I just gently put one hand in the first glove— and promptly got stuck. The nurse, trying to help me get farther in, pulled up. I pushed down. She stumbled. I stumbled.

"Mr. Younker," Dr. Martinez said quietly over my shoulder as the nurse and I waltzed in place. "You have done surgery before, have you not?"

Dr. Martinez had scheduled a joint surgery for that morning on a horse that had a chip fracture called a "joint mouse." The horse also had a good deal of periosteal new bone growth on the knee. Working smoothly, Dr. Martinez lay open the troublesome joint and carefully removed the chip. Then he ground away the extra bone growth with a high speed surgical drill. "Good," he sighed with satisfaction when he had sewn the incision back together. "Now for 1000r of X-ray therapy and he will be just fine."

"Won't that much radiation slow down the healing of the skin incision?" I was trying to recoup. Maybe I could show a little advanced knowledge from up north.

I should have known better. Martinez, who spent a good deal of time traveling around the world to study new techniques, looked at me just a big quizzically. "Not at all, my friend. It takes more than a thousand r to do that. What this will do is prevent recurrence of periosteal new bone growth."

Dr. Martinez had scheduled no surgeries for the following day so that he could call on some of his clients in the countryside. He invited me and Uriel to go along.

Shortly after dawn the next day we took off in Dr. Martinez's private four-seater airplane and flew to the Cordillera del Norte. We stopped at his farm, a several hundred acre spread in a lush green valley. He wanted to show me his private surgical suite and the fifty-yard swimming pool used to exercise horses after surgery. Then we rode off into the mountains. He had to call on a nearby breeder of Arabians.

The manager of the ranch, a tall, blue-eyed, well-built man, came out to greet us. At Dr. Martinez's introduction, "This is Mr. Younker and Mr. Rosenfeld," I thought I could see a shadow pass over his face. "I am Velsh, you know," the manager said almost immediately in a decidedly non-Spanish, non-Welsh accent. "I came here from Vales."

That, I thought, was very interesting. But why was he making such a point of telling us about his allegedly Welsh background? Though still friendly, he was guarded as he showed us to the stables. Only when he brought out the ailing horse Dr. Martinez was to treat did I get a clue to his strange behavior. As he was describing the animal's symptoms to us, the animal jerked its head up. Because he was holding onto the halter around the horse's head, his arm also jerked upward. The sleeve on the arm fell back and there on the flesh of his forearm was a tattoo of a skull with a dagger imbedded in it. . ."My God!" I thought. "A real honest-to-goodness SS man!"

Later, as we flew back to Caracas, I mentioned my theory to Rosenfeld. "It could be," he said. "I thought he acted kind of strange when Martinez introduced us." He thought for a moment and then laughed. "He probably thought we were Israeli commandoes coming to kidnap him."

Chapter Eleven

The few days I had spent with Dr. Martinez made me restless to begin my own work with horses. During my senior year, I unleashed a storm of phone calls and letters to virtually every horse farm in Kentucky. All to no avail. By the time June rolled around and I had diploma in hand, I still had not landed a job as a horse doctor.

Thus, shortly after graduation, I was on an airplane, heading for California with a fellow student who wanted company, to take the Veterinary Board exam (which would determine whether or not I would be allowed to practice out there) and to test the job market. California, like New York and Florida, reputedly has an extremely difficult board exam. (Everyone, it seems, wants to practice in those states. Or at least that's what licensing boards in those states think.) I wasn't sure that I could pass the exam, but I had nothing to lose by making a run at it. In any case, I had never been to California and, at the very least, the trip would give me a well-deserved vacation before I began full-time work.

After taking the exam (I had the feeling afterwards that I had done well) I headed for San Francisco. My cousin Susan was living there. I knew a medical student there who had dropped out of school to spend time in Central America experimenting with Indian psychedelic drugs. And, judging from notices I had seen posted on the bulletin board at the University of California at Davis (where I had taken the exam), there were some job opportunities in the Bay area.

The medical student, whom I had met on a trip to Mexico two years earlier, had told me that he could always be found at a coffee shop called the Golden Goose. When I got there, there was no one in the dimly lit place except for the owner, who was sweeping the floor with half-hearted strokes, and a girl who was sitting at one of the tables, drinking an espresso.

"Never heard of him," the owner told me in a decidedly unfriendly manner. "But then, I've only owned the place for a year. If you want to, you can leave a note for him on the bulletin board by the door."

"Great," I answered. "Can I borrow a pen?"

"Jesus Christ! Now you want a pen?"

I was about to write off San Franciscans when the girl at the table chimed in. "Here. You can borrow my pencil."

I wrote the note, tacked it in among the scores of other notes and index cards and came back to join the girl (Mimsi was her name) for some coffee. "Where are you staying?" she asked after we had talked a while.

"With my cousin and her husband."

"That sounds kind of dull." She laughed. "Come stay at our house."

"Our house," it turned out, was an urban commune Mimsi shared with three other women and four men (the men were gay) in a six-bedroom house. They all worked so it was not exactly a poverty-stricken let's-live-off-the-land kind of commune. And it was tightly organized. While some of the members were assigned to keep the place clean, others were assigned to cook. Not only was the place spotlessly clean, but they were all very well fed. Everyone seemed to be a gourmet cook. During the time I stayed with Mimsi, I ate one gourmet meal after another—nice respites after long days of trekking around the San Francisco area talking to countless veterinarians. I was very tempted to stay and join up.

"A friend of mine has to take her dog to the veterinarian tomorrow," Mimsi told me after dinner one night. "Want to come with us? I don't know if he is looking for any help. But at least you can talk to him."

I had my first inkling that there was something different about this veterinarian when I saw the house where he lived and where he had his office. It was an old, three-story Victorian house—and it was painted bright red, with blue and yellow trim.

When we stepped in the front door, it was as if we had slipped back seventy years in time. His secretary was dressed in a long 1890's dress. Her hair was done in the style of the time and she was wearing high-button shoes. The furniture was all authentic Victorian. Off in the corner there was one of those hand-cranked movie machines.

I looked around the small reception area and then joined Mimsi and her friend who had taken a seat next to a very little old lady who had a small Shih Tzu on her lap.

Because I had come to California directly from a school where regulations about short hair, shaven cheeks, and "proper" dress were strictly enforced, I looked "clean" enough to be taken for a drug salesman from one of the pharmaceutical companies.

The little old lady looked me over very carefully and then leaned toward me. "Is this the first time you've been to see Dr. Summers?" she asked.

I admitted it was.

"Well, now," she whispered confidentially, glancing over to make sure the secretary could not hear me. "I don't want you to be alarmed when he comes out. He does look a little strange."

"Really?"

"Yes. But he just loves my little Bonnie. She had never been to a vet before we came here and she sure does like Dr. Summers. So don't be shocked when you see him because whatever else you think of him, he'll be very good to your pet."

Just as she was finishing her little warning, the office door opened. The first thing that came into view was this huge mass of hair that frizzled out in every direction from the man's head. His face was almost completely covered by a massive beard. A stethoscope, coming out from somewhere in all that hair, hung down to his chest. He was wearing a very conventional physician's white coat over a pair of leather pants, a leather shirt and a leather vest. He had turquoise rings on every one of his fingers and other assorted pieces of Indian jewelry on his wrists and neck. If you can look like that and still maintain a practice, I thought, I'm moving to California for sure.

The old lady with the Shih Tzu and Mimsi's friend were his last clients for the day and after he had locked the front door, he gave us a tour of the house. The Victorian theme in his office was echoed throughout the old mansion. Many pieces of furniture dated back to the late 1800's. Even the windows were 19th century. When several old mansions had been torn down in Oakland, Summers had bought up their old stained-glass windows and had them installed in his place. The house was filled with a vast collection of Indian jewelry and Indian clothes.

Summers and I got to be good friends and during the next few days, I spent a good deal of time with him and his wife. Recently he had been in England and he had seen a 1936 Rolls Royce Phantom II limousine for sale. He had bought it and had it shipped back to San Francisco. At every opportunity, we would pile into the car (it was originally built for one of the Barrymores) and would drive around Golden Gate Park, enjoying the unbelieving stares people would give the freaky hippie driving such a luxurious car.

"Look," he said one day as we were on one of our cruises. "I'm ready to slow down a bit. If you'd be interested in practicing with me, I could really use someone."

I was tempted to accept, but did not. I still had my heart set on working with horses and Summer's practice dealt exclusively with small animals. I wanted to give southern California a try because I had heard that it was good horse country.

The fact that I did not want to join him did not stop Summers from carrying out his plans to ease himself out of his practice. Not too long after I had been in San Francisco, he and his wife bought a house in Big Sur. At first they went down there just on weekends—Saturday and Sunday. Then, they started to leave San Francisco on Friday. Soon, he was working only three days and "retiring" on four. Finally, one day he bought himself a VW, put the Rolls into the garage, locked the front door, put up a sign that said "GONE CRAZY" and never came back.

Although I was enjoying my stay in San Francisco, I had to cut my visit and make my way to southern California. A Dr. Peacock near Los Angeles had advertised for help on the U.C.-Davis veterinary school bulletin board and I had already called him to make an appointment with him.

I flew into Los Angeles International airport, borrowed a car from a friend who had moved to southern California and headed south on the San Diego Freeway. I had left San Francisco only two hours earlier but I felt as if I had crossed half a dozen time zones and cultures during my

Sadie had a bad case of mange and the owners wanted her put to sleep. Dr. Younker got the mange under control and adopted her.

With a young mockingbird (above) who came to visit and with a crow (below) that he went to visit.

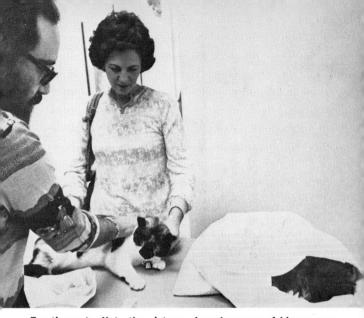

Treating cats. Note the pictures done by some of his younger clients (below).

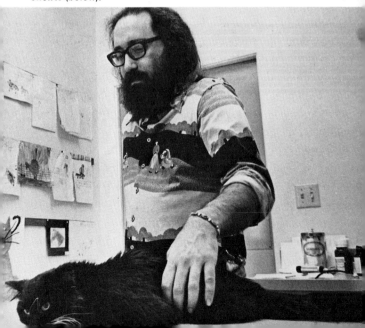

With some of his own pets: a red-tail hawk (above) and a barn owl (below).

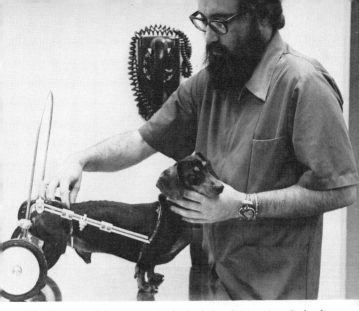

Adjusting a cart for a paraplegic dachshund (above) and checking a patient's X-rays (below).

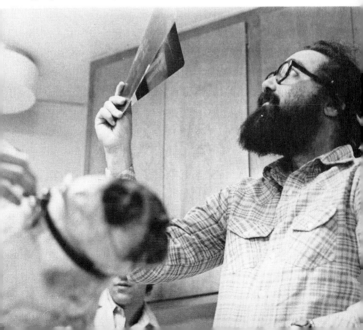

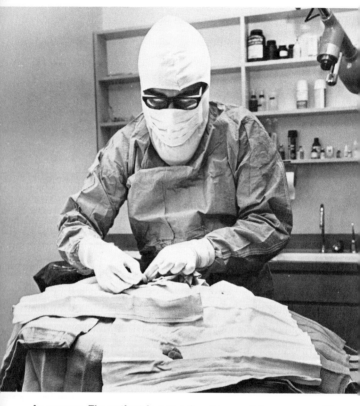

In surgery. The patient is a poodle whose gallstones are on the towel in the foreground.

Checking an acupuncture chart while the patient waits for treatment.

Giving acupuncture treatments. Note the placement of the needles.

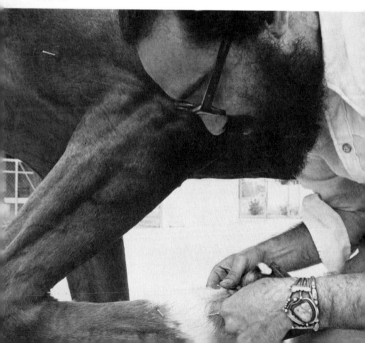

trip. I had left a cool, sparkling, charming city behind me and, suddenly, here I was speeding seventy miles an hour down an eight-lane freeway. Cars all around me whisked by, seemingly impatient with my snail's pace. On each side of the freeway there were sprawling commercial and industrial areas with little outward signs of human life. It was still fairly early in the morning, but southern California's fabled smog was already covering the blue sky and the bright sun with a sickly yellowish veneer.

I might have turned right around and gone back to the airport, but just as my mood was reaching its lowest point, I turned off the freeway and into the road leading to the coast. Beautiful, gnarled old oak trees marked the small hillocks that framed a canyon. The scenery which, near the freeway, had been desertlike, grew greener and greener as I approached the sea. The tangy smell of salt hit my nostrils just as I drove out of the canyon. Almost immediately, the ocean appeared in front of me and, nestled along its shore, the village.

If I had any hopes that I would get to practice in the charming little village with its large population of artists and writers, those hopes were soon shattered. I found the old Spanish-style building in which Dr. Peacock had his office. Peacock himself came to the front door.

When I introduced myself, he shook his head. "I'm sorry," he said. "I guess I should have gotten in touch with you. I hired someone right after you called."

I was angry (I still am when I see him on occasion at a meeting) because he might have had the courtesy to call me and let me know. And I was slightly depressed. On the ride out, I had seen a few houses with corrals where a horse or two stood quietly munching grass. I had even seen a number of ranches—nothing overwhelming, but ranches nevertheless—where at least half a dozen horses had been in evidence But my hopes that my life's ambition was about to be realized were suddenly in pieces.

Since I had come all the way down here, I decided, I might as well stay and scrounge around for a job. But the next few days did nothing to lighten my mood. Every doctor I called had "just" hired someone or was not interested in taking on an associate. But on the day I had marked as my departure date, one of the veterinarians I called gave me the name of another doctor who was looking for help. I telephoned Dr. Forrest immediately.

At first glance, Dr. Forrest did not look like the kind of man with whom I would get along. He had a trim figure. An angular face was topped off by a blond crew cut. He wore mirror sunglasses similar to those worn by cops. And, as it turned out, he had once been a policeman. Two rifles hung on an office wall. A sign on his bulletin board declared, "SOCIALISTS IMPERIL OUR FREEDOM." Lucas, I said to myself, welcome to legendary Orange County.

But as Dr. Forrest showed me his facilities, I warmed quickly to the idea of working with him. He had built a modern, Spanish-style building and had installed superb treatment facilities. Since he specialized in the treatment of horses, he had a modern surgical suite designed for equine work. There was a special stall where horses recovering from surgery could be placed until they were out from under their anesthetic. There was even a large room that allowed him to examine and treat horses indoors on the rare rainy day that sometimes strikes southern California.

"I have a bit of a small animal practice too," he told me as he guided me around. "Whoever comes in with me would have to take over that part of the practice and the work with the pleasure horses. I have a lot of work at the race track I want to concentrate on."

I wasn't all that excited about working with small animals, but at least I would have something of a horse practice if I got a job with him. The arrangement, I said, sounded fine to me.

Forrest nodded but did not commit himself. "Want to make a call with me?" he asked after a while. "I've got to go out and call on a lady who boards about fifteen horses. One of them is lame and four have to be wormed."

We drove out and pulled into an old brick yard that had been converted into a stable. The owner, a plumpish, twenty-five-year-old woman dressed in riding clothes, came out to greet us. She nodded at me when Forrest introduced us, showed us to the horses Forrest was to treat and went back to her office. Just as Forrest was finishing with the last animal, the woman reappeared.

"Doc, after I called you I found out that I had one more horse that needs deworming. Is that okay?"

From the angry scowl that immediately crossed Forrest's

face, I could tell that it was very obviously not at all okay. "Look here, Mrs. Hobner, from now on when you call, you tell me exactly how many animals I am to treat," Forrest lectured her. "I don't want to come here to treat five horses and find that you have six that need attention."

The woman was taken aback and was about to say something, but Forrest did not stop in his tirade long enough to give her a chance to protest. "I have to schedule my day," he went on through drawn lips. "And this sort of thing throws me off. Now I'll be late for my next call and every one after that and God knows when I'll get finished."

"Gosh, I'm sorry," the poor woman finally managed to squeeze in.

"It's fine to be sorry," Forrest shot back, determined not to give her any quarter. "Just don't do it again."

Completely flabbergasted, the woman retreated to the safety of her office while Forrest worked on the horse without the appointment.

At first, Forrest's tirade had embarrassed me. But as he made his way through it, it convinced me that if Forrest did offer me the job, I should take it. The man, I thought, had to be one fantastic and indispensable veterinarian to be able to talk to his clients that way.

And, a little later when Forrest offered me a job over lunch, I accepted with alacrity. (He had asked me to lunch. I envisioned a fancy meal in a good restaurant to mark the occasion. I got a thin hamburger and a coke at a local coffee shop.) I was anxious to start.

Chapter Twelve

"Okay. But if a really BIG," the tinny voice coming at me emphasized *big*, "earthquake does strike, is it possible that Los Angeles could slide into the ocean? I mean it happened to Atlantis, didn't it?"

Very slowly, I opened my eyes and without moving, looked around. A second or two passed before I realized that there was no one in the room with me, trying to put fear of California's earthquakes into a newcomer to the state. (It wouldn't have been hard. The state was in the throes of one of its periodic paranoia trips about earthquakes. Predictions of a major disaster were coming from every clairvoyant. Fundamentalist preachers were moving their congregations to safer states. University news bureaus were hard pressed to crank out news releases denying that earthquakes could be predicted, that California would split away from the continent at the San Andreas Fault and slide silently into the Pacific Ocean.) Dawn was breaking and the alarm clock radio had flipped itself on to wake me up to the banter of an early-morning talk show.

"No, not at all," a condescending voice answered (probably a local geophysicist). "You see . . ."

I reached over and slapped at the turnoff button. For me, a dedicated sleeper and late-riser, it was an ungodly hour. But today I was making my first solo call for Dr. Forrest and I did not want to be late. Mrs. Glover's house, I had been told, was way off in the hill's. Since I had never been out there and since my written instructions were filled with a dozen "turn lefts," "turn rights," and "circle arounds," I wanted to get as early a start as possible. Just in case I had to stop and call a few times for further guidance.

Even at that time of morning, the Santa Ana Freeway leading north to downtown Los Angeles was full of cars, streaming along at their seventy-plus miles an hour. I turned off and followed Broad Avenue, which narrowed down to snake its way through some orange groves and then up into the hills. I had been in southern California for only a short time and its peculiar checkerboard organization—alternating dense metropolitan areas with stretches of deserted country, vast vegetable fields and fruit groves—still amazed me.

The instructions I had been given, it turned out, were good enough to get me to the Glover house without a hitch. The house itself, a sprawling California ranch house, stood high on a hillock. I looked around and spotted a corral. Three or four people were leaning on its rails, watching a group of horses slowly eating their way through alfalfa hay in their corrals.

As I approached, a small woman broke away from the group and took a few steps to meet me. She was a woman with a well-wrinkled face. She was in her forties, but her figure was trim and youngish and she looked at me with sparkling eyes. "I'm Granny Glover," she said, thrusting out her hand. "Are you the new vet with Forrest? What's your name again?"

I told her. I glanced at the corral. "Are those the horses that have to be dewormed, Mrs. Glover?"

Without looking back, she nodded yes. "And, call me Granny," she said. She stared at me another second or two. "You sure look like hell, Lucas."

I was startled. "I do, Mrs. Glover?"

"Granny! You sure do. Have you had breakfast yet?"

"No," I admitted. "I haven't had a chance. I was going to stop for something after I made my call here."

Granny shook her head. "Well, that's why you look so bad. Don't want you working on my horses without having had breakfast. Hike on up to the house and get something to eat first. Tell Bessie I sent you up."

If I looked bad to Granny at the bottom of the hill, I must have looked absolutely terrible to the cook as I staggered into the kitchen after climbing the hundreds (or so it seemed) of steps to get up to the house.

"Mrs. Glover said I needed breakfast and to ask you to

fix me some, if you don't mind, ma'am," I wheezed, trying to catch my breath.

"You mean Granny?"

"Yeah. Granny. Right."

"You look like you need a whole lot more than that, boy," Bessie said. "Well, what you want? You can have anything you want."

"Great." I stopped and thought. "What about French toast?"

"Don't do no French cookin'. How about eggs and pancakes?"

I settled, gladly, for the pancakes, the eggs, and the sausages she piled in front of me. My decision to come out to California was looking better all the time.

The hearty breakfast braced me for the work ahead. Not that deworming horses is a hard procedure. I had done it a hundred times at school. But I did not have my own equipment yet and I was working with tools Dr. Forrest had given me. Unfortunately, it was all old equipment he did not want any more because it was well past its prime. I wouldn't have been surprised if I had bloodied a nose or two trying to pass the old, hard, and brittle stomach tubes (which I had to use to administer the deworming medication) through the noses of the animals.

I drove back to the clinic, stopped in the reception room to glance over the latest anticommunist, antisocialist and antiliberal tracts that had been posted, and then walked back to the office Forrest and I shared. His morning calls were apparently finished because he was already back when I strolled in. He was standing by our side-to-side desks, the loaded 30–30 and 30–06 rifles hanging on the wall behind him. He was wearing his customary well-starched and well-tailored cowboy outfit. When he heard me walk in, he lifted his face from the sheaf of papers he had been reading. I saw my distorted reflection in the mirror sunglasses he still had on.

"How'd it go?" he asked. "Any bloody noses?"

"No. Everything went fine."

Forrest glanced back at his desk and turned a page on the calendar. "I've got to go out and do a soundness exam," he said after a moment. "Want to come along?"

I sure did. During my visit for my job interview with Forrest, I also had gone along when he had made a call to examine a horse that one of his clients wanted to buy. I had been impressed with the thoroughness with which he examined the animals for flaws. "When you do a soundness exam," he had told me then, "the prospective owner is paying you to find something wrong with that horse and you damned well better find something if there is something for you to find."

I wanted to learn Forrest's techniques because I knew that the soundness exam is one of the most important and most difficult duties a veterinarian has to carry out. It is not always easy to spot a subtle lameness in a horse, especially if you might be dealing with an unethical horse trader who may have medicated the horse to make it look good temporarily. If you are to protect your client, you have to do more than walk around the animal, lift its tail, or stare at its teeth. Some people buy a horse the way they might buy a two-dollar puppy at the local pound. But for most people, the purchase of a horse represents a substantial investment. If the client is buying a pleasure horse for his family, the several hundred dollars he might have to pay for the animal represents months or even years of hard-earned savings. If he is buying a horse to race or to breed, the thousands of dollars he will pay represents an important business investment.

I had been working for Forrest for about two weeks or so, when I made my first (and almost last) soundness exam. The client was a woman who was buying her first horse. I was to meet her at Sam the horse trader's place.

When I pulled into Sam's yard, a very sophisticated woman in her late thirties was standing next to a Lincoln Mark IV, leaning away from a bedraggled old man who looked to be well past seventy and who was forcefully chewing a giant wad of tobacco. He was unshaven and was wearing a dirty cowboy shirt, old faded blue jeans, and dusty, scuffed cowboy boots, very much down at the heels.

I introduced myself and Sam went off to get the first horse he had offered the woman, Mrs. Lubner. Even as the animal cleared the corral gate, I could see that it was lame. Forrest, being the fanatic he was, would have turned on his heels and walked away, terminating the exam before it had even started. But since I was new, I thought that I should at least go through the motions. I looked into the horse's eyes. I parted his lips and looked at the teeth. I got out my hoof tester—a giant set of pincers—and picked up the front foot on the near side. As I applied pressure to the "frog," the V-shaped spongy part of the bottom of the foot, the horse showed obvious discomfort and tried to pull the leg away from me.

"I'm sorry," I said to Mrs. Lubner. "I'm going to have to turn this horse down. He probably has navicular disease, a form of arthritis of one of the bones of the feet."

I could tell that Sam was not happy. He called over to a young boy who had been standing by the corral. "Bring out that mare," he yelled.

The horse the boy brought out was, simply, a disaster. She was overweight, had swollen knees and lacerations that ran across the knee joints as if she had run into something sharp or had gone down on her knees on some rocks or pavement. "I'm going to turn this one down too," I said. "Those lacerations go clear into the joint capsule. The joint is infected. I'd be amazed if she isn't permanently crippled, even if we could get the infection cleared up."

"Aw come on, doc," Sam protested. "There ain't all that wrong with that there horse. All she has is them little scratches on her legs. They ain't nothin'."

I shook my head. "Sorry, Sam. I can't agree with you."

Sam's face turned a bright red. "Now listen you son-of-a-bitch. I tell ya there is nothing wrong with them horses!" He was virtually screaming. He turned to the boy. "Get me my gun, boy."

The boy ran off and I began a retreat to the old truck Forrest had loaned me. Before I reached the door, the kid was back with a shotgun. Sam ripped it out of his hands, cocked it, and aimed it at me. "Now you get your ass out of here and don't you never come back. Next time I'm gonna get me a decent vet like Forrest to do the job."

Within seconds I was in my truck, speeding out of the driveway. The Lincoln, I saw in my rear-view mirror, was right behind me.

A few weeks later I got a call from Mrs. Lubner. (It was her second call to me since our confrontation with Sam. The first time, she had called to apologize for the incident, even though it was not her fault.) Could I come out and take a look at a horse she was thinking of buying from a neighbor, a woman who bred Arabians?

When I arrived at the designated place, it was obvious

that her neighbor was wealthy as well. The house, which was in an exclusive part of Orange County, was large. A beautiful stable graced the grounds. It housed four impressive Arabians.

I looked at the horse Mrs. Lubner wanted to buy. It was not exactly unsound, but there were some minor things wrong with it. I didn't want to call it sound either. "You wouldn't buy it then?" Mrs. Lubner asked.

I shrugged. "It's up to you. But I can't in all honesty tell you that this horse is in perfect health."

There was a momentary silence. I glanced at the breeder, Mrs. Beverly. "I hope she's not going to get her gun," I said to Mrs. Lubner, trying to break through the awkwardness of the moment.

"My what?" the startled Mrs. Beverly asked.

Mrs. Lubner explained, telling her of our run-in with Sam. Mrs. Beverly laughed. "I didn't like losing the sale, but what the hell. At least you're honest."

From then on Mrs. Beverly became one of my steadiest clients.

Chapter Thirteen

By the time fall arrived, I had settled comfortably into my new professional life. After a few weeks in Dr. Forrest's practice, I had even learned to do all the little, mundane things I had learned to do in school and then forgotten. I had been trained to pin complicated fractures, to do delicate orthopedic surgery, to treat fertility problems and exotic diseases. But from those four years of advanced education I had brought very little about helping small animals with their more routine problems.

Much of what I had to know to be a day-to-day veterinarian, in fact, I learned one day when I faced my first full morning of in-patient cases.

The first patient I was to treat that day was a scrappy little terrier. The chart Sarah, our secretary, handed me said the animal had a long history of skin diseases. Quickly, I reviewed in my mind some of the problems the dog might be having with its skin, their causes, and some possible cures.

"Alfred is here for his teeth cleaning," Sarah sang out as she left the room.

I knew I was in trouble. In four years of schooling, I had done no more than half a dozen cleanings—and then only by hand. Forrest owned a modern ultrasonic tooth scaler. I had no idea how to use it.

Luckily, Sarah came back into the room, carrying some freshly sterilized instruments. There was no way out of the situation. I had to ask her how to use the tooth scaler. Patiently, Sarah explained the procedure while I concentrated on following her instructions.

When Sarah brought in the next patient, a grossly overweight boxer, I thought that I might be out of the woods for the day. According to Daisy's chart, she had a heart murmur. Maybe the medication she had been on hadn't been working. Maybe I'd have to find something new to prescribe for her. I also started to prepare a lecture I would give the pet's owner about the animal's weight problem. . . .

"Ear cleaning, doctor," Sarah sang out once more and left the room.

I could feel a blank expression creep across my face. I had no idea where to start. There was a box of Q-tips in the room, but surely a quick pass with one of those would not do. I followed Sarah out. "By the way," I asked as casually as I could, while making a show of looking for something on the shelves where Forrest kept his stock of drugs, "does Dr. Forrest have any special way in which he likes to have ears cleaned?"

I held my breath, hoping that an "oh-no-not-really" would not be my answer.

Although I was not facing her, I could feel that Sarah was looking intently at me. "Dr. Forrest likes to fill the ear with an antibiotic and then massage it around," she answered. "Then he takes a Q-tip and cleans the inside of the ear. He does that over and over until the ear is clean."

I started to go back to the room, but Sarah was not through. "Of course, Dr. Patterson, the man I worked for last, used to like to put Cerotic in the ears and then leave it there for several minutes while it dissolved the wax. Then he'd flush it out with a bulb syringe, using Phisohex and water first and then just plain water."

"Is that what they taught you at school?"

"Yes," I said, reaching for a bottle of Cerotic and a bottle of Phisohex. "That's exactly what they taught us in school. The very first year of clinics."

When I had finished, I had forty-five minutes until the next appointment. With a cautious glance at the two ominous rifles poised behind my desk, I started to do some paper work.

Rifles and guns were one of Forrest's obsessions. He told anyone who came into his office that the rifles on the wall were always loaded because a man had to be ready to use them at all times. Forrest also carried a third gun with him, ostensibly because the racetrack where he served as veterinarian was located in a bad neighborhood. But Forrest seemed to relish the idea that something might happen that would enable him to use one of his rifles. "I just want someone to try something so I can blow the son-of-a-bitch away," was a litany I heard frequently.

The rifles, however, made me nervous. Forrest had a terrible temper and I was worried that one day he would use them in anger against someone he knew, not, as he hoped, against the hordes of communists or the gangs of criminals he was afraid were out there roaming the streets.

I decided that instead of writing out charts, I was going to put my little plan into action. About a week earlier, I had asked Mrs. Forrest, who also worked in the office, how to load and unload the rifles. Trying to look as innocent as possible, I explained that I wanted to know how they worked—just in case. She had shown me gladly and now, with both Forrest and his wife away from the clinic, I took down the rifles, emptied them and put the bullets in the bottom drawer of my desk.

I breathed a sigh of relief.

About a week later, Dr. Forrest brought a group of friends to the office. Beaming proudly, he pointed at the rifles, telling his buddies all about them. Moving smartly, he snatched the 30–30 off the wall and pulled the bolt back to show his friends the bullets. The gun, of course, was empty.

Forrest virtually leaped at the 30–06 and tore it off its supports. It too was empty. I could see a whole range of emotions—from anger to dark suspicion—sweep across his face. On the one hand he was mortified to find that he was not as ready for Armageddon as he had thought. On the other hand, a delicious possibility occurred to him. Could there be a conspiracy in the making against him and other patriots?

"Ed," I said. "It was me. I took the shells out."

Forrest did an abrupt right face. "You?"

I launched into my cover story. "Yeah. I've been hearing and reading all this stuff about how we are going to have an earthquake one of these days and I was afraid that during the shaking one of the guns could fall off the wall and I'd get shot in the back. So I unloaded them just to make sure."

Forrest did not know whether to be mad at me or to feel sorry for me for being so stupid. Suddenly, one of his friends, then the other, started to laugh. Forrest, convinced now that I was really afraid that the San Andreas Fault would shoot me in the back, joined in the guffaws. "That's idiotic," he said when he could finally stop laughing. "Look. The safety catches were on. They could never go off."

"Still," I insisted. "I'd feel better if there weren't a loaded gun at my back."

Because Forrest gave local breeders a discount, many of the small animals I treated were dogs and cats used for breeding. The balding man in the dirty khakis and the plaid shirt who was waiting for me as I walked into the examining room a day or so after the rifle incident was typical of some of them.

"Well?" he asked as I came through the door. I had taken a vaginal smear on one of his prize bitches and had just spent a few minutes studying the smear under the microscope to determine whether or not she was ready to be bred.

"I don't think she's quite ready to breed," I told him. "I'd wait a day or two."

"What do you mean a day or two," he exploded. "I don't want to know what *day* she might ovulate. I want to know what time she'll ovulate and how many eggs she will produce."

"You want to know right down to the hour?"

"That's right. A big gun vet from back east came out and talked to our dog club and he said you can tell exactly what time they will ovulate and when they will ovulate the most eggs."

I decided to humor the man. "Okay. Let me go back and check that smear again."

I went back to the laboratory, puttered about a bit, sat down to have a cup of coffee, and then went back to the examining room.

"I have studied this very carefully," I said, taking on a professorial tone. "Now. Today is the thirteenth. She will probably ovulate on the fifteenth, roughly between 3:45 and 3:50 a.m. I'm sorry, but that is as close as I can pin it down."

"How many eggs, doc?"

"Fourteen."

The man's face relaxed. "That's better, doc. I don't want that day or two stuff." He stopped for a while and thought something over. "But, I don't know. Fourteen eggs. That's too many. I don't want that many pups in a litter."

"Yes, of course. But some of the eggs will die, some won't be fertilized and some will be fertilized and will be reabsorbed or not implanted properly on the uterine wall."

The man listened in rapt attention. "Well, all right. I'm sure glad you got on the stick and spent a little time with that smear and figured it out."

He shook my hand and turned to walk out.

"Hey, wait a minute," I called out. As much as I enjoyed the thought that he would stay up half the night to make sure that his bitch would be bred at just the right time, I didn't want to leave him with a scientific misconception (so to speak). "You didn't believe all that stuff, did you?"

The breeder looked at me suspiciously. "You mean that wasn't true about her ovulating at quarter to four in the morning?" The man did not give up easily.

"No. The whole thing. Everthing I told you and everything that big gun supposedly told you is a bunch of bullshit. There is no way in the world that anyone can tell you exactly what time an animal will ovulate. The best anyone can do is tell you within twenty-four hours or so. But that is as close as anyone can get."

Although breeders are, by and large, nice people, their obsession with fertility, sterility, estrus cycles, coloring, and configuration was sometimes a little unsettling. There had to be something in life besides the size of the next litter your Siamese cat was about to produce. I was glad to see other people whose animals had more conventional problems—even if those people, on occasion, were not thrilled to see me.

I had just finished working with a golden retriever whose pregnancy had been giving her trouble and walked into the reception room to see who was next.

"Mrs. Sweetzer's terrier is having trouble with its foot, doctor," Sarah told me, as she handed me a chart.

Mrs. Sweetzer, I vaguely knew, was an aged silent screen actress. She had not given up the illusion of glamor and now looked like a caricature of the slinky woman she might have been once. She had a big chest and, although she was seventy-five years old, wore low-cut dresses. She wore very red lipstick, huge false eyelashes and thick, green eye shadow.

She looked at me, alarm evident in her face. "Oh, my," she stammered. "Now, there is nothing personal in this, young man, but you are so young. . . . Maybe I should come back when Dr. Forrest is here."

"He's a very capable young man," another client who had come in to pick up some medicine chimed in. She was a breeder who had also balked the first time she had drawn me on an office visit. Forrest had straightened her out, soundly excoriating her for believing that he would hire someone who was incompetent.

In the examining room, Mrs. Sweetzer glued herself to my side as I looked over her little Timmy.

"It looks to me as if Timmy has an abscess between his toes," I said. "He probably picked up a foxtail some place and now the foot is infected."

Mrs. Sweetzer looked at me, anxiety still on her face. "Are you sure, dear?"

"I'm sure. We'll have to take it out. But I'll have to give him general anesthesia to get at it."

Mrs. Sweetzer paled visibly beneath her rouge. "Oh, my goodness, no. That is very dangerous."

"There is a risk always, Mrs. Sweetzer, but I would not say it is dangerous. We have never lost a dog to anesthesia. Believe me."

I was almost afraid that she would cry. "Maybe we should wait for Dr. Forrest to come back," she pleaded. "Timmy could die, couldn't he?"

If I insisted on giving Timmy a general anesthetic, I decided, I would never get the foxtail out. Forrest would not be back that day and I did not want to take a chance that the infection would get worse while she waited for an appointment with my senior associate. "All right," I relented. "We'll just give him a little tranquilizer. Would that be okay?"

"Like my Valium?" Mrs. Sweetzer sniffed.

"Very similar."

"But then the operation would hurt him, wouldn't it?

"He might feel it, yes." I was getting a little antsy.

"Couldn't you give him Novocain as well?"

"All right, I'll give him a tranquilizer and the local anesthetic."

She was still skeptical, but finally gave in.

The operation, even with Mrs. Sweetzer hovering all too closely, went well, as it should have. After that call and on the strength of that simple operation, I became, in Mrs. Sweetzer's eyes, the world's greatest veterinarian. From then on, I was her Timmy's doctor.

Chapter Fourteen

Although I loved my work, I think that in those early days of practice, I probably overdid things a little. During the day I was either tearing around Orange County treating one horse after another or I was in the clinic treating small animals.

But my nights were as hectic as my days. When I had begun to work for Forrest, it never had occurred to me (or to him) to suggest that we share answering emergency and nonemergency night calls. I just assumed that the burden of after-hours medical treatment should fall on the junior associate's shoulders. Thus, many midnights and dawns found me treating dogs hurt by cars, horses with colic, mares starting to foal or mares having trouble foaling.

All in all, I really didn't mind. I was young and reasonably healthy. The nights were warm and pleasant and there was little discomfort to accompany the loss of sleep.

The inane calls, however, were the ones that began to get to me. When I had first started working with Forrest, I got myself, like every physician I had ever known back in Cincinnati, a listed home phone number. "You are crazy to do it," Forrest warned me. "People will start calling you at all hours of the night for the most idiotic of reasons."

Forrest was proven right. On many a night I was hauled out of a deep sleep by clients who did not hesitate to call me when the mood moved them. "Doc," I must have heard a dozen times. "I know it's one o'clock, but I was wondering: Is it too (cold, warm, late) to give my dog a bath now?"

"Why the hell are you giving your dog a bath now?" I decided to ask one caller one night.

"Well, Johnny Carson just went off the air. So I got the

time now." The voice very definitely implied that I was a fool for asking. I probably was. But I had only been in California a short time and had not yet grown accustomed to the fact that people out here live disjointed lives. Supermarkets stay open twenty-four hours a day. Midnight movies draw around the block lines. Toy stores stay open until midnight. There is no reason not to call a veterinarian at one o'clock to ask him a silly question. He's probably up too.

It took me a little while too to realize that the telephone in southern California, more so than anywhere else, is the prime means by which people in this sprawling metropolitan area interact with their fellow human beings. In Cincinnati, the telephone is used to make a quick call—to make a date, to order something, to get information. In southern California the telephone is used in a much more complicated fashion. On the one hand, it is used to avoid entangling relationships. A weekly thirty-minute call puts off the necessity of having to make an appointment for a troublesome get-together—one that would entail leaving one's home or, worse, one's car. Conversely, it is used to reach out when no one wants to bother getting together with you. People may hedge in response to a request for a lunch date, but they'll never hang up on you.

Mrs. Sweetzer was an accomplished telephone user. I soon came to suspect that her frequent visits to our office and, more so, her frequent calls to me meant that she probably had few or no friends. Her husband Tommy, I knew, was a director. Although he was also well into his seventies, he apparently traveled a good deal when he was working on a production.

One night at two o'clock, the telephone's rings jarred me out of my sound sleep. A hysterical voice was screaming something about a stroke. After a second or so, I realized it was Mrs. Sweetzer calling. Timmy, she repeated once more between her sobs, had had a stroke.

With sleep still clouding my mind, I had trouble making out the story. Moreover, because she always talked of Timmy and Tommy as if they were of equal importance to her, in my stupor I could not remember if Timmy was the husband and Tommy the dog or whether it was the other way around. I didn't want to add insult to hysteria by asking which one she was talking about. "What happened?" I stammered, hoping noncommital questions might elicit some clues. "How do you know it's a stroke?"

Mrs. Sweetzer was not about to help me. "I looked into his eyes and they were all bloodshot," she said, the words accented by hiccups.

It was still possible, I reasoned, that it was her husband she was talking about. She might have been staring into the set eyes of a dead man. If she called me, I thought, I must be the only friend she has left in the world.

Still, I wanted to be sure before I drove over or roused the police or fire department. I decided to risk my good relationship with her. "Mrs. Sweetzer," I asked cautiously. "Is there anything else wrong with him?" I took a deep breath and went on, "Will he come to you if you call him?"

"Oh yes, he scampers right over."

I was relieved. "Mrs. Sweetzer," I told her, trying to reassure her and calm her down. "Dogs seldom have strokes. And, if they do, they are usually paralyzed by them. Bring him in first thing in the morning. He'll be all right until then."

Mrs. Sweetzer was at the clinic at nine. Timmy, except for a little conjunctivitis, was in perfect health.

At nine-thirty I called the telephone company and had my number changed and requested it be unlisted. An answering service expert at screening calls for a doctor, I reasoned, would help me give my clients emergency care when they really needed it. It would also allow me to get the sleep and rest I now desperately needed to rid myself of the infection that was, I thought at the time, responsible for the swollen glands in my neck, the congestion in my chest and the constant, hacking cough that was always with me.

The exhaustion that was part and parcel of my days was also rooted in a stormy romance I was having with Jennie, a girl I met at pool side in my apartment building.

Most of my friendships with women had been fairly stable. But this one helped turn me into an emotional wreck. Jennie was a beautiful girl who was most attractive to men. She enjoyed the attention and, without trying, managed to be rather flirtatious. She wanted to be totally independent and her desire to be independent seemed to conflict with my dependent nature. Rather than accept her as she was, I became more and more dependent and possessive of her,

149

which did nothing but drive a wedge between us. I was really quite irrational.

Of course, the more possessive I grew, the more intent she was on proving her independence. "I won't be here this weekend," she announced one Thursday evening. "I'm going skiing with Dave Peters."

Friday and Friday night were almost unbearable for me. I could think of nothing save Jennie and Peters. By Saturday morning I was so knotted up with anxiety that I knew I would have to take a tranquilizer—something I had never done before—if I were to make it through the morning's appointments at the clinic and through the rest of the weekend.

As soon as I reached the office, I looked through our drug stock to see what animal tranquilizers we had on hand. Because tranquilizer dosages are calculated according to body weight (among other things), I couldn't very well take a tranquilizer tablet that was meant for a ten-pound cat or one meant for a fifteen-hundred-pound horse. But, since some animal and human drugs are made from the same basic ingredients, I could check our *Physician's Drug Reference*, a manual that lists all human drugs manufactured, their use, and their effective dosages to see what human tranquilizers corresponded to those drugs we had available. I could then calculate how much of the animal tranquilizer to take to calm myself down.

On the shelves I had found Trifluomeperazine, a tranquilizer supplied us by the Nordon Company, a subsidiary of Smith, Kline and French. In the *PDR*, I found a listing for Trifluoperazine. I was so upset and nervous that I did not notice the slight difference in the spelling of the two drugs. The dosage recommended for Trifluoperazine in the manual was fifteen to forty milligrams. Because, unthinkingly, I thought the two drugs to be the same, I decided to take three of the ten-milligram pills of Trifluomeperazine we had in stock. Thirty milligrams, I thought, would be enough.

In reality, I found out later, the animal drug is ten times more powerful than the human drug. Thus, the effective dosage I had washed down with a quick glass of water had been equivalent to almost three hundred milligrams.

By the time the first client had come and gone with her horse, I was calming down a bit. But then strange things began to happen. I looked at the next horse and felt that I had to run from the room. I was sure I had forgotten how to worm a horse. I had to force myself to treat the animal and two others that followed. At any moment, I was sure, I was going to make a mistake and kill one of my patients.

Finally, I could stand it no more. I hurriedly put down a stomach tube I was holding and walked quickly out of the treatment area and into the clinic. "I'm sick," I told Sarah as I virtually ran past her desk. "I've got to get home. Cancel all my appointments."

"Wait," I heard her call after me. "Lucas! You can't do that. You've got twenty patients waiting already."

I lunged for the door. "I can't, Sarah. I've got to get home."

Light-headed, dizzy, I stumbled to the car. I managed to get to Orange Grove Lane without incident. But suddenly Orange Grove left the ground and turned itself into a long ribbon floating and twisting high up into the air. I gripped the steering wheel with all my strength, struggling to keep the car on the narrow ribbon as it looped, turned, and twisted roller-coaster style three hundred feet above the ground. From time to time I would glance out the door window and stare with horror at the roofs below me. At any moment I would lose control of the car and crash to my death on one of the buildings.

I managed to keep the car on the ever-narrowing ribbon until I pulled into the parking lot of my apartment building. Groping along the walls, I made my way through the narrowing and widening corridors, found my apartment, almost tore the door of its hinges and staggered into bed. But sleep would not come. Instead, people started to run through my bedroom, screaming at me, threatening me, hauling me out of bed and chasing me from room to room. Shapes, colors and flashes of light filled the apartment for almost twenty-four hours.

Finally, almost a full day after I had taken the tranquilizer I managed to fall asleep.

By Thanksgiving, my emotional state had reached its lowest point. I had been invited to my cousin Herschel's house to join his family for the traditional turkey feast. But almost from the time I arrived I said little to anyone. When dinner was served, I sat at the table, staring into space, eating nothing. "You've got to do something for yourself,"

Herschel (who is also a rabbi) finally said. "Call Ben and ask him to see you."

Without a murmur of protest, I went to the phone and called Dr. Ben Goodman, Herschel's psychiatrist friend, at his home in Santa Barbara. "Come up right now," he told me. I got in my car and sped the ninety miles up the coast to see him.

Because Ben maintained a part-time practice in Los Angeles, I was able to see him on a weekly basis. Slowly, I began to battle my depression, to fight my obsessive need to own and control Jennie. I measured my progress over the ensuing weeks and months by how far I could get from Ben's office before turmoil set in once more. At the beginning, I would feel good only until I got to the coffee shop next door to Ben's office. Soon, I was feeling well until I got to the entrance to the Santa Monica Freeway. After several sessions the good feelings lasted the entire course of the Santa Monica Freeway. Eventually, I managed to get through the Santa Monica Freeway *and* the Santa Ana Freeway before I started to feel sorry for myself again. After six months with Ben, I was almost able to survive through most of the week between my appointments with him before I started to feel the depression pulling on me once again. Within a year I was able to stop seeing him altogether.

Best of all, the therapy sessions were giving me the wherewithal to concentrate fully on my work again. And, in the process, I began to question more and more my association with Forrest.

Forrest was a good veterinarian and he could have taught me a good deal, particularly about horses. But he was seldom around and I did not have much of a chance to consult with him when I faced a serious animal illness with which I had not had much experience.

One day, a client brought in a cat that had, in his words, been going "downhill." The cat was not eating, it was lethargic and just generally acted sick. The abdomen felt swollen to me and, using a syringe and needle, I managed to bring some suspicious straw-colored fluid out of the peritoneal cavity. I X-rayed the cat and saw that the abdomen was filled with fluid. I suspected peritonitis but since I had not treated many small animals yet, I was not absolutely sure of my diagnosis. I tried to reach Forrest at the track, first calling him by conventional telephone, then trying to raise him on his mobile phone. When all my efforts failed, I called Dr. Dieter, a famous veterinarian in the area, and asked him if he could take a look at the X-rays. The cat, Dr. Dieter confirmed, had feline infectious peritonitis. When Forrest returned later in the day, he was very hurt that I had not waited for him to get back to discuss the cat with him. But neither that incident nor a few others like it encouraged him to take more time to give me the help I needed. Since I was being left to my own wits anyway and since I could always call on other veterinarians in the area for advice when I needed it, I decided I might as well have my own practice.

When I had gathered enough nerve to do it, I gave Forrest notice.

Chapter Fifteen

Even though it was February, the temperature on that Tuesday morning had already reached 82° by eleven-thirty. I was living in a large singles apartment complex but because it was a weekday, I was the only one in the pool area. My apartment was on the ground floor, facing the recreation area and I had run the long extension telephone out to my chaise lounge. Except for the whirring and bubbling of the Jacuzzi next to the pool (I had just taken the third hot bath of the morning) and except for the twitterings of the birds, it was nicely quiet.

California-style, I was trying to put together a practice. When I left Forrest, I did not notify any of our clients that I was striking out on my own because to do so would have been unethical. Some of the people whose animals I had treated, however, did seek me out and served as the nucleus of my very small budding practice. To increase my clientele to a level that would enable me to make a living, I had to wait for these clients, acquaintances, and friends to refer me to people who had animals and for word to get around that there was a new vet in town.

But to build a successful practice, you have to act and look successful. Nothing is more suspicious to people than a doctor, lawyer or veterinarian with time on his hands. Thus, I hit upon a simple stratagem to give the appearance that I was a much sought-after animal doctor. I had my answering service screen all my calls. Clients calling with routine problems—vaccinations, dewormings, castrations—were automatically told that I was busy and that there were no appointments available until the following Thursday. Anyone who had to wait two to six days for a routine appointment could surmise that I was a busy man.

But making all my appointments for one day served another purpose: It left me with six free days in which I could give immediate attention to any emergencies that came up. When the service received an emergency call, they put the client right through to my poolside "office." "Gee, I'm booked solid," I would lament after hearing the story, "but I'll tell you what. I can change around some of my appointments and get right out there." Other veterinarians in the area—the ones who were established and truthfully booked solid all the time—sometimes took two or three days to get to an emergency call. I could get there within minutes. As a result, many people, who had found me when they could not reach their own veterinarian or when they felt they could not wait for him, were impressed by my response to their emergencies and would often use me later when their animals needed routine care.

About noon, the telephone rang. "It's a Mr. O'Keefe. His horse has gone lame and he's worried," the woman at the answering service told me. "And, a Mr. Erehart said his horse is no better. A Mrs. Grimshaw wants to have her horse dewormed and vaccinated."

"Call back Erehart and Mrs. Grimshaw and tell them I can squeeze them in late Thursday. Put O'Keefe through if he's still on." From what O'Keefe told me, it didn't sound as if the hourse needed immediate attention. But the man seemed genuinely worried. I decided to see him that afternoon.

Larry O'Keefe was waiting for me by the fence of the small corral in the back of his house when I arrived. With a glum expression, he was watching the bay gelding peacefully eating hay.

"I bought that horse for my daughter about ten days ago or so," he told me after we had introduced ourselves. "I had a vet give him a soundness exam. He said the horse was in good shape. He was all right for about a week but the last two or three days he just seemed to get sicker and sicker. This morning I just couldn't get him to move at all. You can tell he's favoring that right front leg."

I bent down and squeezed through the rails of the fence. By the way the horse was standing there, I guessed that he had a front leg lameness. Speaking softly to the horse, I approached his left shoulder. When I picked up the foot, I could see the badly contracted heel and wasted frog. And,

156

when I applied pressure to the foot with my hoof tester, the horse flinched.

I didn't like the thoughts forming in my head. "It's probably navicular disease, an inflammation of the bones of the foot," I told O'Keefe. "You say the horse had a soundness exam?"

O'Keefe nodded.

"Who did it?"

O'Keefe kicked softly at the grass. "The man I bought the horse from said I could use the vet that had been its regular doctor. Said he was reliable."

"What did he say he had been treating him for?"

"You know, regular stuff. Floating teeth. Vaccinations. That sort of thing."

I vaguely knew of the veterinarian and called him from O'Keefe's kitchen. The doctor was not in, but his partner was. I decided to play a hunch. "If you have X rays on a horse I'm seeing," I said, describing the horse and giving the previous owner's name, "I'd appreciate it if you could tell me what he's been seen for before."

The partner went to get the X rays. I could hear them crinkling as he held them up to the light. "Looks to me like he's got navicular disease," he finally said. "Why?"

"Because your associate just passed him on a soundness exam, that's why," I said.

I told O'Keefe what I had learned. "I paid twenty-five hundred bucks for that damned horse. Guess I got took."

I didn't say anything. Silently, I agreed with him.

"Is there anything you can do?" he asked after a while. "My daughter fell in love with him at first sight. I wouldn't want to pass him off on anyone else either and it seems a shame to put him to sleep."

I recoiled at the idea of putting the animal down. "You don't have to put him to sleep. I can sever the nerves that supply the back part of the foot so he won't feel pain when he walks. He'll be usable for a while."

On the way back I decided to try to avoid performing soundness exams for my clients when they sold a horse. It was obvious that the situation was rife with potential conflicts of interest. It would be just as easy to recommend another veterinarian to conduct the presale exam. Over the years, I have learned that most veterinarians have the same

157

philosophy and I certainly have not run into a similar case since I called on O'Keefe.

As I pulled into the Erehart driveway late Thursday, I vaguely wondered why he had called me again. I had been there a month or so earlier to worm his horses on the recommendation of a client that had come with me when I left Forrest. One of the horses, I had noticed then, had lacerated his leg just above the hoof. The cut, which ran through the coronary band, was already a few days old and had not been sutured. There was already the beginning of some "proud flesh," an excessive buildup of the tissues of healing.

"That laceration is in a bad place," I had told Erehart. "Are you using anything on it?"

"Scarlet oil."

"Scarlet oil?" I echoed. "That's fine for some wounds because it does promote healing. But you have to be careful if the wound is below the hocks or the knees because there is a tendency for 'proud flesh' to form in those areas where the skin is stretched real tight. I wouldn't recommend scarlet oil for that wound."

Erehart had been very offended that I had presumed to advise him about the treatment of his horses. "I own a feed store, young man," he had said. "And I treat a lot of my customers' animals. I was at it before you even thought of becoming a vet and I know what I'm doing."

I got out of my car and walked back to the stable. When I found the horse, it was obvious why he had called me back. The foot was a mess. The proud flesh had proliferated and the hoof was now badly deformed.

"Can you do anything about it?" a voice behind me asked.

I turned to face Erehart. "Nothing," I said. "Nothing at all. But I'll be glad to refer you up to the veterinary school at Davis if you want."

The doctors at the veterinary school at Davis, it turned out, couldn't do anything either.

Things went better at the Grimshaw stable. I gave the horses their vaccinations, wormed them, and, because a couple of horses needed it, floated some teeth. (Horses, when they chew food, are hard on their teeth. The chewing motion grinds the molars into a fine edge. In the upper molars, the sharp edge develops on the outside of the teeth, next to the cheek. In the lower molars, the sharp edge develops along the side toward the tongue. Filing off these sharp points is called "floating the teeth.")

When I was through, I washed up at an outside faucet and went into the house to present my bill. Mrs. Grimshaw was sitting at her kitchen table with another woman and a man. The other two people looked terrible. He had not shaven in days. They were both in wrinkled, dusty clothing. "This is my sister- and brother-in-law," Mrs. Grimshaw explained, noticing my gaze. "They've just come back from a camping trip."

Mrs. Grimshaw looked at the bill. "I haven't got the cash," she said. "Will a check for seventy-five dollars do?"

The brother-in-law grabbed the bill out of Mrs. Grimshaw's hand. "Let me see that thing," he snorted. He put down his beer can and studied the bill for a moment. "Jesus Christ! This is ridiculous."

Since I hadn't been in practice alone very long, I was still not sure of myself when it came to money matters. I took the bill out of his hands and looked it over. "I only charged ten dollars to come here," I said defensively. "I charged $7.50 a piece to worm the horses. The damned medicine cost me . . ."

"Hey wait, wait a minute," the man interrupted. "Don't get so upset. I didn't say what was ridiculous about it."

I was puzzled. I looked at the bill again. "I don't see anything ridiculous here at all. This is not a ridiculous bill."

"It sure as hell is ridiculous to me," he said, snatching the bill back. "Look, I'm in the t.v. repair business—here, have one of my cards and if you ever need a t.v. come see me—and the men who work for me make house calls. Now those guys are tops in their field but they got only six months' education. They get $14.95 for a house call. You got eight years of college, right? And you only get ten bucks. That's ridiculous."

"Oh," I said, much relieved. *"That's* ridiculous." I grabbed back the bill, scratched out the ten dollars and wrote in fifteen. "There, now I make five cents more than your guys."

I left, wondering if the brother-in-law had reimbursed Mrs. Grimshaw for the five dollars his big mouth had cost her. Every other veterinarian in the area was still charging $7.50 or $10. But I was damned if I was going to make less than a television repair man.

Because I was now on my own—away from Forrest's conservative ideas about personal appearance—I decided to let my hair grow long and my beard to come back.

The long hair and beard, I soon found, dictated the kind of clientele I drew. When I looked "straight" some of the people were hassling me about paying their bills, about laboratory tests I would perform on their pets, about my refusal to put animals to sleep when they simply did not want to be bothered with them anymore. After my hair grew long, my clientele was made up of people who were more relaxed, people who cared more for their animal than the money or the inconvenience the animal cost them on occasion. I was not making as much money as I might have made had I sported a crew cut, tie, and jacket, but I didn't care. I had no use for the kind of person to whom my appearance, my color or my religion was important.

The hassles from people who sought my services were so few and far between that I was taken aback when someone did say something about the way I looked.

One man who made it a point to let me know that he did not approve of the "new" me was Al Hyatt.

I had gone to Hyatt's place to deworm some of his horses. I drove into his yard and began to unload my tools. Hyatt, a short, heavy man, spotted me from the house and waddled out to greet me. He looked at me for a moment, rubbing his sunburned neck with one hand. "What the hell you got that goddam beard for?" he asked. "With all that goddam hair and them funny clothes you wear you look like hell."

I took a deep breath and started to put everything back in the car.

Hyatt's eyes widened. "Hey, what the hell are you doing?" he asked, alarm suddenly replacing the bantering tone.

"I'm leaving."

"Are you crazy, doc? You haven't even started to worm my horses yet. You can't go any place."

"It's too bad," I said, throwing things into the trunk.

160

"I'm not going to worm your horses. I don't like the way you talk to me."

"You're a new vet," Hyatt tried to reason with me. "You can't walk away from a job."

"I sure can. No one talks to me like that. If you want to give someone shit about the way they look, go up to Hollywood Boulevard and find someone up there. Don't do it to me." I slammed shut the trunk lid. "And don't worry, you won't even have to pay for the call."

Hyatt decided to back down. His horses needed attention and he would not be able to get another veterinarian for weeks. "I'm sorry," he finally said. "I was just jokin' with you, that's all."

I gave him a hard look, opened my trunk and slowly took out my tools.

Eventually, I even gave up being mad on that rare occasion when someone felt compelled to give me a hard time. Rather than argue the point when someone started to say something, I would just refer him to another veterinarian.

One man, Joe Allen, started to grumble about my "unclean, un-American" appearance almost as soon as he laid eyes on me. I took out my prescription pad and wrote down the name of one my colleagues. "Go see Dr. Haynes," I told him. "He's extremely competent. He has a haircut just like yours and he even has a little moustache just like you do."

Allen, very much surprised, took the paper.

I thought I had seen the last of him, but one day a few months later there he was again. "I guess I was a little hard on you last time," he told me by way of apology.

I thought that would be the end of it, but Allen just could not give up without a fight. "It's just that I'm not used to dealing with hippies for doctors. I mean, I still don't know why you got to have all that goddam hair."

I sighed. "Look, I didn't ask you to come back. I really don't like your attitude. I don't understand why you did come back."

Something, it was obvious, was tearing at Allen. "I got a lot of problems at home. One of my kids has long hair, too, goddam it, and I hate it. Maybe that's why I act like I do toward you."

So that was it. Taking out his anger on his kid didn't satisfy him. He had to take it out on someone else as well.

161

"Your kid is probably going to end up thirty years old, looking just like me," I said. "Is he in any kind of trouble? Is he stealing hubcaps or sniffing airplane glue?"

"Nah. Basically he's a good kid."

"Then why don't you just lay off. Let him have his long hair. Leave him alone and he may just cut it himself."

"I doubt it. He's just the hippie type. And it's a reflection on me. I have an image to uphold in the community."

"Bull. My dad is a successful contractor in Cincinnati and he's got as big a reputation to uphold as you do because his family has been there for three generations. He doesn't like my long hair and it still upsets him. But I've been fighting with him about it since I was six years old. Maybe if he hadn't bugged me continuously about it, I wouldn't have it now. You want to make things worse, you just go ahead bugging your son. He'll probably do the opposite of what you want him to do."

Allen was silent for a moment. "I don't go for all this psychology crap. But maybe you are right."

Allen must have decided that I was right because he remained my client and never said another word about my—or his son's—appearance to me.

Although I had convinced Hyatt, Allen, and a handful of other skeptics that my appearance was my business, my hair, beard, and clothes became a major, new source of contention between Jennie and me. She no longer had to be on the defensive when I started to carry on about her behavior. Now she could launch a counteroffensive, castigating me for the way I looked. I had become a hippie, someone who was in no position to make judgments about *her* way of life.

Although I was no longer falling victim to deep depressions over Jennie, our relationship was not the healthiest for either one of us. I really had difficulty handling it when she would take off for the mountains for a few days with other friends. By September of 1969 I decided that for her good and mine I should really take a stand so I told Jennie that the next time she went off for the weekend with someone else she didn't need to come back to me.

Jennie laughed at that and four days later was off with her friend Dave Peters to his mountain cabin for the weekend.

The next morning I decided to put an end to the situa-

162

tion. A few days earlier, I had received a letter from Martine, a young woman from Mexico I had met on a vacation I had taken in Cozumel four years earlier. Martine was beautiful, rich, and brilliant. Among other things, she spoke seven languages and worked as an interpreter at international medical conferences. I had just received a letter from her—the first in almost a year. She had been out of touch, she explained, because she had been in Russia for a year. Could I now come down to Mexico for our first reunion in four years? Considering I'd been madly infatuated with Martine since the first day I met her I could hardly turn her down.

Before Jennie got back to the apartment, I called Martine, asked her if the invitation was still open (it was), canceled all my appointments and got on the next plane for Mexico City. Jennie or no Jennie, I needed the vacation anyway. I had not had a break since I had left school and I was, even with an answering service, still constantly tired. More important, nothing I had been able to do so far had helped me rid myself of the cough. All the antibiotics, all the codeine, all the other cough suppressants I had prescribed for myself were doing nothing for me. Maybe a couple of weeks of peace and quiet would do the job.

Martine picked me up at the airport and, after spending a few hours in Mexico City, we drove down to Acapulco.

The last time I had been in Acapulco, I had gone there to meet my parents, my younger brother, and sister for a brief vacation.

This time, however, my stay in Acapulco was anything but relaxing. My cough was so bad that I could not control it. With Martine looking on anxiously, I plied myself continuously with medicine.

"Lucas, have you seen a doctor?" We were sitting at an outside café in Acapulco. I was leaning back in my chair, my neck bent back, my face to the sky.

"No," I squeezed out between coughs. "I think I've been afraid to find out what it is."

Martine called for the bill. "You are terribly sick. You are going back right now and seeing a doctor." I protested but Martine insisted. We drove back to Mexico City and she put me on a plane back to Los Angeles. I called Jerry Schuler, a friend of mine who is an M.D., and made an appointment to see him early the next day.

Jerry listened to my chest, carefully felt the swollen glands in my neck and marched me to the X-ray machine. Ten minutes later we walked into the dark room to look at the pictures. Jerry took one and held it up to the viewer with one hand. Almost simultaneously he took a deep breath and crushed out the cigarette he had been smoking.

"Hey, Jerry," I asked, "what the hell is that mass in the mediastinum. Animals don't have that."

Jerry turned to me, a stricken expression on his face. "Shit! That is either a substernal thyroid tumor or a tumor of the thymus gland. You're going to the hospital."

For a moment I was too dazed to talk. "No shit," I finally said. "I just signed a lease for office space and everything. I'm supposed to move in in less than three weeks. And now this."

Within twenty-four hours I was back in Cincinnati. My brother picked me up at the airport because my parents were on vacation on an island off Portugal. (I didn't want them to know that I was sick, but Uncle Izzy, a family friend as well as a doctor, convinced my brother to call them at their hotel. There was only one flight a week off the island and, because it was the height of the season, all flights were booked weeks in advance. But they were put on stand-by and when a couple from New York heard why my parents had to get back, they relinquished their seats.) We drove to the hospital. After a fight with the admitting office—they didn't want to let me in because I did not have five hundred dollars cash I could deposit with them, but finally agreed to let me in on the strength of a credit card—I made it to a bed.

When the time for the biopsy approached, a tall, blond man came into my room. Thoracic surgeons, I think, are a cold breed anyway. But this man—his name was Sterling—could have frozen water with his glance.

"How do you want this?" he asked. "With a local or a general?" I chose the local.

He nodded. "Cut off that goddamned beard before you come into surgery," he commanded and walked out.

I shaved off enough to give him a clear view of my neck. But when I was on the table, he looked at me with disgust in his eyes.

"Tell me," he asked as he cut into the lower part of my

164

neck, "what's the beard for anyway? What are you trying to prove?"

I said nothing. Sterling bent over me, cutting, snipping, and muttering orders to his assistant. "You doubt your masculinity, Mr. Younker? Is that what it is?"

"Listen," I whispered. "You may have a great reputation as a surgeon, but you are one shitty psychiatrist."

Sterling said nothing. A sharp pain ran through me as he zapped me with the cautery to stop the bleeding. "Stop wriggling," he ordered every time he jabbed me. "If I had known that you would be so much trouble, I would have knocked you out."

Later in the day, Sterling threw open the door to my room and stood framed in the doorway. His eyes were glacial. "It looks as if you have a mixed thyroid carcinoma," he announced. The words hammered at me. "Do you know what that means?"

I knew. "Six to eighteen months, right?"

"That's right," Sterling answered, turning on his heels to leave.

"Wait a minute," I called after him. "Hold on."

"I have surgery to do, Mr. Younker."

"Well just hold on a second. What are you going to do?"

He was having a hard time controlling his impatience. "We'll cut out what we can. That's about all we can do." With that he vanished, allowing the door to swing closed behind him.

I was glad that he would not be the head and neck surgeon who would be doing the big operation.

Somehow, the death sentence that now hung over my head did not concern me very much. Eighteen months seemed like a long time and I was not afraid to die. I just felt badly for my family. My family, of course, was shattered and I later found out that my father had tried hard to bargain with the doctors for my life.

"Izzy," my father said to the general practitioner who was our family doctor as they stood outside my door one day. "They say Lucas may have eighteen months to live. Right?"

"That's the *best* we can hope for, Myron. That's right."

"Now isn't it conceivable, and this is just hypothetical, that he could live nineteen months as well?"

"We don't really know. But it's possible, yes."

"All right, now let me ask you another question. If it's possible that he could live nineteen months, isn't it also possible that he could make it through twenty months?"

"Myron. Listen. I know you want Lucas to live. But Myron, you are not negotiating with the Teamster's Union here. Let's just stop, okay?"

As it turned out just a few days later, they did decide to give me a new lease on life.

I was reading a magazine when one of the hospital's pathologists came into my room, wearing a decidedly happy expression. "We've had a chance to study the stained sections a little longer," he told me. "We don't think any more that you have a mixed carcinoma."

"What then?" I could scarcely speak.

"We think it's a papillary adenocarcinoma. It's a much slower growing form of cancer. You could have another twenty years at least."

The night before the operation to remove the tumors, the anesthesiologist, a refugee from the British national health service, came to see me about the anesthesia arrangements for the next day. Instead of explaining to me what he would be doing, he surprised me by giving me a choice of anesthetics. "You are a doctor, after all," he explained.

"I want to wake up as fast as possible after the surgery," I told him, "so how about fluothane as the general?"

"Fine. Now how about the pre-anesthetic, something to relax you?"

"I'd like to try Innovar. But does it do to people what it does to dogs?"

"What does it do to dogs?"

"It makes them shit all over the place."

He laughed. "No, it works quite well with us humans."

The next morning the nurse came into my room at 5:45 and read the chart where the order for the Innovar had been entered.

She looked up at me. "I'm not giving anyone Innovar. A guy on 4-west died from it two days ago."

"I'm not getting a pre-anesthetic then?"

"No," she answered and walked out.

I had asked that no one except Martine come and see me before the operation (she had flown up as soon as I had called her and had told her the reason for my cough. Now she was spending every day at the hospital). I didn't want

166

to see a lot of people struggling to repress tears. But as they wheeled me to the operating room, I spotted my father in the doctor's lounge, sitting on a couch. When we passed a linen closet, I saw my mother and brother hiding inside, looking out for me through the partially closed door.

Because I did not have my pre-anesthetic, I was stone cold sober when they wheeled me through the double doors into the operating room. The room was ice cold to boot and I lay there shaking like a leaf. I could think of nothing except the coincidence that the surgery light above the table was the same as the one I had purchased a few years back at a government auction (even during my school years I had begun to look for, buy, and save equipment for the veterinary office I would someday open) and which I had stored in my dad's warehouse in the intervening years. I hoped that the rest of their equipment at the hospital was not that old.

"What's with you?" a voice accented with British intonations said behind me. "Are you scared or cold?"

"I'm scared, cold, and I didn't get my Innovar."

"What the bloody hell," he yelled. "Good Lord, why not?"

"Because the nurse said that a guy had died from it and she wouldn't give it to me."

He grabbed the telephone, called the nurse's station, and cursed her hard enough and long enough to warm up the operating room by several degrees.

"We'll have to do without it," he said, slamming the phone back on the receiver and turning to me. "I'll give you a short-acting barbiturate to get you on the road to sleep . . ."

The pain I felt after I came out of the anesthesia was more than I could believe. All the nurses and doctors who cared for me in the days that followed liked me because I complained little. But I was not being a hero. The pain was so incredibly intense that I had no way of expressing the way I felt. Since I could not possibly communicate what I was going through, I simply kept quiet.

Slowly, things began to improve. People around me rallied to give me support. Martine spent eighteen hours a day at the hospital. Dr. Tripp, the surgeon who operated on me, paid me nightly visits just to talk. My private night nurse, who had been private nurse to Eisenhower and Patton during World War II, regaled me with her war experiences.

"Once I beat a German soldier to death with my trenching tool," she told me.

"Why?" I lipped. I had a huge tracheal tube in my throat and could not talk.

"Because the bastard shot me in the leg, that's why," she replied as she busied herself straightening out the room. "Say," she went on after a few minutes. "I'm going to have a visitor a little later. Hope you don't mind."

I shook my head no. "Who?" I asked, again silently moving my lips.

"Christiaan Barnard. Good friend of mine."

I laughed silently, thinking she meant to entertain a boyfriend. A couple of hours later, Christiaan Barnard, who was in town for a speaking engagement, walked into my room, sat down, and chatted with her like an old friend.

As I slowly put the operation behind me, my greatest problem was the constant tests to which I was subjected—particularly the blood tests I had to have every six hours. During the operation to remove the massive tumor that had invaded me, the blood supply to my parathyroid glands had been destroyed. Because I now had to get calcium by injection or tablets, blood tests had to be done four times a day to make sure that I was getting enough to stay alive.

During the day I did not mind the blood tests, which were performed by skilled technicians or interns. Even though my veins—after a week of these tests, intravenous feedings, and assorted injections—were as bad as those of the woman prisoner I had tested years earlier, the day personnel always managed to extract the amount of blood they needed with a minimum of trouble. But at night the task was left to the nurses and they were not up to the job. (Not that they were incompetent. But I was in a teaching hospital where interns often did blood tests. The nurses, therefore, were simply out of practice.) I shuddered every time I saw a white skirt float up to my bedside at two in the morning.

I think my unwillingness to complain about my pain made the staff more sympathetic to me. After I had joked with one of the interns about the way the midnight nurses handled the needle, he suddenly began to show up at two in the morning to do the test himself. I was thankful enough that he could find the time to do the test on the nights when he was on duty. But he also showed up on the nights that he was off duty. He was so concerned about me that he would get out of bed, come do the test, take the blood to the laboratory, and then go back to bed. I think he is practicing in Minnesota now. If so, a group of very lucky patients there is getting unequaled humanitarian care.

After six weeks in the hospital, I began to feel hemmed in. While I was slowly improving, Dr. Tripp had allowed me to come along with him when he made visits to other patients and even had arranged for me to come into the operating room with him when he had surgeries scheduled. But on the forty-second or forty-third day I was overwhelmed by the feeling that I would go crazy if I stayed in the hospital one more day. I got dressed and started to walk out. Halfway down the corridor, I ran into Tripp.

"Where are you going?"

I told him I was going home.

"I don't think they'll let you out of here until the radioactivity in your urine is down to a safe level," he told me. (I had received radioactive iodine treatment as a precaution against any live cancer cells that might have gotten by the surgeon.)

"It's all right. I promise I won't piss on anyone. But I've got to get out of here."

Tripp smiled and stuck out his hand. "Go ahead. I'll sign you out."

I stayed with my parents a little while, but my restlessness grew. A few days after I had checked out of the hospital, weak as I was (down to one hundred and twenty pounds from my normal weight of one hundred and fifty), Martine and I got back on a plane and headed back to California. I wanted to get back to work and we wanted to start our life together.

Although I did manage to start my professional life going again, Martine and I were not able to establish a relationship even though we loved each other deeply. In the end, our cultural differences proved too great and we had to go our separate ways.

PART TWO

Chapter Sixteen

The raccoon was a mess. It was so weak it could not maintain a standing position when I propped it on its feet on the examining table. Its thinning fur was dirty and matted. A good portion of its obviously malnourished body was covered with decubital ulcers, ulcers that form when an animal (or human being) lies down and stays in the same position for too long a time. The ulcers themselves were infested with maggots.

"Did you find this one in the fields out behind your house?" I asked Mrs. Holden. I had operated on the family dog recently. As a matter of fact, they still owed me money for the surgery.

"Actually, we found him on the back doorstep one morning five years ago," she replied, looking down at the inert, slow-breathing animal.

I waited for an explanation for the state the animal was in. None was forthcoming.

"I'll do what I can, Mrs. Holden. However . . ."

"We don't want you to do anything, Dr. Younker," she snapped. "Just put it to sleep. You can add the charge to our bill if you want."

The animal looked as if there were nothing to do but put it out of its misery. But I had done no tests yet, had hardly examined it. I was not sure that it had to be killed. Just because they wanted me to kill their pet—and from the look on Mrs. Holden's face I could see she was determined to get rid of the raccoon—was no reason for me to comply. My personal feeling is that my first commitment is always to the animal. If I can save its life, I will do everything I can to convince the client. In fact, I have been known to lie, even to steal an animal to save it from certain euthanasia. I can always treat the animal at my own expense and find more benevolent owners for it.

Without waiting for an answer to her command, Mrs. Holden left the examining room. I took the raccoon to the back, X-rayed it, drew blood for tests and spent the better part of the next two hours cleaning the maggots out of the ulcers and removing what dead tissue I could. When I was finished, I put the raccoon on intravenous fluids and went back to my other patients. Since it was already Friday, I would not get the results of the blood tests from the laboratory until Monday morning. I could decide then on what course of action to take with the raccoon. If the tests showed an incurable problem I'd have to put it to sleep. If not, I would keep it until it was healthy again.

"No, not yet. Yes, ma'am, I will," I heard Susan, my secretary, saying into the phone when I walked into the office early Saturday morning.

"Yes, ma'am. No, ma'am, what?" I asked.

"That was Mrs. Holden. She wanted to know if you had put their raccoon to sleep yet. I told her not yet."

I was annoyed that Susan had told them that the raccoon was still alive. By and large, clients are understanding if you cannot carry out a routine procedure right away. But for some reason, when they ask that an animal be put to sleep, they want it done immediately, as if there were no time to spare. I suspected there would be trouble with the Holdens.

Within forty-five minutes, I got it. Mrs. Holden's son-in-law and two of his friends stormed into the office.

"What's going on here?" he shouted. "You were told to put that animal to sleep. Why haven't you done it?"

I held my temper. "It was your mother-in-law's opinion that the raccoon had to be put to sleep," I told him. "But I won't put anything to sleep until I'm sure there is no way to heal it. And I'm not sure yet the raccoon is beyond help. I won't get test results back before the beginning of the week."

"Test results?" The son-in-law screamed. "What test results? Who the hell authorized you to do tests? Who the hell do you think is going to pay for them?"

"Listen, nobody has to pay for them. I'm going to pay for them."

The son-in-law glared for a minute and then stomped out. His buddies followed him.

Twenty minutes later, Mr. and Mrs. Holden came back. "You give us back that raccoon," Mrs. Holden said as she came in. "Just give us back that raccoon if you are not going to follow orders."

"Gee, I already put it to sleep."

"Prove it!"

"It's already done, Mrs. Holden. Now . . ."

"We are going to stay right here until you prove you did what we wanted," Mr. Holden snapped.

With that they marched out to the parking lot.

What could I do? I certainly was not going to kill the raccoon now just to get rid of them. I had told them the animal was not there. And they just seemed crazy enough to maintain a long vigil until I proved that I had done as they had asked.

Inspiration struck. I picked up the telephone and called Andrea Cannon, a friend of mine and a veterinarian with whom I often collaborated on horse cases. "I'll be there as soon as I can," Andrea told me when I had finished explaining the situation to her.

Almost before I knew it, Andrea's car was pulling into the parking lot. She opened the door of the car, flipped back the front seat and took out a cat carrier. Very casually she strolled to the office and opened the front door. "Hi, doc!" she yelled out cheerfully. "I'm here to pick up my cat. How's the old bugger taking to getting fixed?"

We went to the back, put the raccoon in the cat carrier and came back to the front. After a few minutes at the front desk where we made a great show of discussing something or other concerning the cat's convalescence, Andrea walked out the door. "Thanks for taking such good care of Dandy, Dr. Younker," she called out, waving simultaneously with her free hand. "See you soon."

I watched Andrea back out of her space and pull out to the street. I went out and called to the stake-out party.

"If you are unhappy why don't you file a grievance with the veterinary association?" I said to them.

Within a few days it became evident that while I had won my battle with the Holden clan, I had lost my war against the raccoon's afflictions. The blood tests indicated that damage to the kidneys was irreversible. There was no hope for the animal and finally I had to put it to sleep.

(The matter was investigated by a member of the grievance committee. The committee, after discussing the case, decided the client was right and I was wrong. They reasoned that my first obligations was the verbal contract that I had made to put the animal to sleep. I felt that my first obligation was to the animal and not the people. The committee felt that the fact that I had not charged the client was irrelevant.)

The Holdens were part of my growing small animal practice in those early days after my return from Cincinnati. For a while after I had come back to southern California, I had hoped that I would be able to spend most of my time with horses. But as time passed, it became more and more obvious to me that my goals and ambitions in veterinary medicine were changing. By opening an office, I had expanded my ability to treat small animals. And, almost as soon as I opened my doors, I found a procession of cats, dogs, birds, and other assorted small creatures finding their way to me. Moreover, I found myself welcoming this increase in small animal patients because my doctors had ordered me not to work with horses for at least a month or two to avoid unnecessary strain.

More important, as the weeks and months began to fly by, I slowly grew more and more dissatisfied with the conditions surrounding my horse practice. As I looked at my situation objectively, I could see that I was spending only half of my time looking after horses. The other half I was spending behind the wheel of my truck, covering the vast distances that separated my clients. I didn't want to spend half of my life on southern California freeways, speeding from appointment to appointment.

I was also forced to admit to myself that I just could not deliver the kind of medical care to horses that I wanted to give them. Forrest had managed to set up facilities that allowed him to take very good care of his horse patients. He had a large clinic, a modern surgical suite, and a convalescing area geared to large animals. I had nothing of the sort. If I wanted to perform even minor surgeries on horses—castrations, denervings—I had to do them in dusty, dirty backyards.

Every veterinarian has to do some backyard operations.

Often there is no alternative. But I did not want to do them routinely. And, although the veterinarians to whom I referred complicated surgical cases allowed me to scrub in and assist them during the surgery, I did not relish the thought that for years to come I would find myself in the assistant surgeon's role.

I really did not mind the addition to my practice because I was growing uneasy with the kind of medicine I had to dispense when treating many of the horses in my practice. Somehow, when some people buy a horse they fail to consider that they will have to spend quite a bit of money for routine medical care. They forget that food is not the only thing that is important to a horse. A horse needs foot care. It needs routine dewormings. It needs help against the "dangers" that sometimes mark its outdoor life: Give me a horse and give me a small nail in a pasture fence and I will make an even bet that nail and horse will find each other— even if the pasture covers three acres.

More important, some people are seldom prepared for the "catastrophic" medical problems that can afflict horses. Thus, when faced by a four-hundred-dollar operation to save a colicky horse, some owners, forced by financial considerations, choose to put the animal to sleep.

For many race-horse owners, the animal is no more than a living racing machine. Often, when the horse breaks down, it is just patched up—even if the patchwork will enable the horse to run no more than one additional race. If a horse suffers a minor injury—to the knee, for example—it often should be laid up for a month. But to retrain a horse after a month's lay-off can cost thirty dollars per day or more for still another month. Many race-horse owners are not willing to spend that much more time and money on a minor knee injury. Instead, they ask the attending veterinarian to inject cortisone in the affected joint and keep the horse running until it finally can no longer compete and must be put out to pasture or put down.

I just like horses too much to find real pleasure practicing a medicine dictated by economic necessity.

On an otherwise quiet day, I received a frantic phone call from a man who had found my name in the *Yellow Pages* after he had been unable to reach his own veterinarian. His dog, he told me, had lapsed into unconsciousness.

By the time the man arrived at the office, the dog was in a coma. I suspected diabetes and ran a quick blood test. His blood sugar was a whopping 560 mg percent—way above the normal count of 100. "Your dog is in a diabetic coma," I told him. "It's a very long shot at this point, but if you are really attached to him, I'll be glad to try to pull him through."

I reached for a syringe and vial. The man's eyes widened. "I don't want you to put him to sleep, doctor. He's been with us a very long time." It was almost as if he had not heard a word I had just said. "I don't understand why you can't put him on insulin or something like that."

"This is insulin, Mr. Horning."

He looked at me, a look of bewilderment on his face. "I was told you couldn't use insulin in animals."

"You can use it," I said, plunging in the needle. "But it takes a lot of work to get diabetes under control. Sometimes the treatment works and sometimes it doesn't. But the main thing is whether you want to try or not."

I kept the dog in the office and for days gave it various doses of insulin and ran continuous blood tests to determine just how much of the hormone the animal needed to metabolize its sugar properly. Because diabetic animals have to be fed precisely at the same time and because they have to be fed the same amount of food every day, I outlined a rigid feeding schedule for Mr. Horning to follow. I also showed him how to give the dog his daily insulin injection and how to test the dog's urine to make sure the sugar levels were at their proper level. Between the two of us, we managed to keep the dog alive and well for another two years before it finally did succumb to its disease. It would have been easy to write the dog off, to administer that shot of Euthanol when Horning had first brought the dog in. But for the man, his family, and the dog, those two additional years were important enough to have warranted the effort to prolong the animal's life.

It is not always possible to win the battle against having to put an animal to sleep—even when you desperately want to help someone whose animal seems to be the only comfort in life.

"The other doctor, he had Pedro on antibiotics for three, four weeks, but they don't help," Mrs. Gonzales, a small, thin woman, was telling me as I examined her mastiff. It was apparent from the way she gently patted the dog, talked to him, and just stared at him while I examined him that she was very fond of the dog.

Because Pedro had been limping and because I had detected a swelling in the carpal area, I decided to take X rays. When I looked at the film a little later, I felt a familiar and bitter pang in my chest. The dog had an osteogenic sarcoma, a virulent, fast-growing cancer.

I broke the news. "We can amputate the leg," I told her, "but that probably would not be the end of it. This kind of cancer spreads like wildfire, usually to the lungs, and we'll probably have to do some chemotherapy as well to try to get at the other cancer cells. But it will be very expensive."

Mrs. Gonzales was close to tears. "Doctor, I am widow. I have only the Social Security checks."

"You said you had a son. Can he help?"

For a moment she said nothing. "He has got no job. He is a drug addict and he is on probation."

I had a feeling I was fighting a losing battle. If I had been practical, I would have suggested putting the dog down then and there. "Look," I said instead. "Let me amputate the leg so we won't get a farther spread of disease. I'll try to figure out something about the drugs."

The only chance, I thought, might be the University of California at Davis. I got through to a man I knew was working on drugs to battle osteogenic sarcomas. I explained the situation to him and asked if he would be willing to take the gentle mastiff on as a charity case.

"I can't do it," he told me simply but firmly. "I haven't got the funds to do that sort of thing.

I was defeated. The drugs available were astronomically expensive and although I could afford to undertake surgeries free from time to time, I did not have the money myself to subsidize a protracted chemotherapy program. I put the animal to sleep but could not rid myself of the bitterness I felt. If it had been a human being, the money for the drugs would have been found.

Although there are times when I am faced by a situation in which I have no choice but to put an animal to sleep, there are often times when I can prolong or save an animal's life—not because I have the medical knowledge but because I can help people decide against euthanasia. The veterinarian's role is especially critical when a client is faced by a life or death decision. The doctor, because he is vested with an air of authority, can easily influence the decisions people make. If someone brings in a sick dog that has been with the family for years, that has protected the house, and has grown up with the children, the veterinarian's hang-dog expression in the face of a seemingly desperate situation can be enough to tip the client toward a decision for euthanasia.

When Al Scott brought Motley in to be put to sleep, I could have readily agreed with the decision. Motley was an old dog. The aged animal was far more lethargic than he should have been—even at his age—and his abdomen was filled with fluid.

"Doc," Scott had told me. "Motley's been with us for a long time. But it looks as if he's had the course. Can you put him to sleep today? I hate to do it because the children really love him. But . . ."

"Hold on. If the kids love him so much, why put him down if you may not have to?"

"I don't know, doc. . . . It just seems as if he's at the end of his rope, that's all. Why bother him more?"

I could sense that Scott was not set in his decision.

"I don't want to impose my values on you," I told him, "but I think we should try. If we can make him comfortable, he could have another year. And if we can do it, I don't feel my conscience will allow me to put him to sleep. If you have your mind made up, I'm sure I'm not going to change it. But I don't want to put Motley to sleep just like that."

Scott thought things over for a minute. "What should we do?"

"Let me run some tests and see what the problem is and what can be done about it. Then we can decide whether or not it's necessary to put him away."

Scott had twelve kids and, although he had a good job, money in the household was probably scarce. The decision to start on the road of a possibly costly treatment weighed heavily on Scott. Nevertheless, with just a bit of prodding, he decided to spend some of the family's money to prolong Motley's life. Motley was, when Scott came right down to it, the fifteenth member of the family.

Scott left Motley, and I went to work on him. After I had taken almost two gallons of fluid out of his abdomen, I started the tests. Although congestive heart failure could have been responsible for the fluid buildup, the tests exonerated his heart. They did reveal, however, that Motley had a cirrhotic liver and that it was the villain in the piece.

Spotting the cause of the problem turned out to be only half the battle. Motley would not respond to any of the many diuretics I had available. Only when a friend recommended a drug I had not known about did Motley come around. With the drug to flush fluids out of his body and with other drugs to support his liver, I kept Motley alive for another nine months. It wasn't all that much, but it was enough to make the kids happy and enough to make Scott feel that he had made the right decision.

To save an animal from a premature or unnecessary mercy killing, the veterinarian must have the cooperation of the client. The veterinarian cannot save an animal when he is dealing with a person who considers a dog or a cat just another disposable good to be replaced when it breaks down.

From time to time I get someone—usually not one of my steady clients but someone who has picked my name out of the *Yellow Pages* or who has seen my office from the street—who demands that I kill his pet rather than take even the most moderate steps to cure its ailment. "Hell," I hear every once in a while. "Why should I spend fifty bucks for medicine if I can get me another dog at the pound for two dollars?"

Because I know there are people like that around, I find special gratification in having clients like Mrs. Davis, who can commit themselves to saving a pet they have had only for a short time.

Mrs. Davis was sitting on the edge of one of the high-backed chairs in my reception room when I came back from an emergency call to treat a mare that had been having trouble foaling. In her arms, Mrs. Davis was cradling a small kitten.

Susan ushered her into one of the examining rooms and handed me the chart she had prepared. The kitten, the note clipped to the chart said, had injured its eye.

I looked up from the chart to find Mrs. Davis staring at me, anxiety in her face. "Doctor, I don't believe in killing things," she said. "I was told to put him to sleep and I don't want to do it."

I examined the cat's eye. The cornea had been scratched and the eye was completely collapsed and infected.

"I don't think the eye can be saved," I told her after I had finished my examination. "But there is no reason to put him to sleep."

For the first time, Mrs. Davis relaxed. "Go ahead and do what you can," she said, caressing the kitten. "And, don't worry about the cost."

I removed the kitten's eye, kept the kitten in the office until I had cleared up the infection and then sent him home. The cat looks as if he has a permanent wink, but otherwise he has led a perfectly normal life.

Not long after Mrs. Davis had brought her kitten in, the Sherman family—man, wife, two kids—trooped in with a cute eight-week-old cairn terrier.

"We just got her a few days ago at the pet store," Mr. Sherman explained as the boy gently put the puppy on the examining table. "But she won't run around or nothing. She just sort of lays there, breathing real hard."

One good look at the small puppy told me that she had probably been born with a heart defect known as patent ductus arteriosus. In any fetus—be it a human fetus or a dog fetus—a small vessel known as the ductus arteriosus links the circulation system connecting the heart with the lungs to the circulation system leading to the rest of the body. Under normal circumstances, the ductus should close up after birth. But sometimes, it does not. And when it stays open (or "patent") it interferes with normal circulation around the body because it detours blood away from its normal course. The ductus is a small vessel and the rush of blood through it after birth sets off visible and audible vibrations. The terrier's chest was heaving ferociously under the drumming of the unnatural flow of blood through the patent ductus. When I listened with my stethoscope, I could hear the familiar "machinery" murmur given off by the patent ductus.

The best way to treat a patent ductus is to operate—to open the chest, find the small vessel and tie it off. But surgery, especially because it is risky when performed in young animals, is not a happy choice. Only recently, another puppy with a patent ductus had died while I was operating to repair the defect.

That puppy had been sent to me from Arizona. A veterinarian I know in Phoenix had called me because clients of his had left the puppy to be put to sleep. He had done only one patent ductus before and that operation had failed. Since he knew that I would perform surgeries free if I saw a chance to save an animal, he had brought the puppy to my attention. I told him I would try to save it. He found a friend who had a private plane and asked him to fly the puppy to Los Angeles.

When the puppy arrived, I called Dr. Chadwick, a friend of mine who has excellent surgical facilities in his animal hospital, and asked if he would talk me through the operation since he had done it many times before. He had agreed quickly and even worked with me to close the ductus. Everything went well during the main part of the operation. But, just as we started to close the chest, the heart began to fibrillate, to beat wildly. We managed to restore its normal beating pattern and once more started to sew up the chest. Again, the heart began a wild erratic beating. But this time, instead of responding to our drugs, the heart stopped completely. We could not start it again and the pup died on the table. Chadwick and I were heartbroken.

Now, I faced the Shermans. "Did you get the dog at a store where they guarantee their animals?"

"Yes," Sherman answered. "They said they would take it back if there was anything wrong with it."

I hated to take the next step. "If I were you, I would take her back and get another puppy."

The family was crestfallen. "But we've really gotten to love her, doctor," Mrs. Sherman said. "What will the pet store do with her anyway?"

I didn't want to say anything in front of the children so I just let silence speak my answer.

"Doctor?"

"Well, I could try to operate. But there is no guarantee of success. And it's expensive. It would cost you another one hundred and fifty dollars to three hundred and fifty dollars."

Now, the Shermans were faced by a hard choice. They wanted to save the dog, but the sums I had mentioned were beyond their means.

"We could try medication," I told them. "But again, there is no guarantee the dog will live long. And you are going to face a problem if she reaches maturity. Surgery to spay her would be risky considering she has a bad heart. She could survive a pregnancy or two but they would be risky too. We could try an intravaginal device to keep her from getting pregnant. . . . ."

The Shermans were happy to settle for that. They loved their new puppy and wanted to save her. She'd never be a frisky dog because she would tire easily, even with moderate exercise. But at least she would live—and she would make a nice companion around the house.

Chapter Seventeen

The basset hound looked at me with the sad eyes characteristic of his breed as I took the thermometer out of the sterilizing solution.

"He might have a slight upper respiratory tract infection," I told the dog's owner, Mr. Norman, as I gently inserted the thermometer in the animal's rectum. "Let's check his temperature and that will . . ."

The door to the examining room flew open. "Emergency, doctor," Susan called out. "She's in the other room."

With barely an "excuse me," I ran to the second examining room. A papillon was lying on the table, breathing very hard. Even at first glance it was obvious that the little animal was struggling to stay alive. Next to her stood a small, thin woman who seemed to be in her seventies.

The woman looked at me sharply as I came into the room. "Young man, I just want you to know I would not be here except that my dog is so sick and I don't think she'd make it to our regular veterinarian over in Compton. He's the only veterinarian she has ever abided. I know she is not going to like you and so I probably won't come back."

I didn't feel like arguing the point. One look at the labored way in which the animal was breathing was enough to convince me that dog was indeed in a lot of trouble.

"How long has she been having problems breathing?" I asked as I quickly began to look her over.

"I don't really know, doctor. Bonita hasn't been eating well for about a week, but otherwise she was all right until about an hour ago. She drank an awful lot of water this morning and then just collapsed."

I hurriedly put on my stethoscope and listened to the small chest. I detected a murmur characteristic of a heart in which one of the valves is malfunctioning. Worse, the other sounds that came at me from the chest told me the dog was in the throes of congestive heart failure.

I ran to the drug shelves and found a vial of Lasix, a diuretic. The diuretic did not help. I hooked the papillion to an EKG so I could monitor her heart and started digitalis treatment. When Bonita's condition seemed to be stabilizing, I hurried back to the room where I had left the basset hound.

"I have an emergency and can't finish your dog now," I told Mr. Norman. "If you will make an appointment with the receptionist, I can see you later this afternoon."

"But . . ."

I let the door swing closed and hurried back to Bonita. The little dog was still breathing hard, looking out at the world through fearful eyes. Mrs. LaVerne was standing by the table, gently petting her, murmuring words of assurance.

Gingerly, I ran my fingers along the bony body. I suspected that the heart problem was not Bonita's only affliction.

"Has she been spayed?" I asked Mrs. LaVerne, just to start the process of elimination somewhere.

"No. As a matter of fact, she was just in heat last month. But she has had an awful lot of trouble with her cycles."

Suddenly, as I pressed the abdomen, the dog yelped. The abdomen seemed tender and distended. "She might have some fluid accumulating as a result of the heart failure, but I'm not sure," I told Mrs. LaVerne. "It could also be an infected uterus. Can you leave her here so I can run some tests?"

Mrs. LaVerne's eyes opened widely. "You mean hospitalize her? Leave her here alone?"

"I'm afraid so. This dog is in very bad shape. She may not live anyway. But I'll have to keep her here if I am even going to try to help."

Mrs. LaVerne's hands trembled slightly but after a moment of agonizing, she relented.

After she had taken a tearful leave from her dog, I took Bonita to the back and X-rayed her. My suspicions were confirmed. The twelve-year-old dog had a huge, pus-filled uterus.

What to do now? If I did not operate to remove the organ, the raging infection would surely kill the dog. If I operated, I would be taking a substantial risk that the dog's weak and failing heart would not withstand the rigors of general anesthesia.

I decided the uterus had to come out. But I was short-handed at the office and would need good surgical help if I were to pull the dog through its hazardous surgery. Luckily, it was Sadie's day off. I tracked her down at a friend's house at the beach and twenty minutes later her low-slung sports car roared into the parking lot. (I had met Sadie's dog before I met Sadie. A few years earlier, Sadie, too busy with her nursing chores at a local doctor's office, had asked a friend to bring her golden retriever to me because the dog was, according to Sadie, "panting too much." When I saw the dog he seemed fine. Sadie, who I was sure was a ding-bat to be worried about such a healthy dog, came in a few days later to pay her bill during a quick lunch break. When I saw her, I decided she could not possibly be a dingbat, assured her the dog was just fine, and asked her out.) Sadie scrubbed in and joined me in the operating room.

Instead of giving Bonita a general anesthetic, I pumped a local anesthetic along the midline of the abdomen and opened her up. Working as fast as I could, I removed the uterus. Much to my relief—and perhaps my surprise—Bonita survived the operation.

I gave her some more diuretics to help her rid herself of the excessive fluids that had collected in her lungs. When I was sure she was in a stable condition, I started to go to lunch. It was Friday and the traditional luncheon at which a dozen or so veterinarians gathered every week at the Twin Dragon to discuss their cases was already underway.

As I passed the front desk, the telephone rang. I should have kept going but I stopped when I saw Susan wince as she listened to the caller. She covered the mouthpiece and handed me the telephone. "Boy, is he mad!"

"Younker," a voice yelled when I said hello, "you are by far the dumbest, worst veterinarian I have ever run across."

"Wait," I protested, trying to recognize the voice. "What did I do?"

"Where the hell did you ever get the idea you were a

competent animal doctor, you idiot? Do you know what you did this morning? Do you?"

My gosh, I thought, could this be Mrs. LaVerne's regular veterinarian? Was he upset because I had talked Mrs. La-Verne into leaving her dog with me just this once?

"You sent me home with a dog that had a *Goddam thermometer up his ass!*"

Relief swept through me. I had forgotten about Mr. Norman and his dog. I was embarrassed. But it wasn't as bad as he made it sound. After all, he could have just taken it out himself when he realized what I had done. I apologized, honestly told him that I had forgotten all about the thermometer when the emergency had occurred, and hung up.

Dave Kaplan was at the bar, sipping a coke.

"What kept you?" he asked, never taking his eyes off a foxy Oriental girl at the end of the bar.

I told him about Bonita and what I had done to the basset hound.

"You just don't have enough experience yet," he said, spearing a green olive from one of the containers behind the bar. "When they call and are all heated up about the thermometer, you have to know what to say."

"It's happened to you too?"

Kaplan laughed as we walked to the table to join the others. "Oh sure, lots of times. Happens to everybody. But see, the conversation should go something like this:

"You: 'What! You didn't take the thermometer out, did you?'

"Them: 'Yes, why?'

"You: 'I told you to leave that thermometer in another thirty minutes after you got home and I bet it's only been twenty minutes.'

"Them, sounding kind of hurt: 'You didn't say anything like that, doctor.'

"You: 'I forgot to mention it? Gee, I'm sorry. That's our new disposable thermometer and it's supposed to stay in that long. You're supposed to take it out and read it and call me to tell me the temperature and then throw it out. You didn't throw it out already, did you?'

"Usually, they'll put it right back in and call you ten minutes later to give you the reading. You've got to learn to handle these things, Lucas. They're the difference between an amateur and a pro."

"And you are the pro's pro, right Kaplan?" someone across the table asked.

"Nah," Kaplan answered with modesty. "Everybody learns these things in time. Dave May really knows how to handle his little 'situations.'"

Dave wasn't there to tell his tales, but Kaplan, never one to shy away from a good story, launched right in. "They were doing some remodeling over at Dave's place last summer and everything was in a big mess.

"But it was business as usual and they had a few animals in the hospital, including one very mean cat. Someone opened the cage to feed the cat one day and it jumped out, got on some boxes on a table and from there jumped right into an air-conditioning duct that one of the workers had left open.

"No one wanted to reach in there to pull the cat out. So Dave tells them to put a sandbox up there and some food and water and then to refer the owner to him when she comes in to claim the cat.

"Two weeks later, the lady comes back from vacation and comes to pick up her cat. Dave greets her at the door. 'Mrs. Green, so nice to see you,' he tells her. 'I'm so glad you came in just at this moment because just a few minutes ago we put your cat in our brand-new overhead exercise run. Your cat is the first one to use it.'

"She's all excited because her cat is initiating this new concept in animal care. So he says to her, 'We are all terribly busy right now, so would you mind stepping up the ladder there, we don't have the steps put in yet, you know, and calling Kitty. She'll come right out to see you and you can take her home.'

"So the lady climbs up the ladder, calls Kitty and takes her home. Next thing Dave knows, some of his clients are asking him if their animal is going to get to use the new overhead exercise run."

"Not everyone gets away with stuff like that." It was Chadwick at the other end of the table. "Friend of mine went on vacation last year and left the practice in the hands of the receptionist and a relief veterinarian. While he's gone, a lady comes in to claim her dog, a dachshund she had boarded there for a couple of weeks. It was an old dog, it had teeth missing and it was already getting gray around the muzzle.

"The receptionist goes to the kennels in back and comes out with this three-year-old dachshund. 'That's the wrong dog,' the lady says.

"The receptionist knew it was the wrong dog because she also knows that the lady's own dachshund is missing and no one knows where it is. So she brought out this other dog that had a slipped disc and which had been paralyzed and which the owner had left to be put to sleep. The staff, rather than put it down, had kept it as a pet and the animal eventually recovered after a few months of "cage" rest.

"They actually convinced her to take this other dog home. Of course, as soon as she gets home, she thinks things over. When my friend got back, he fired everyone because no one would tell him the truth about what happened to the lady's dog."

I put my two cents in. "Well, you have to be smart.

"I knew this old German veterinarian back in Cincinnati. One day a lady brings in a big, white duck to be dequacked because the neighbors had been complaining about all the noise it was making.

"Hellenstein had never dequacked that kind of a duck before and because he was a very conscientious doctor, he decided he had to practice first. He goes out to the local duck farm and buys himself a duck, the same color, the same breed, the same size. Everything is the same except that it's a wild duck, not one that has lived with a family. He takes it to the clinic and does the operation.

"Everything went fine in the practice operation so they put the lady's pet duck on the table. But the pet duck has a hemorrhage during the operation and dies. Everybody is all upset, but not the old man. 'You vill let me handle ziss ven ze lady comes,' he tells his staff.

"When the time comes for the lady to pick up her dequacked duck, there was Hellenstein to meet her. 'Ah, Mrs. Smith, I am zo glad to zee you,' he tells her. 'Let me please tell you about your pet. You vill notice zat zere has been a slight change in ze perzonality of ze duck. Ze duck had to undergo anesthesia for zis operation and zometimes it iz found zat ze duck undergoes a zlight perzonality change in zese cases. You vill notice alzo in your duck zat he has become a bit more excitable, and you vill find that he will be very excited to zee you. He vill flap his wings and jump around a lot.'

"They bring out this wild duck that's thrashing around, flapping its wings and madder than hell because in addition to all the other indignities it has suffered away from its pond, it now can't quack to boot. But the people loved it. They just thought it was great that they had this duck that didn't quack any more and that had, as kind of a bonus, a brand new personality."

There were a few appreciative chuckles—just enough to reward me, the relative newcomer, for my effort to contribute to the prebusiness entertainment.

"Hey, Kaplan," someone called out after a minute during which everyone went back to the Sizzling Rice Soup. "Any women offer you anything interesting lately?"

Women seemed to be very interested in Kaplan. His encounter with "The Breast" was, by now, Orange County folklore.

An attractive (according to Kaplan) young woman had brought her Labrador retriever to him because the animal had been scratching incessantly. Kaplan suspected ringworm and prepared to examine the dog for signs of the disease. Ringworm, despite its name, is caused by fungus, not by a worm. And one way to diagnose ringworm is to turn off all the lights in the examining room and shine an ultraviolet light on the afflicted area. Under UV light, some ringworm infections will fluoresce bright green.

Kaplan took his ultraviolet light and its accompanying five-inch magnifying glass and started his inspection at the dog's tail. Working slowly and carefully so as not to miss anything, he moved the light up the dog's long back, looking for the tell-tale green.

He finished the back and then the neck. He got to the dog's head and down to the snout. With a start, Kaplan suddenly realized that he was staring down at a gigantic nipple, human variety. He looked up from the magnifying glass to see his client cradling her well-endowed breast in her hands. "Doctor," she asked, looking into his eyes. "Do you see any of that stuff there?"

"I've got ethics, you know," he told me later. "Man, I started back-pedaling fast, telling her 'put that back,' and yelling for my receptionist to get her ass into the examining room."

Kaplan took a bite of the Moo Shu Pork that had just arrived and shook his head, no, nothing like that had happened recently.

The disappointment around the table was evident. "Something like that did happen to me last week," I volunteered. Everyone looked over in anticipation.

"This woman came in," I started. "I think she was about thirty or thirty-five. Tall, really good-looking. Great body. First time she'd been in.

"She had this old dog that had slipped a disc and was in pain, dragging its feet, the whole bit. I told her that one thing that might help would be a laminectomy.

"She looks at me and says, 'What's that going to cost?'

"About two hundred or three hundred dollars," I tell her.

"She thinks a couple of seconds then says to me, 'Doc, I haven't got that kind of money and I really like the dog. Do you think I could take it out in trade?' "

I waited for the hooting and the clapping to die down.

"Well, I got all flustered and embarrassed. 'Like what?' I finally got around to asking her.

" 'Well,' she says. 'I do ironing, Dr. Younker . . .' "

After the laughs died down, we started on the serious business of discussing the tough cases we had each worked on during the week and seeking each other's advice on problems some of our patients were facing.

Chapter Eighteen

For a moment I just stood there and stared at the poor animal. Her head was so swollen, she scarcely looked like a horse any more. She could barely chew, could hardly breathe. Discharge flowed from both nostrils. Her eyes were swollen shut. If she had keeled over and died on the spot, I would not have been surprised.

"Is your mother home?" I finally asked the young girl who was sitting on a corner of the fence, looking glumly at the motionless horse.

"Yeah, here she comes now," she answered, a slight tone of hostility breaking through the studied flat tone of her voice.

I turned toward the house nestled among the avocado trees, and watched Mrs. Christian walk slowly toward us.

"Get in the house," she barked at the girl. After watching the girl go off, she turned to me. "What do you think, doc?" There was something in her question that told me she really didn't care very much, that the mare's illness was just another of the day's nuisances.

I walked closer to the horse and gently patted her on the forehead. "I don't know yet. It looks like a reaction to something. Do you have any rattlesnakes around here?"

"There's no rattlesnakes around here," she said with some impatience. "And she hasn't been away from the property for a week."

Maybe, I thought, the mare had eaten something. My eyes roamed the property. "Was she out of the corral?"

"Yeah, sure. She's out all the time. Yesterday, the kids let her out and she was in the avocado grove." .

It was possible, I thought, that the mare had munched

on the avocado leaves on the trees and had suffered an allergic reaction to them.

"Oh yeah?" Mrs. Christian said in an uninterested tone when I mentioned my theory. "Well, just go ahead and treat her, doc, and send us the bill." And with that she shuffled back to the house in her black fur-trimmed house slippers.

I went to the truck to pick up some more equipment. When I got back to the corral, Linda, the girl who had been sitting with the horse when I arrived, was back on the fence. She watched me sort out my things. "Is she going to be all right?"

"I don't know yet," I said, gently pushing a stomach tube through one of the mare's nostrils. I wanted to get some mineral oil into her stomach to cleanse out what might be left of the avocado leaves and to coat the stomach and intestines so nothing else toxic would be absorbed. "I hope so. Is she your horse?"

"Sort of. I mean, she belongs to me and my brothers and sisters. My folks don't ride."

There was again something in Linda's behavior, something in the way she said "folks," that had an edge of uncertainty about it. There was something on her mind besides the horse. But whatever it was, she wasn't ready to come out with it. She watched quietly as I finished administering the oil and started to give the mare anti-inflammatory drugs, antibiotics, and vitamins.

"Why are you giving her all that stuff?" Linda asked, alarmed.

"Well, because I have never treated a case of avocado poisoning before and I'm not sure what will do the job right now," I said, trying to explain my shotgun approach.

When I packed up and walked back to my car, Linda, her hands tucked into the back pockets of her jeans, followed me. "Doc, are you coming back?"

"Tomorrow. She's not going to get better overnight."

When I returned the next day, armed with advice from a colleague with whom I had consulted (I had not been able to find anything about avocado poisoning or its treatment in any of my textbooks or journals), the horse was no better. In fact, she looked even closer to death.

"She sure ain't better, doc," Mrs. Christian said behind

me. And, unless I was wrong, she was slightly tipsy. "What are you doing to do now, doc?"

"I'm going to give her some anti-inflammatory drugs," I explained. "It's going to take a while to get her over the reaction."

An alcohol-accented "Oh," was Mrs. Christian's only response. She stared at me for a second, turned, and ambled back to the house. I got busy with the horse.

"She's bombed again." It was Linda, standing at the fence.

I was embarrassed and didn't know what to say.

"She always is," Linda went on, bitterness now openly creeping into her voice. "By lunch time she can't even see straight."

I started to answer, but Linda stormed off without giving me a chance.

When I returned the following day, Mrs. Christian was not around. Linda met me at the corral. "Doc, I'm sorry about yesterday. I shouldn't have bothered you with that stuff."

"You didn't bother me. If something is on your mind. . . ."

"I hate it, doc. And she's hassling me all the time. She's on me every minute. . . ." The words came pouring out.

I prepared another injection of anti-inflammatory drugs for the mare. "What does she hassle you about?"

"Oh shit, you know. Everything. My clothes. My hair. Because she thinks I'm taking drugs."

"Are you?"

Linda was struggling with herself. There was a lot she had been bottling up.

"I've tried some."

"Like what?"

She shrugged as if it were of no importance. "LSD. Mescaline. Mushrooms."

"Do you like that stuff?"

"It's better than what goes on around here. Her drinking. Her and my old man arguing about money all the time. Anyway, they're getting a divorce. One of these days I'm going to split."

Linda's tale had a familiar ring to it. It was a rare day when I did not hear of a family torn apart by alcohol, drugs, battles among parents and children, separations and divorces.

A while back, Meredith Chase, a client, had greeted me with a long face when I had come to examine her gelding.

"It's Allan again," she told me. "They caught him smoking grass in one of the school's bathrooms. I just don't know what to do with him. He drinks. He smokes marijuana all the time. He is continuously getting into fights. I am at the end of my rope."

I knew Allan and, outwardly at least, he seemed to be a nice kid. Whenever he had the opportunity, he would talk to me about animals. His face lit up when I talked to him about some of my experiences with horses.

"What are you going to do, Meredith? Can you get some help?"

"I'm not going to do anything any more. I'm going to have him declared a ward of the court and let someone else worry about him. I'm fed up."

A few days later, on my way to treat a horse that had navicular disease, I saw Allan shuffling along. I pulled up next to him. "I'm on my way to treat a horse. Want to come along?"

Allan jumped into the car. "Where are you headed?" I asked.

"Nowhere," he said, resting his head on the door window. "Just walking. Mom's drunk again and I can't stand to be home when she's been hitting the bottle."

From that day on, Allan spent three to four hours every afternoon at my side. He was full of questions and I was glad to answer them. Slowly, Allan started to turn around. His relations with his mother didn't improve, but he started getting better grades in school, started getting along with other people. Just a bit of positive attention was enough to get him off the jail-bound road he had been traveling.

As a youngster, I had spent many hours unsuccessfully trying to find a veterinarian who would allow me to spend time with him, watch him work, to help him around the office by doing nothing more than cleaning cages. I had sworn to myself that if I ever had a practice of my own, I would have an open-door policy for kids who wanted to spend time with me. And, even though Linda had never expressed an interest in veterinary medicine (aside from the bit I practiced on the family horse) I decided that I

196

would suggest that she join Allan in looking in on things for a few hours a week. I didn't think that I could solve her problems for her, but at the very least, spending time with me in my practice would give her some relief from the oppressive atmosphere at home. Somehow, I never got the chance to mention the idea.

For a while drugs came to play a greater and greater role in Linda's life. One day she was picked up by the police, wandering around in a daze in the middle of a busy intersection. But then, she somehow straightened herself up. Sadly, three years later she went hiking in a national park and while clambering at the edge of a high cliff, fell to her death.

I hurried back to the office because Mrs. Holcombe was due in with her Great Dane, Duke. I had been taking care of her animals—one dog and several horses—since Mrs. Holcombe had moved to Orange County a year earlier. Mrs. Holcombe had moved away from one of the fanciest and most exclusive areas in Los Angeles County because much to her disgust one black family (headed by a veterinarian, I later found out) had bought a $250,000 home there.

"Mrs. Holcombe is in examining room one," Susan announced as I came through the front door. "But I think you'd better take a look at the patient in the other examining room first."

Susan looked a bit strained, but I didn't say anything and walked into the second examining room. On the table was a five-foot boa constrictor.

"She's been acting sickly the last day or so, doctor," the man standing by and stroking her said. "She won't eat and looks kinda droopy."

I walked around to the front of the table and looked at the snake's head. She was blowing bubbles out of her nose.

"From that nasal discharge, I'd say she's got a respiratory infection," I explained. "I'll give her some antibiotics."

I gave the snake an injection, told him to bring her in the next day, and stepped back to admire the reptile. "That is one beautiful creature," I said. "Can I get a picture of her?"

"Better yet. Let me take a picture of you and Shelly together."

I went to the back, picked up my camera and, after

draping the snake around my neck, walked out into the waiting room where the light was better. Mrs. LaVerne, who had brought one of her other papillons in for a shot, took one look and fled. The boa's owner snapped off a couple of pictures of me and Shelly and left. I stepped into the first examining room where Mrs. Holcombe, who had been told that I had just had a quick emergency, was patiently waiting.

Mrs. Holcombe, looking her Junior League best, stood quietly by the examining table as I worked on Duke.

"Say, Dr. Younker, isn't it terrible, that business about Angela Davis?" she said after a while.

Because I make it a rule not to discuss politics with my clients, I said nothing. In any case, the last thing I wanted to do was discuss the slaughter at the San Marino courthouse in northern California.

Unfortunately, Mrs. Holcombe took my silence as encouragement. "I just knew it, you know. If you encourage communism and radicalism, that's the kind of thing that will happen. The nerve of that woman, anyway. You give them the best opportunities in life, allow them to go to some of your best universities, and what do they do? They preach killing you and burning down your houses."

Before I knew it, I found myself violating my rule. "Maxine, if I were black, I'm sure I wouldn't be your veterinarian."

The apparent non sequitur left her quiet for a moment. But she decided to pursue it. "Dr. Younker, that would not make any difference. If you were black, I would still come to you."

"That's not the point, Maxine. The point is that I probably wouldn't be a veterinarian if I were black because at the time I went to veterinary school, they didn't take many blacks. That would have made me mad enough to be a Black Panther or another kind of revolutionary because all I ever wanted in life was to be a veterinarian. There would have been nothing left but to be a militant."

"Oh goodness, you are much too smart to really believe that. Besides, she got into all the best schools. Brandeis, the University of California."

"I don't think that makes a difference. Obviously she doesn't think that what happens to her alone is the important thing, but what opportunities are available to her people as a whole. I think it's that attitude that 'we let them into our universities' that probably annoys people like Angela Davis. The connotation is that we have the right to bestow the blessing of a good education on just a handful of blacks or Chicanos or whatever, and that they should be thankful for that. A couple are 'allowed' to get into school and the rest waste their lives on ghetto street corners."

I stopped and cooled down. "Anyway, you don't even know if she was involved in the shoot-out. You just have the police's word for it."

Mrs. Holcombe said nothing to counter my argument. I finished examining Duke while she chitchatted about other things.

"It may be his hip," I finally said. "You'd best leave him here. I want to get some X rays and see how he does for the next few days."

Mrs. Holcombe said a cheery good-bye to Duke and left. I picked him up and started to carry him to the back. But as I stepped out of the examining room and into the hallway, the subtle, distinct odor struck my nostrils.

"Susan, is he?"

Susan slowly nodded her head in the affirmative. Harry was indeed in the office.

As word had spread that I welcomed kids in my practice as observers and volunteers, high-school counselors had started to call me, asking me to accept problem children. Harry had been one of the troublesome youngsters referred to me. He was slow in school, had trouble getting along with his classmates. He came from a poor family. Like many people whose low income forces them into a cheap diet of starches and carbohydrates, Harry was grossly overweight. Harry, finally, had a terrible body odor problem. Within a few minutes of his arrival, the entire clinic reeked with his scent.

This was Harry's fourth day with us and I could not take it any longer. But how to teach Harry about hygiene without telling him he smelled bad, without hurting his feelings?

Harry was in back mopping the floor in the kennel area and after I had put Duke in a clean cage, I casually turned to Harry. "Hey, Harry, did you have your shower yet today?" I asked point-blank.

"Sure. This morning."

I wasn't so sure. But then, maybe no one had ever taught Harry about soap. Or maybe they only had cold water at the apartment and Harry couldn't stand to stay under it long enough to get really clean.

"Okay, that's fine. But I just want to tell you that I usually take a shower twice a day because when you are around sick animals, you have to be very careful about germs. These animals are weak and if they get other germs from us they could really be in trouble. So what I want you to do is go to the back room and take another shower and use a lot of that special soap we have there."

From them on, Harry took a hot shower every day as soon as he came into the clinic. We also got him to stop wearing the same clothes day in and day out. I don't know if he noticed, but people stopped taking detours to avoid his presence.

Chapter Nineteen

As I passed the Holcombe house on the way to Christine Miller's, I got a little surprise: Dr. Collingwood's pickup truck was parked in the Holcombe driveway. I hadn't seen Maxine Holcombe in six to eight weeks—not since I had done pregnancy examinations on her four mares a day or so before she had picked up Duke after I had operated on his hip. I had been wondering about the long silence. And now I knew the reason. She had gotten herself another veterinarian. But why?

Maybe, I thought as I drove on to the Miller place, I had screwed up one of the pregnancy exams. Once in a while when I palpate a mare in a very early pregnancy (less than thirty to thirty-five days) I am not always sure. But I had not had any trouble with Maxine Holcombe's horses and I had been convinced at the time that one of the mares was pregnant and that the other three were not.

I pulled into the Miller driveway, parked, and walked past the big house to the stables. Christine Miller came out of the back door, and walked along with me.

"You look preoccupied, Lucas," she said. "What's the matter?"

"I just came by Maxine Holcombe's place and saw Dr. Collingwood's pickup there. What did I do to her horses, Chris? Did I miss one of the pregnancy exams I did?"

Christine opened the door to the stable and let me in. "You didn't do anything wrong to her horses." She paused for a moment and scrutinized my face. I began to feel a little bit uncomfortable. "You really don't know?" she finally went on.

What the hell was going on? "Know what? What should I know?"

"You didn't hear about your famous Black Panther statement?"

I had no idea what she was talking about. "My famous Black Panther statement? What Black Panther statement?"

"Every once in a while we have a big luncheon in the neighborhood for all the ladies who own horses. Anyway, at the last one about three weeks ago, Maxine stood up and said that she had evidence from statements you had made to her that you were a Black Panther. She said that you were just here to get our money and channel it to the Black Panthers. She said we shouldn't use you. I think some of the people there believed her."

I told Chris about the conversation I had had with Mrs. Holcombe about Angela Davis. She took a sip from her beer can. (She was never without one.) "And from that she got the idea that I actually belong to the Black Panthers? I met Huey Newton once, but I really don't think that I qualify for the organization."

"I'm sorry, but what can I tell you? Did you lose anyone else in the last few weeks?"

"Not that I can tell. I only see some of these people once or twice a year when I vaccinate or deworm their horses."

Chris shrugged. "I wouldn't worry about it. That's probably the end of it anyway."

The last thing I was going to do, I thought to myself as I drove to the last call of the morning, the Janeway place, was to worry about silly things like that. I would have been devastated if I had done something wrong medically. But if people want to boycott me because of my political beliefs, well, I was not about to change my life for a couple of dollars. And, as far as Maxine Holcombe was concerned, I was sure that once day she would have an emergency when the other four or five doctors who treated horses in the area would either be busy or gone for the day. I'd enjoy seeing her face and discomfort while I looked after her sick animal then.

I drove slowly to the Janeway Stables, girding myself for the battle I knew would come. I was scheduled to deworm some horses there, including one little mustang that was absolutely one of the great manhaters of all time. The little animal loved young girls, but he didn't seem to like me at all. Whenever I had to work on him, there was a major battle. Every time I got into his stall, he would try to bite, kick, or strike me. I could only work on him if he had a lip chain on or had been tranquilized—but accomplishing either of those things was in itself a life-endangering event. Of course, I was too proud to tell the owner to get himself another veterinarian. No matter how much trouble that horse gave me, I always came back for more.

Dan Fisher, the owner of the stables, walked over and met me as soon as I got out of my truck and unloaded my equipment. "Should I make your day and tell you they sold the mustang?"

"No such luck, I'm sure."

"You're right. Want to start with him first? I already asked a couple of the fellas to give us a hand."

The minute I appeared in the stall doorway, the mustang laid back his ears. While I filled the syringe with a tranquilizer, Fisher, who was holding the halter, approached the horse. He entered the stall and in a moment of luck, Fisher managed to get the halter on the mustang's head and hold him fairly still. I moved in quickly and gave the mustang the injection. When the drug had taken its effect, I started to deworm him. When I was done, I went on to do, without incident, the other horses that had been scheduled for treatment.

A couple of hours later, I was walking along a row of horses that had been tied to a fence. They were all standing parallel to the fence and I didn't pay much attention to them because I was looking for a specific horse that I knew was over in another part of the property. Suddenly, out of the collection of horses, one hind leg lashed out at me with lightning speed. A searing pain shot through my knees and I crumbled to the ground. I looked over just in time to see the mustang, a glint of triumph in his eye, casually turn his head away. The son-of-a-bitch had been waiting patiently, waiting for an opportunity to get me.

Dan Fisher came running over while I was trying to stumble to my feet. "Jesus! Are you all right?"

My knees felt as if a dentist were drilling into them with an old, slow drill. "I guess so," I managed, trying to catch my breath. "But that's it, man. You're going to have to get yourself another veterinarian for that mustang. I'll be damned if I'm going to let that mother kill me."

With Fisher's help, I made it back to my truck. Gritting my teeth against the pain, I put it in second gear and drove the fifteen miles home with my legs stretched out in front of me as far as possible. To avoid moving my legs or bending my knees, I did not shift into another gear or stop for a sign until the truck wheezed into the apartment building parking lot. I edged out of the cab, got to my apartment, put on a bathing suit and dragged myself to the Jacuzzi for a couple of hours of hot-water massage before my afternoon appointments. Fortunately, I haven't managed to get hurt since then.

I opened one eye and stared at the telephone. Eight o'clock on a Sunday morning and it was already lashing out at me. I propped myself up, took the receiver and mumbled a distinctly uncheerful "hello."

"Lucas?" It was Andrea Cannon. "I'm sorry to call so early but I've got a horse from down your way coming in because the lady can't get hold of her own veterinarian or anyone else around there. From what she says, it sounds like the horse has an impaction in the colon."

"You want me to come and help?"

"Would you? The horse is on its way and by the time you get here, I'll have it prepped and on the table. But get here as quick as you can."

Andrea didn't have to encourage me to be quick. The emergency situation was enough to get my adrenalin going, even on an early Sunday morning. A blocked intestine, after all, could kill the animal at any moment. But the chance to work with Andrea always is enough to propel me out of bed (or my office, if I'm not overly busy) and into my truck for the race to Chino. Andrea, in my opinion, is one of the best veterinary surgeons in the country and I accept every opportunity to assist when she does equine surgery. Because working with Andrea is an educational experience, I never charge for my time while I am in the operating room with her. Or, as it was about to turn out, almost never.

I ran into the prep area and came skidding to a halt. There in front of me stood Maxine Holcombe. "Dr. Younker! Are you the fine surgeon who is coming to assist Dr. Cannon?"

I had, I have to admit, to work to suppress a smile of satisfaction. The Black Panthers were home to roost. "I don't know how fine a surgeon I am, but I sure am the one who is going to work with Dr. Cannon."

Maxine's studied appearance of composure, I could see, was under severe strain. "You don't know how much I appreciate your coming out on a Sunday to work on Starlight," she babbled. "I'm sure that . . ."

"Oh, don't worry," I told her, giving my surgical mask a final adjusting tug, "I'll send you a bill."

As soon as I walked into the operating room, Andrea began to cut into the horse's abdomen. Slicing first through the skin and then through the subcutaneous tissue and the linea alba, she made her way into the abdominal cavity as I handed her whatever instruments she asked for and as I sponged away the blood to give her a clear view of the field in which she was working.

When she finally reached the interior of the abdomen, I whistled softly into my mask. Starlight's intestines were severely inflamed, acutely distended, and dangerously close to rupturing.

"Another few minutes and we would have had another real mess on our hands," Andrea said. Recently we had done an operation on another colicky horse. In that case, the intestine had already ruptured by the time we had been called and we had found a bellyful of manure when we opened the abdomen. Undaunted by what should have been a virtually hopeless situation, Andrea asked for a garden hose, cleaned it, stuck it into the horse's belly and ran water through its entrails until the water ran clear. Then she quickly repaired the ruptured intestine by doing an intestinal resection and anastomosis. She poured what must have been half a gallon of antibiotics into the animal to fight the deadly, widespread infection that would come as a result of the rupture and closed the abdomen. Against astronomical odds, the horse recovered.

Now, Andrea reached into Starlight's belly up to her elbows and palpated the many loops of the bowel, trying to find the obstruction.

"Here we go," Andrea said after a few minutes. She pulled the left dorsal colon into the incision, exposing a large mass that was completely obstructing the segment of the intestine. After packing off the area with sterile drapes, she cut into the distended intestine and exposed what seemed to be a stone about six inches in diameter. Actually, it was an enterolith. The horse had probably swallowed a small wire that had made its way into the intestine. Over a period of time, minerals in the animal's intestinal tract had been deposited over and around the wire. The deposits formed the rock—the enterolith—and in time, the rock had grown big enough to block off the intestine and trigger the crisis.

As we were sewing the horse back up, I told Andrea the Black Panther story. "I usually don't send your clients a bill when I help," I told her, "but for once I'm going to do it. I'll give the money to charity, but I want to charge that lady for the call."

Although I did plan to give the money to charity, I had made a strategic mistake in telling Andrea that. I had planned to sign Maxine Holcombe's check over to the Black Panther Milk Fund. Their hot-breakfast program for ghetto children seemed honorable enough, and besides I wanted the satisfaction of imagining Maxine's face when she saw the endorsement on the back of her check.

Unfortunately, Maxine had called Andrea to complain about my bill, and Andrea, to placate her a bit, had told her that I would be turning my fee over to charity.

"It's a good thing that money is going to a good cause," Mrs. Holcombe told me when she called to complain about the bill. (I had charged her more than Andrea had. But then, Andrea doesn't charge as much as she should.) "Now, who do you want me to make the check out to?"

I was foiled. There was no way I would be able to get her to make a check out to the Black Panthers herself. I had to abandon the plan and suggested she send the money to an experimental animal acupuncture program I was helping to organize.

Chapter Twenty

Dave Kaplan did not seem to be in a very cheery mood when I called him to ask him if he had had any experience with a new drug a detail man was trying to convince me to buy.

"You haven't seen this morning's paper?" he asked somewhat mournfully when I asked him what was bothering him. "Go on and take a look. I'll hold on."

I went to the front desk and rummaged through the morning's mail—the bills, the magazines and the junk mail—until I found the local paper. I leafed through it quickly and then I saw it: "CHIMP MAULS VETERINARIAN," the headline screamed. In the very first paragraph, I spotted Dave's name. Without reading the rest of the story, I ran back to the phone in my office.

"Wow! What happened to you?"

Dave sighed. "Oh, it's too long a story."

"Don't worry about it, I've got the time." I untangled the phone cord and backed over to the waterbed I-had just installed for the times I spend all night at the clinic to look after a critically ill animal.

"Well, about a week ago, this reporter was driving by Anaheim Stadium a few hours after an Angel game. When he gets to his car in the parking lot, he looks back at the stands and sees this chimp wandering around. He goes back in and finds the chimp staggering around, emptying beer cups. I mean this chimp is getting blotto.

"So this *meshuggener*, instead of calling the humane society or something, takes this half-grown, drunk chimp, puts him in his car and drives over to my place. Wants us to take care of him while he tries to find the owner. Luckily, he was a happy drunk.

"A couple of days later someone had him out of the cage and was just letting him roam around the kennel room. I guess he didn't like beards because when I walked in, he freaked out. He really went bananas. He starts screaming and running around, knocks me flat on my ass and runs out of the room.

"This chimp, let me tell you, is making time, turning locks, opening doors, making a mockery of my escape-proof hospital. He's just hauling tail to get out of there. I'm running after him and just as he gets to the front office, I get between him and the front door.

"He wasn't going to let me get in his way, so he grabs me in a bear hug and starts squeezing. His muscle fibers, of course, are eight times as powerful as mine, so it's like being squeezed by a five-hundred-pound man.

"I'm hitting him over the head, he's scratching and squeezing me. Just about that time, one of the kids that's helping me out after school opens the door from the kennel to see what all the screaming and yelling is about. The chimp takes one look at the open door and runs through it and right back into his cage."

"So how'd the story get in the paper?"

"The reporter came in just as the chimp was letting go of me. He got a good look at my torn and bloody clothes and went to write his story.

"How come nothing like that ever happens to you, Younker?"

Kaplan was soon proven wrong. Not too long after that conversation, I was included in a television special on pets. The day the film crew came in I had a rare list of appointments. A parrot, an opposum, and a mountain lion. Later, to publicize the special, the producers asked me to pose for still pictures with the mountain lion. On the appointed day for the photography session, the mountain lion and I gamboled in a pastoral area near my office. But after a while, when the cougar started getting a little bit too rough, I asked the photographer to stop shooting. I got up from the grass and started walking away. Casper, the cougar, waited until I was about fifteen feet away, took a giant leap and, mouth wide open, grabbed my buttocks with his teeth. "Oh goddam, doc," the photographer wailed. "I just put my lens away. Would you mind doing that again?"

For the moment, however, Kaplan was right. The only

animal I had in the clinic at the moment that could be classified as "exotic" was a red tail hawk. One of my clients, a man who knew I treat wild animals—be they hawks or pigeons or field mice—for free and then release them back to nature, had brought the hawk in to me. Someone had shot it in the wing, blasting away the elbow joint. Between the time it had been shot and the time the bird had been brought to me, the humeral and radial bones had fused together.

I could not imagine how the hawk had survived without being able to fly. But I did not want to set the bird free again in its crippled condition because it would not survive much longer. Since it could not fly to hunt, it would almost certainly die. On the other hand, I did not want to keep it in a cage for the rest of its life if I could possibly do something to help it. How to get it into shape so it could go back to its natural environment was my problem for the moment.

Hope came that night over dinner at Granny Glover's house. Granny's husband is a well-known orthopedic surgeon. Although his specialty is human surgery, he is knowledgeable enough and imaginative enough to help me out from time to time when one of my patients has a tough orthopedic problem.

"That stuff about the six million or whatever dollar man may be a lot of hogwash in a lot of ways," Dr. Glover was telling me over dessert. "But in principle at least it's not that far off. We're using more and more and better and better prosthetics every day to help people handicapped by orthopedic problems do things they thought they'd never be able to do again."

"Are the artificial hips I've been reading about really that good?"

"Good? They're terrific!"

"Well, actually, I'm not surprised, seeing it was developed by a doctor of veterinary medicine," I kidded.

Inspiration suddenly struck. Orthopedic surgeons were also using artificial knuckle joints to replace real knuckles crippled by arthritis. The human knckle joint, I calculated, is about the same size as the elbow joint in the wing of a large bird.

"Could we use an artificial knuckle joint to restore the elbow joint in a bird wing?" I asked Dr. Glover.

He looked at me over his ice cream. "I don't know. I've never thought about it. But I can get one and we can try it." Within a few days, Doc had the artificial joint. I had borrowed a high speed surgical drill from my friend, Al, the local representative of an orthopedic equipment company, to take apart the illicit joint that had formed between the two wing bones. Between the two of us, we managed to fit the artificial knuckle in perfectly.

I was in back checking the hawk's progress two days later when Richie, the boy who was doing volunteer work that afternoon, came running in. "Mrs. Kepler's mother-in-law's dog got hit by a car," he yelled.

I hurriedly washed my hands and ran to the examining room. Mrs. Kepler and her mother-in-law, Mrs. Meza, were huddled over a small form on the examining table. The dog was badly hurt. The distal tibia had been fractured, half an inch above the hock. The car must have pulled the little creature along, dragging its broken leg over the pavement because the exposed part of the tibia looked as if it had been ground with a file.

"There isn't anything I can do for the leg," I told Mrs. Meza, who was fingering the large cross she wore around her neck. "But I can amputate it and the dog will do just fine."

"Oh, *Dios,* no! A dog with three legs? *Que cosa!*"

I appealed to Mrs. Kepler. "Three-legged dogs do fine. I can even give you the name of one of my clients who has a three-legged dog. You can go visit her and see that he is perfectly normal in every other respect."

"No," Mrs. Meza broke in. "That is a terrible thing. If you cannot fix the leg, then, then . . ."

"Put Buffy to sleep," Mrs. Kepler finished for her.

The last thing I wanted to do was put an otherwise healthy animal to sleep and, against my better judgment, I agreed to do the surgery to repair the leg. "Okay, I can try to fix it but you are going to have a big problem with an infection. There has been a lot of trauma to the leg and it's badly contaminated. The break is right at the joint and it's going to be practically impossible to heal. And its going to be expensive besides."

"We don't care how much it costs," Mrs. Kepler said. "Go ahead and fix it."

I wanted to try one last time to convince them that amputation was a better alternative. "It would be cheaper to amputate it. I guarantee you that in two or three days the dog will be up and running around."

Although I could not budge them, I was not surprised at their stubborn refusal to permit the operation. People see men and women who have lost a limb struggle to get around on crutches or to make painful adjustments to an artificial limb. They conclude that the loss of a leg will be as crucial to an animal as the loss of a leg to a human. They cannot accept the fact that a dog or a cat get along beautifully with one leg missing.

Some animals, in fact, can manage marvelously with just *two* legs. Returning late one night after an emergency call to treat a horse, Andrea Cannon found a dog lying in a field, just off the side of the side of the road (she had spotted it only because in coming around a curve, her headlights had been reflected in the animal's eyes). The dog had apparently been hit by a car because both of its front legs were badly mangled. Andrea, like many veterinarians, always has a humane killer with her, just in case she finds an animal so badly hurt by a car that it must be put to sleep. But in this case, she decided she could do something for the dog. She took it home and removed both legs at the shoulder. It took the dog a little while to get used to its new condition but now he gets around beautifully by hopping around like a kangaroo.

When Mrs. Kepler and Mrs. Meza had left, I went to look for Richie. I needed him to help me in the operating room. For the last year or so, Richie had been one of my special "projects." Some kids who come in to volunteer think they can take over for me two days after they walk in the front door for the first time. Not Richie. The boy had so little confidence in himself, he was so afraid that he would hurt an animal, that he refused to do anything around the clinic except the most menial work. I had given him his way for a few months, but recently had begun to press him to take on more responsible duties. I started by taking him on horse calls where he could stand off to one side and could get me what I needed from the truck. In time—even though I had to hold his hand the first few times—I managed to get him to do things like adjust the flow of an intravenous setup I had hooked up to a cat or to run a Q-tip around a dog's ear.

Now, I decided, it was time for him to start monitoring the anesthesia machine during surgery. "Come on Richie," I told him when I found him in the kennel where he usually retreated when he suspected something was at hand. "We've got to operate on Mrs. Meza's dog."

Richie turned his back to me and opened one of the empty cages. "Gee, Dr. Younker, I still have all these cages to clean and then I've got to scrub the floor."

I tapped him on the shoulder and fixed him with as severe a stare as I could muster when he turned to face me.

"Right now, Richie."

"But . . ."

"Now! Richie."

Richie stood by the operating table, staring at the anesthesia machine as if it were a time bomb ticking away its last ten seconds. "Richie, just keep an eye on the rebreathing bag and make sure there is enough oxygen in it. If it gets empty, turn this knob at the top of the flow meter so that more oxygen enters the system. If we need to turn down the concentration of anesthetic, I'll tell you what level to turn it to.

"And don't get in a panic! I'm watching the equipment, too. I'm watching the dog and I'm watching the heart monitoring machine. I'm not going to let anything go wrong."

Richie nodded without taking his eyes off the anesthesia machine and the dog (I had also told him to keep an eye on the dog's reflexes). In fact I don't think he looked away or blinked more than necessary until we finished the operation ninety minutes later. When we walked out of the operating room, he looked as tired as if he had just completed twenty-four hours of duty in a county hospital emergency room. Even so, there was something about him afterwards that told me that he had gotten over a big hump. The next time it would be easier for him. And I would not be surprised if I had another budding pre-vet student on my hands. (It had happened before. And one of my early volunteers had, after only a year of work after high school, just become the manager of a large animal hospital in Newport Beach.)

Between Mrs. Meza's dog, Buffy, and the hawk, I had my hands full. The day after I operated on Buffy, the hawk started to claw at its bandages and before he was through, he had torn everything apart. Doc found another artificial knuckle and once again we operated. But like before, the hawk tore apart our handiwork, this time so severely that I was forced to amputate the wing. I retired the hawk to the aviary of the house I had recently bought, where he still lives, completely content.

As I expected, Buffy developed a severe infection that would not allow the maimed leg to heal. We gave the dog expensive antibiotics, we drained the wound, changed bandages and splints regularly. Nothing helped. For three months the infection raged. Despite it all, despite all my arguments and enticements, Mrs. Meza would not give me permission to amputate. Only when the dog's kidneys, exhausted from fighting the infection, were on the verge of failure and the dog was dying, did she finally agree to let me take the leg. Since then, Buffy has lived a very normal life.

Chapter Twenty-One

'I'm going to have to put a muzzle on her," I told Mrs. Schiff the minute I laid eyes on her one-hundred-pound German Shepherd. Just one glance at the dog told me she didn't like me and that she was a fear-biter to boot—a dog that will bite anything or anyone it is afraid of. I was not about to risk losing a hand.

"Oh no, absolutely not," Mrs. Schiff protested. "I can restrain her. Don't worry."

I was not persuaded. The dog was staring hard at me. At the same time she was struggling to get away from Mrs. Schiff, not so much to get to me as to run away. "I can tell this dog is very afraid of me," I insisted. "I want to listen to her heart and to feel her abdomen and I don't want to get bitten doing it. If you can't hold her, I'll have to muzzle her to give her a tranquilizer."

"Don't do that! The last time she was tranquilized, she didn't wake up for weeks. Go ahead and examine her. She'll be all right."

Mrs. Schiff embraced the dog and I crouched to begin the examination. The moment I started, the dog turned, and sunk her teeth into Mrs. Schiff's arm, clear down to the bone. Mrs. Schiff's screams brought everyone running into the examining room. In the ensuing confusion, someone managed to muzzle the dog and get her out of the room. I helped Mrs. Schiff to my truck and rushed to her doctor.

Because I had little time before I was due over at the university to make one of my periodic checks on the experimental animals used by the psychology department, I called Susan from the doctor's office to make sure everything was quiet. It wasn't. "Mrs. Chase called," Susan told me. "She's got a horse that's sick and wants to know if you can come by. And oh, Sadie called. Wants you to call her."

"I'm having a terrible day," Sadie told me when I reached her at her office. "Can you pick something up for dinner?"

"Sure. I've got to run up to Hollywood later for something. You want me to stop at Hsu's?"

(Hsu's Szechuan and Hunan Taste Restaurant in Hollywood is our favorite eating place.)

"That'd be great. I'll call them now and order. Maybe they have some Camphor and Tea-smoked Duck ready today. How about some Pinecone Fish, Hot and Sour Soup and some Eggplant in Black Bean Sauce?"

"You got it all figured out, eh?"

"I've been thinking about it all morning. . . ."

Mrs. Chase had not given Susan any of the particulars but as I drove over, I bet myself a new part for the 1936 Buick I was trying to rebuild that I knew what the problem was.

I had gone out to Meredith's place a few months earlier to treat a cut horse. "When was the last time he had a tetanus shot?" I asked Meredith when I had finished suturing the laceration.

Meredith was very offhand. "I don't give my horses shots. It's not worth it. I've had horses for more than four years and I've never had a horse get sick on me once."

"That's crazy, Meredith," I had told her. "Horses get tetanus much easier than people because they get cut more often. And they are very likely to pick up influenza or distemper from other horses when your kids go riding—which they do all the time. Why take a chance?"

"I'll worry about all that when the time comes. I'll be damned if I'm going to spend twenty dollars a horse to get them vaccinated."

The mare Meredith had just called about had a heavy discharge from her nostrils. Her eyes were running. Her mandibular lymph nodes were swollen and abscessed and the horse could hardly breathe. She looked severely depressed.

"She's got a full-blown case of distemper, Meredith," I

told her very evenly. "You can bet on it that the other young horses are going to come down with it as well."

Meredith didn't say very much as I treated the mare.

I turned at the sound of feet running up the corridor behind me. It was one of the graduate psychology students. "I was hoping you'd be here today, Dr. Younker. We're going to start some sleep studies with eight-week-old kittens and we want to implant some electrodes in their brains."

"What are you going to use for an anesthetic? You don't have any anesthesia equipment around here."

"Yes, well, that's what I wanted to talk to you about. How about if we just give them some phenobarbital? Do you think that would do it?"

"It's awfully easy to kill a cat with that, especially eight-week-old kittens. You should really use gas if you want to do it humanely."

He ran his fingers through his beard. "Let me think about it, then. I'll catch you later."

I let myself into the University laboratory. The rabbits were healthy and the pigeons, which I had been treating for a parasite infection, also seemed to be on their way to recovery. But the colony of wild blue-eyed cats was having ear-mite trouble. I had the time that afternoon so I decided to start treating them before things got out of hand.

When I first had been offered the job of helping out with the animals in the laboratory, I had felt some conflicts about the matter. I was not opposed to original research with animals, research designed to elicit new information about physiological processes, about a disease, or about an experimental drug that could be beneficial to human beings. But I didn't like the fact (and I still do not) that many of the experiments conducted are not really necessary. There are experiments that are done again and again for no other purpose than to teach students about psychological phenomena already well described in a hundred different textbooks. I had a hard time getting myself to accept the fact that experiments that cause an animal pain or that lead to the animal's sacrifice had to be repeated by every class that swept through the psychology department. On the other hand, I knew that those experiments were going to be carried out whether I was there or not. The least I could do, I finally told myself, was to make sure that the animals were as comfortable as possible as long as they were subjected to the experiments.

On my very first visit to the laboratory, I found good reason to be thankful that I had been able to put some of my doubts aside and had agreed to look after the experimental animals. Almost every one of them had some minor health problem.

Because the beagles seemed to be the worst off—they were plagued with ear mites and were going crazy scratching themselves, trying to get some relief—I had decided I had better start with them. A chart on one of the laboratory walls briefly noted what work was being done with what animals and which professor was supervising what experiment. I went to look for the man who was running the experiment with the beagles.

"I'm sorry," Professor Berman said when I located him and told him of the trouble his animals were having. "But I cannot permit you to do anything about it."

"But it's not a dangerous procedure," I argued. "It's not going to kill them or anything."

"That's not the point. You have to knock them out to get at the mites, you say. Very well, that in itself could be a variable and could affect the beagles and in turn the whole experiment. We could lose a whole semester's work."

"It's not humane to keep them and not treat them. How would you like to have little bugs running around inside your ears, chewing at your ear canal and not being able to do anything about it?"

"I'm sorry, but the answer is still no. In any case, it doesn't much matter. We are going to sacrifice them all in a few weeks anyway when the work is completed."

Late in the afternoon two or three days later, Karen (one of my assistants) and I skulked into the laboratory. We knocked out every beagle in the place, cleaned every ear and treated them with Canolene, a medicine that just happens to have a very bright green coloring.

The next day the office telephone rang. "You'd best come over right away," a very disturbed Professor Berman told me. "All the beagles have something green oozing out of their ears. Do you think it has anything to do with the ear mites?"

"Wow," I said, trying to sound genuinely alarmed. "I bet it's a pseudonomas infection, secondary to the mites."

"Oh my God, that's all I need. What will happen?"

"Well," I said clearing my throat, "they might get a secondary ear infection, which would certainly be a variable on an experiment."

"Can you come right away?"

I gathered up Karen and went back to the psychology department. The beagles, of course, were already rid of their ear mites, but with Professor Berman looking anxiously on, we put on a great show of giving the beagles "emergency" treatment.

By the time I had finished working on the blue-eyed cats, the student who had asked me about the sleep studies with the kittens came back.

"What did you decide?" I asked as I packed away my equipment.

"We decided to forget the experiment. Thanks for the advice."

I was indeed happy that I had taken the job.

When I got back to the office late in the afternoon, Mrs. Van Den Kamp was waiting for me, her one-year-old black cat, Cassie, lying listlessly in her lap. Cassie, she told me, had not been eating and, for the last day or two, had refused to leave her box. Mrs. Van Den Kamp, whose broad Dutch face was usually graced by a smile, looked solemn and drawn.

I had treated Cassie for minor problems before and knew her to be a spunky little cat. But as I carried her into the examining room, she hardly stirred. I was very much afraid that I had a dying cat on my hands.

As I lifted Cassie's tail to take her temperature, I heard a soft crackling sound, almost as if there were Rice Krispies under her skin. The thermometer said she had a temperature of 106° (it might have been higher, but the thermometer's top reading was 106). I looked closer at Cassie's back end, softly running my fingers over her back, her hind legs, and tail. Wherever I touched, I set off the Rice Krispies sound.

"There is gas in those tissues," I told Mrs. Van Den

Kamp. "Right now, I'd say that Cassie has a bad infection. Was she out earlier in the week?"

"Before she got sick? Yes. She wanders out at night."

I guessed Cassie had been bitten by a tomcat she had been trying to escape. Usually, cat-bite infections stay localized. But, in this case, the infection had spread. I prescribed antibiotics for Cassie, but warned Mrs. Van Den Kamp that there was a good chance that even with medication things could still take a turn for the worse. In fact, I was worried that the skin on the cat's legs would just slough off.

"Do you want to keep her here?"

"Well, not if you can bring her in every day for the next few days. I know that could be hard . . ."

"Oh no. It wouldn't be a bother at all. I'd rather keep her at home."

"Me too. I like to keep pets in their own surroundings. I know how I felt when I was in the hospital. I would have felt a lot better if I had been in my own house, with my friends and my people around. I don't think that throwing an animal into a small cage does anything to make it feel better and I like to avoid that whenever possible."

Mrs. Van Den Kamp took Cassie home. For three days, the cat's condition did not change. But on the fourth, things took a turn for the worse. As I had feared, the skin sloughed off. Nerves and muscles were exposed. The infection had been devastating because there was a good deal of dead tissue and pus in the area.

Cassie was in a lot of trouble because the skin is a vital organ. If I could not get the skin to regenerate, her body would lose fluids and she would die. But then, inspiration struck. Only a month earlier, I had gone into the drugstore next door to ask the pharmacist a question about the thyroid medication I had been taking since my operation. He could not answer me. But when the detail man, Al Kinard, representing the manufacturer of the drug came around, the pharmacist sent him over to my office to answer my query.

Many doctors don't like detail men because they consider them a nuisance. But I like these salesmen because I find them a great source of information about drugs. Besides, I have a soft spot for them because I was a salesman—of sorts—myself at one time.

During one summer break from college, I could not find any kind of a job dealing with animals. No veterinarians wanted to hire me just for the summer. I couldn't even find something on a farm for just my room and board.

In desperation, I turned to the want ad pages. But even here I met with frustration. I answered dozens of "Salesman Wanted" job ads, but could not pin down an offer because I failed all the tests that were invariably given to applicants for sales jobs. Disgusted, I finally called the man who had given me the last aptitude test that showed that I should not be hired.

"I don't understand," I pleaded with him. "I got everything right on the test. Why do you say I flunked it? Why didn't I get the job?"

The man apparently took pity on me. "You're right, you did get everything right. But to us that is 'flunking' as you put it. In the first place, the test showed that you have too much education to be selling our product, you wouldn't be satisfied with that kind of a job. In the second place, the test showed that you were, well, let's say, too idealistic, too nice . . ."

I took the hint and when I applied for a job with Kaminer's Alclean Corporation, I steeled myself to suppress both my knowledge and my finer instincts. I forgot who Napoleon was. When they asked me something like (and I'm being facetious) would I rather eat ice cream, have sex with a beautiful woman, or knock down an old lady on the street just for laughs, I answered that I would rather knock down the old lady. I got the job.

I was a smash in training school because I had taken drama in school and could do a little bit of acting. I got the tones of voice, the pitches down just right. They thought I was going to be the greatest Alclean Vacuum Cleaner salesman of all time.

Unfortunately, I was not as ambitious as the company would have liked me to be. We used to get a sixty-five-dollar commission for every vacuum cleaner we sold. That was a lot of money to me, so I would sell just one machine a week, usually to people who, I thought, really wanted it and needed it.

One day, though, the president of the firm, a Mr. Kaminer, called me into his office.

"We're very disappointed in you, Younker," he said,

looking at me as if I had just betrayed a life-long friend-ship. "You were one of our more promising students. What happened?"

"I guess I just don't want to sell vacuum cleaners to peo-ple who can't really afford them."

"What do you care if they can afford them or not? We sell them on time and then resell the paper anyway. You're just making excuses. I'll bet you double commis-sion that you couldn't go out and sell two vacuum cleaners tomorrow."

The next day I went out and the first call I made was on a seventy-eight-year-old man who was living on Social Se-curity payments of eighty-two dollars and who had just bought a brand new Hoover. I sold him an Alclean. On the next call I missed. On my third call I found a laid-off auto assembly worker who hadn't worked in three months. There wasn't a carpet in his place. I sold him an Alclean because it had a floor waxer attachment.

At the sales meeting the next day I was the big hero. They asked me to come on stage to give a blow-by-blow account of how I had accomplished my big feat. Mr. Kami-ner came on stage and the company photographer took my picture as Kaminer handed me a check with my two-hundred-and-sixty-dollar commission. I said thank you, handed Kaminer my demonstrator, formally resigned, and walked out.

Being a detail man, Kinard could not resist the urge to try to sell me a new drug or two. "Ever hear of Travase?" he asked after we had finished talking about my thyroid medication. "Great stuff. It's a new enzyme in ointment form. It's terrific for abscesses and burns."

"How much is it?"

"Eight dollars for a half-ounce tube."

"Eight bucks for half an ounce? That's a bit high to pre-scribe for animals. Thanks, but if I ever need it, I'll let you know."

The man was not to be dissuaded. "I just got a tube back from next door because it had expired. But the ointment is still good. Just put it in your refrigerator and if something comes along, try it."

The Travase, I thought, could be Cassie's last hope.

The ointment required a lot of work—it had to be put on under a wet dressing that had to be changed every six hours—but in almost no time it rid Cassie's back end of all the necrotic tissue. When a base of new tissue had formed after five weeks, I skinned Cassie's tail, used the skin for grafts to the legs and amputated what was left of her tail. Some of the grafted skin, much to my amazement, even sprouted a good coat of fur. In fact, Cassie's back end healed so nicely that she was able to participate in a cat show—and to take first place in the "pet" class.

Chapter Twenty-Two

At six feet four and, as far as I could estimate, two-hundred and fifty pounds,——looked every bit as formidable in the confines of my small examining room as he did within the boundaries of my nineteen-inch television set on Sunday afternoons.

"It's nothing serious, is it, doc?" the professional football player asked. His cat was on the examining table, unconcernedly licking one paw.

"No, it's just a small abscess. I can lance it right now. If you want to, you can go into the reception room and wait if watching is going to bother you."

"Aw, hell no. Go ahead."

I took out one of my scalpels and bent over the cat. With a flick of my hand, I cut into the abscess. I thought I heard a strange noise, but didn't turn around. Using my index finger and my thumb, I gently opened the wound I had created and watched a spurt of green pus come rolling out. This time I heard the sound again and recognized it as a strangled moan. I turned around just in time to see the player falling backwards into a corner and sliding down to the floor into a sitting position. He was out cold.

All I could remember about human first aid was that, in case of a fainting spell, one should force the head between the victim's knees to get blood back into the brain. I rushed over and tried to bend the formidable neck forward. No luck. The room was just too small and he was too big for me to maneuver him into the recommended position. Okay, I thought, let's drag him into the waiting room because there is more space there. I couldn't budge him. The hell with it, I finally told myself, let him stay there until he wakes up by himself. I went back to the cat and finished cleaning out the abscess. When I had applied the last bit of antibiotic ointment, the football player started to stir. I waited for him to pick himself up.

"You all right?" I asked, trying to keep as diplomatic a face as possible.

He grunted.

"Okay, bring the cat back in a couple of days. I'll want to make sure that it's healing nicely."

As he opened the front door, Bill O'Connor stomped by him. O'Connor, the football coach at one of the local high schools, is a jovial man with whom I had always gotten along very well. In all the time I had been treating his Griffon, I had never seen him angry. But now, as I walked into the reception room to give Susan the cat's chart, I could see that he was boiling.

O'Connor stormed to the center of the reception room ignoring everything else and thrust a piece of paper toward me.

"Doc, before I tie in to you, I want to ask you one question. Did you write this?"

He slammed the paper down on the counter. Looking at it more closely, I could see that it was one of my bills. "After all the good that we have done for your animal," a note scribbled across the top of the bill said, "the least you can do is pay your bill on time. L. Younker."

I held up the cat's chart—on which I had just made some notes—to him. "That's my handwriting," I said, pointing to the chart. "I don't know anything about that note."

"That's good," he said, calming down quickly and reaching into his pocket. "Anyhow, here's my canceled check for last month's bill."

I watched O'Connor leave and then leaned over the counter. "Susan, did you write that note?"

"Doctor Younker, last month your accounts receivable went to ten thousand dollars. I was just trying to get some of it in. I'm sorry I made a mistake about Coach O'Connor, but you're going to go bust."

"I don't care if my accounts receivable are one hundred thousand dollars, Susan. A note like that is not very appropriate or very professional."

I took the next chart off the counter and asked Deanne

226

Lawson to bring her little Lhasa Apso into the examining room.

Mrs. Lawson did not waste any time. "We want to put Chrysty to sleep."

I couldn't believe it. "Why? She's a perfectly healthy dog and has a lot of years left. She's so sweet!"

"Sweet dog? Yesterday she went right through the screen door and attacked the newspaper boy. We just have not been able to control her at home. She won't let anyone she doesn't know come near the front door."

I did not see any reason to put the dog to sleep. If she was overly aggressive around the house, it was probably as much the family's fault as Chrysty's. Dogs are essentially pack animals and their role in the pack—whether they are to be subservient or whether they are to lead the pack—is very important to them. For the domesticated dog, the family is its pack. Giving in to natural instincts, the tame dog will try to establish itself in the human "pack" just as it would in its natural pack out in the woods. If the family does not know how to handle a dog properly, especially an aggressive puppy, the dog comes to believe that it is the leader in the house. The family is his to protect—just as the pack and its territory would be his to protect out in the wild.

I explained all this to Mrs. Lawson. "You don't have to have this dog put to sleep. First of all, try to get to the door before she does. I know she can hear better than you can. Nevertheless, try to show her that you are perfectly capable of protecting yourselves. And just try to be a little tougher with her all around. You'll straighten her out."

"I'm not sure I believe all that," Mrs. Dawson said, picking Chrysty off the examining table. "But I guess we'll try."

I walked Mrs. Lawson and Chrysty out, making notes on Chrysty's chart as I approached the front desk. When I looked up from my paper work, my insides trembled. Mrs. St. George was standing squarely in front of me, fury blazing in her eyes. Automatically, I looked down at her hand. As I had feared, she was holding a crumpled bill. "Dr. Younker," the edge of her words could have put my finest scalpels to shame. "Did you write this note?"

"No," I sighed, "I didn't, Mrs. St. George. What does that one say?"

She held up the bill so I could read it. "You put the

make on us and then you tripped us off," I read aloud. "Pay now and change our minds."

I had visions of the practice I had so carefully built crumbling about my head. I mumbled what apologies I could, escorted Mrs. St. George to the door, and went back to the desk. Susan was busily shuffling papers, trying to look very occupied. I was so mad I could hardly talk. "Susan," was all I managed, "the expression is 'rip off,' not 'trip off.' "

There was one client waiting—one of the grubbiest-looking hippies I had ever seen—holding a beautiful Samoyed. The sight of the goregous dog was enough to calm me down.

"Boy that is a great dog," I said, petting its back. "Just a couple of weeks ago or so I had a cop in here with a Samoyed just like this one. Only that dog thinks he's a cop too. He can get really aggressive towards me."

When I had finished the little speech, I looked at the dog's chart to see what this new client's name was. I looked back up at the hippie who was now smiling broadly. "Is it really you, Herman?" I asked, suddenly feeling very foolish. "Christ, I never would have recognized you. Did they make you a narc or something?"

"Yep," Herman said as I closed the door to the examining room. "And I'm doing well too. Man, I look so bad, last week when I went into one of the shops I always go to, they wouldn't take my check, even with an I.D."

"Hey, Herman," I said. "I want to ask your professional advice about something." Something had been bothering me for a while and I wanted to clear it up.

"A while ago, these kids, two of them, come in, really hippie-looking types too. They said they wanted to buy some Promazine. That's a drug used as a tranquilizer. They said that their agriculture teacher at one of the colleges around here had asked them to come by and get it so he could use it on a cow.

"I told them that I couldn't sell it to them without a prescription. But the next day, there they were, asking me for it again. I told them that I didn't believe they wanted to use it for any cow, but that they were going to use it themselves. So they come right out and say, yeah, we want to make Angel's Dust with it. They told me they'd pay me five hundred dollars a month to supply them with the drug. Can you believe that?"

Herman grimaced a "why-not-I-can-believe-anything" look and waited for me to go on.

"Anyway, I said to myself either these two guys are totally freaked out coming in out of the blue like that or they are narcs trying to set me up. Just to be on the safe side, and to kind of check things out, I thought I'd better report what was happening.

"I waited until about ten o'clock one night and walked into the police station looking my scruffiest worst. I had an old pair of blue jeans on and an old work shirt and my hair was all frizzed out.

"I tell the cop at the desk my story, but giving him the minimal amount of information. I also told them that I really had not paid too much attention to what the two guys looked like because I was really busy the days they came in, but that my secretary had talked to them a while and that she might be able to give them a better description. See, I wanted to see if the cops would follow up.

"So what do you think happened?"

"I don't know," Herman said. "I'd guess the narcs would have had a couple of detectives out to talk to you at eight the next morning."

"Is that the way you guys would have done it in Garden Grove?"

"Yea, sure. Especially if they offered you money to keep a steady supply coming."

"Nothing happened, Herman. Nothing. None of the narcs ever showed up. And those two characters never came back to see me either. And, what really made me suspicious later that those two were not real freaks was that when they came in they tried to sound like they really knew how to make Angel's Dust. But I found out that instead of asking for Promazine, they should have asked for phencyclidine which, some real freaks told me, is known as PCP on the street. Pretty strange, huh?"

"I'd say."

"You think it was a setup too, or am I being paranoid?"

"I can't say for sure that they were trying to set you up but it sounds kind of suspicious. Maybe the cops were just kind of testing you. There's not too many hippie doctors in Orange County, you know."

229

"I guess not. Anyway. How's old Snowball here doing? He's due for his shots today, isn't he?"

I gave Snowball his vaccines and sent him on his way. Joe Naylor, one of my colleagues, was walking in the door to take me to lunch.

And walking in right behind him was Julie Donovan. Julie is every inch the lady. She is respected in the community. Her husband is a prominent executive.

Mrs. Donovan did not step all the way into the office. She paused in the doorway, reached into her purse and pulled out a piece of paper that by now had an all too familiar look to it.

"Dr. Younker," she said, holding the paper toward my face. "What the fuck is the meaning of this shit?"

I hardly heard anything Joe had to say at lunch. I was too busy thinking of how I would fire Susan.

Chapter Twenty-Three

Andrea and I had spent the morning working on her horse calls and we had stopped for a bite to eat before going our separate ways for the afternoon. She took a sip of coffee and gave me a mischievous look. "Did I ever tell you my cat story?" she asked.

"The one about the lady who had left thirty-seven cats?" Andrea at one point had ministered to thirty-seven cats, all belonging to one old lady. The lady apparently thought of Andrea as more than a veterinarian because, despite Andrea's urgings to the contrary, the old lady insisted on consulting with Andrea about her own medical problems. One day, Andrea got a call from the woman's husband because he was very concerned that his wife seemed to be having trouble breathing. Andrea told him to call an ambulance but, out of concern for the woman, rushed over to her house to see if she could help somehow. When she arrived, however, the woman was dead. Four days later, the husband died.

Andrea, now worried about the thirty-seven cats, called the Humane Society and asked them to pick up the animals. The Humane Society said they would be very happy to receive the thirty-seven cats but they were not about to go out and catch them. Andrea, they suggested, should do that herself.

Although the old woman had collected the cats, had fed them and had made certain that they received some medical attention when they were ill, she had given them the run of her property. As a result, the cats were essentially wild animals that had less use for human beings than normal, domesticated cats. To catch the cats, Andrea had to throw phenobarbital-spiked meatballs into the yard, wait

231

until a cat ate it, and then stalk the animal until it fell over into a deep slumber. It took her five days to catch all the cats—and far longer to find suitable homes for them all.

"No, not that one," Andrea said. "The cat-in-the-bag story."

That one did not sound familiar.

"A friend of mine and I were coming here for lunch a while back," Andrea went on, "and on one of the side streets around here we see this cat, lying in the middle of the road, thrashing around in agony.

"I figured it had been hit by a car and got out to see if there was anything I could do. Well, the cat was beyond help, so I got out my euthanasia solution and a syringe and put it to sleep. But I did not want to leave a dead cat lying around so I figured I would dispose of it at my office after lunch. I just put it in a department store shopping bag I had in the back seat and my friend and I stopped for something to eat.

"About halfway through, my friend looks up and says, hey, isn't that your shopping bag? I look over and see this very well-dressed, very nice lady carrying a shopping bag just like the one I have in my car. It couldn't be, I said, she probably just went shopping in the same store, that's all.

"She sits down, orders lunch and then very casually opens the shopping bag and looks in. She jumps up, knocks her chair down and runs like hell right out of the restaurant. I guess she really did steal the bag out of my car."

Andrea seemed to be in high spirits so I decided to go ahead and mention the favor I'd been wanting to ask of her. For several weeks now, I had been involved in a state veterinary association study of animal acupuncture. Just recently, I had made contact with some University of California at Los Angeles researchers who did acupuncture with humans but who were also interested in trying the old Chinese techniques on horses. Because Andrea was the veterinarian at the Cunningham Ranch, a large and well-known thoroughbred farm, I wanted to ask her if she had any horses the U.C.L.A. acupuncturists could treat.

"Sure," Andrea answered after I had explained everything to her.

I was taken aback that she had agreed so readily to offer up precious thoroughbreds for what essentially had to be considered experimentation. "Shouldn't you check with Mr. Cunningham first?" I asked.

"Listen, Lucas," she said after I had insisted several times that she check with Cunningham. "The last quack that was out there was playing music up the barren mares with a rectal probe to try to get them in foal. After that guy, a few needles is going to sound pretty tame to him. Really, he won't mind a bit."

"You mean he wired the probe to a radio and then tuned it to a classical music station?"

"That's it, exactly!"

"I don't believe it. Did it work?"

"What do you think? The last we saw of him, he was out on a neighboring farm stringing up loudspeakers in a vegetable field to help them produce bigger tomatoes.

"Just let me know when you want to come out and I'll have something ready for you," Andrea said, reaching for the bill. "Is there anything in particular you want to treat?"

"Anything. Give us something you haven't been able to cure with conventional medicine."

When the U.C.L.A. reasearchers—Sang Choe and Joe Oliviani—and I showed up at the Cunningham Ranch a few days later, a good-sized (and skeptical) crowd was waiting for us. Andrea greeted us and, after we had introduced ourselves all around, disappeared into one of the barns.

When she emerged a few minutes later, I shuddered. She was leading a horse that had one of the worst cases of emphysema I had ever seen. The horse was so debilitated, she had to stop every few steps to rest. In fact, her breathing was so labored you could hear her breathing one hundred yards away. Her chest heaved as she worked to expel breath.

"Andrea, this is not the case you want us to treat, is it?"

"Lucas, you wanted one we have been having trouble with and we have been having trouble with her for five years."

"Don't you have a case that is a little more acute, something that hasn't been going on for years and years? Anyway, why haven't you put this horse down already?"

Andrea looked lovingly at the mare. "Well, she was a good stakes mare in her day and Mr. C. wants to keep trying to get her in foal."

I turned to Choe. "This horse," I told him, speaking slowly, "has emphysema." Choe, a stocky Korean, is an Oriental M.D. who specialized in herbal medicine and acupuncture. He had only recently come to the United States and his English was somewhat stilted.

"Ah, yes. Emphysema. Very difficult to treat in people."

Choe stepped to the horse, whose exhalations after the short walk from the stable made it sound like a Mack truck climbing a steep hill. After palpating the horse for several minutes, he treated three acupuncture points on each side of the horse for one minute each. When he was done, he walked back to where Andrea, Joe, a few observers, and I were standing and began to clean his needles.

I panicked, afraid that the short treatment he had given the mare meant that she was beyond hope. "Look, she isn't any better," I said to him, trying to keep my voice down. "Couldn't you treat a few more points or do something else?"

Choe now began to put away his equipment. "No. That is enough treatment for today."

Several of the bystanders—including two or three of my colleagues who had come to watch the experiment—chuckled. Suddenly, Andrea, who had been looking past my shoulder, yelled. "My God! Look at that horse!"

I was almost afraid to turn around. I was sure the mare's knees were buckling now and she was slowly sinking toward the ground in a final moment of agony. I could just imagine myself being sued for the hundreds of thousands of dollars her unborn (and, of course, yet to be conceived) foal would have brought.

"Ah, what's the matter?" Choe asked, spinning around to take a look.

"The horse is breathing normally!" Andrea said, her voice full of wonder.

I turned and looked at the horse. She was standing there placidly, breathing as if she had never been sick a day in her life, as if she had just come back from a pleasant morning in a pasture full of choice grass.

Choe was not impressed by what had transpired. "Of course," he said, closing up his case and putting on his jacket. "I treat horse. What do you expect. But do not be too excited. Horse will relapse shortly. Horse must be treated again tomorrow."

234

I would have time the next day and planned to come back to watch Choe give the second treatment. "What time will you be here tomorrow?" I asked.

"Oh, can't come here tomorrow. Tomorrow I have other things to do." (I was puzzled, but presumed he had other acupuncture appointments. Later, I found out that the following day was the day on which he served as a box-boy in a supermarket. He had the part-time job because he still did not earn enough as an acupuncturist to support his family. Now, not only is he able to support them as an acupuncturist, but, in addition, the governor recently appointed him to an acupuncture advisory committee to the Board of Examiners in Medicine.)

"Tomorrow," he went on, "you treat horse."

I was horrified at the thought that I should undertake treatment of the horse. "I don't know anything about acupuncture," I protested. "I don't know where the needles go or even how to put them in."

Choe reached down for a box he had not packed away and gave me several long acupuncture needles. "Here," he said, "you hold between thumb and forefinger. Pull fingers up. Push fingers down. Up, down, up down, like doing what you call push-up. Tonight you practice this one thousand times, putting needle into toilet paper roll. I draw x's on horse. Tomorrow, you put needles in middle of each x."

For hours that night—until I could push them into the not-so-baby-soft roll of paper without bending them—I practiced with the needles. The next day, dragging Sadie along for moral support (it was her day off and she protested bitterly having to get out of bed early), I went back to the Cunningham Ranch to treat the mare. Once again, the treatment alleviated the horse's raucous efforts to expel the air from her lungs. This time, however, the effect lasted for almost two weeks. She relapsed, was treated again by Dr. Choe, and was sent off to a breeding farm.

Word of our success at the Cunningham Ranch spread quickly. As more and more veterinarians (and laymen) showed an interest in acupuncture for animals, my personal investigation of acupuncture turned into a more formalized research program. Having seen one case in which acupuncture did work, I wanted to find out precisely how many other horse diseases were amenable to acupuncture, how many treatments were required for each disease, and how long the treatment's effects would last. One full day a week, I decided, would be devoted to acupuncture. I would donate my time. Contributions made by people who brought their horses into the project would be used to pay Choe and Oliviani for their time and to educate and train other veterinarians in acupuncture as Choe, Oliviani and I broadened our own knowledge about the field. Soon, we were treating forty horses—for everything ranging from lameness to facial nerve paralysis—on the day we had set aside for acupuncture.

"Do you think this sort of thing might work on small animals?" Dr. Garvey asked me during one of these acupuncture sessions. Dr. Garvey, a veterinarian, had been bringing in his own horse because he had not been able to cure it of a severe case of hepatitis using conventional medicine. Now, after three or four acupuncture treatments, the horse was recovering.

"I don't see any reason why not," Joe said.

"Do you think then, that you could treat one of my patients, an eighteen-month-old Great Dane?"

"Well, that's a different matter. Theoretically, acupuncture should work. But we don't have any charts here for acupuncture points in small animals. We only just recently got the chart for horses. What's wrong with the dog?"

"He can hardly walk because he has a bad case of hip dysplasia."

"Bring him in, I guess. Maybe we can extrapolate from the horse charts to find the right acupuncture points."

The following week, Dr. Garvey brought in the dog. The poor animal was so crippled by his congenital deformity that he could hardly stand up. But at the end of that first session, there was already discernible improvement. And, after two more treatments, the Great Dane was running around the treatment room like a puppy.

"Lucas," Dr. Garvey said as he watched the dog scamper about, "how does Wednesdays strike you?"

"How does Wednesdays strike me for what?"

"For the day on which Joe or Sang can do acupuncture on small animals in my clinic."

Shortly thereafter we began treating animals with acupuncture in my clinic too on one day each week.

On one of the first Thursdays after we had started acupuncture on small animals, we were asked to treat a miniature poodle named Maria. When I tried to stand the dog on the examining table, the dog collapsed.

"Maria was hit by a car when she was six months old," the man who had brought her in told me. "I've been able to keep her going for six years even though she has been paralyzed. But it's getting harder and harder to cope with."

I put the X rays Mr. Garcia had brought with him on the view box and looked them over. There was a fracture of one of the vertebrae and a severe displacement of the structure. When I looked closely, it was apparent that the shock of the collision with the car had caused a fracture and one part of the spinal column to overlay another part. In any case, it was a dismal situation.

"Very frankly, I think this is a hopeless case," I told Garcia. "I don't even think it is worth it for you to make the contribution to the acupuncture project or to spend the time it will take you to bring the dog in for treatment."

Garcia flared. "It's my time and my money and if I want to come in, I will." Just as suddenly, he calmed down. "Look, doc, the dog got hit by a car three weeks after my wife died. It was her dog. I've been spending money for six years to pay for a baby-sitter to come in and take care of the dog while I am at work. So if I want to spend the money now to try to save her with this thing you are doing . . ."

I relented somewhat. "We'll treat the animal six times. If she responds, we'll go on. If not, we'll stop. Fair enough?"

"Fair enough."

When Bobby Rosen, an acupuncturist who had recently joined the project, stuck his head into the office and announced that "Garcia is here" on a Thursday three weeks later, my heart sank. So far, Maria had not improved at all. After the last two treatments, she had still not been able to take any steps or to stand up on the examining table. There seemed to be no good reason to go on with the three other treatments.

I motioned for Bobby to close the door and come in. "Look, we've got to stop giving this guy hope," I told him when he had stepped inside.

"I agree with you, doc. When you go into the examining room, tell him."

"No, listen, I've got this dachshund to look at right now.

You're the acupuncturist. You go ahead and tell him and tell him I'm sorry."

"Not me, doc. It's your baby."

With a heavy heart, I went to the examining room where Garcia was waiting. Bobby trailed in after me. I smiled weakly, and started to go through the motions of examining the dog. I put my hand under her belly and gently lifted Maria onto her feet. I removed my hand, waiting for her to go down and to give me an excuse for launching into my speech that the time had come to abandon treatment.

Maria, however, stood there. She wobbled. She swayed. But she stayed on her feet. I looked at Bobby. Bobby looked at me.

"That isn't important, is it doc?" Garcia asked when he saw us exchange looks.

"What do you mean isn't it important?" I asked. "Has this happened before?"

"Sure. When we got home from the second treatment, I put her down on her bed and she just stood there. Then, she pushed herself up while she was eating. She hasn't been able to walk, though, so I didn't say anything about it. But, it's important?"

I was overjoyed. "It's damned important."

We treated the dog until she was able to take a few steps without falling over. It was the best we could do—but even that was enough for Garcia.

Word now spread to Hollywood that we were treating small animals with acupuncture. Things had gotten so busy at the Garvey clinic that one of our friends in the Hollywood area had offered us space at his clinic to do acupuncture. There, the acupuncturists treated animals belonging to Doris Day, Lorne Greene, and other Hollywood notables.

Our burgeoning fame, however, was almost the undoing of the acupuncture research program. On one acupuncture day, a reporter from a local television news program called to ask if she could come down with a crew to film us at work. I told her that we were almost done for the day. Undaunted, she said they could be down within an hour. Fifty-five minutes later, there they were.

When I had originally talked to the reporter, I had been hesitant to give permission for her to do a report on our work because I was afraid that it would be too easy to sensationalize what we were doing. But after I had talked some more with the reporter I felt she was a conscientious journalist who would be fair in putting across what we were doing. And, for a while after she and the film crew had arrived, it seemed as if nothing would happen anyway that would give anyone anything very sensational to report. Although she was getting a lot of enthusiastic comments from clients in the office, the crew had nothing to film except a few acupuncturists putting a few needles into small animals unconcernedly lying on examining tables.

Then disaster (as it was to turn out) struck.

At ten minutes to five, just before we were to close the door, one of my clients, a very beautiful, stately blond woman, rushed in. The white sweater she was wearing was covered with blood. In her arms she was carrying a small terrier, unconscious and smeared with blood. Almost hysterical, she told us that the dog had been shot by a neighbor who had been annoyed by its barking. She had come to the office, expecting only to find conventional emergency treatment.

"I'm going to get an intravenous setup to give the dog fluids and blood," I told Bobby after we had hurriedly examined the dog and had found that the shot (a .22 we later learned) had entered through the lower abdomen and had exited through the chest. "It's going to take me a couple of minutes, so why don't you and Joe try acupuncture to control the shock. She's pretty close to being comatose."

I don't think I was gone quite three minutes. When I came to the operating room—where Bobby and Joe had moved her so they could keep an eye on her vital functions with the monitoring equipment I used in surgery and intensive care cases—the dog, wide awake and alert, was sitting on the operating table, trying to bite everyone within her reach. We finally managed to calm her down, sewed up the wounds, and gave her a healthy dose of antibiotics to ward off any potential wound infections.

Even though Jessie had made such a dramatic recovery without the benefit of fluids or transfusions, I wanted to keep her with me to keep an eye on her. That evening, I took Jessie and some intravenous equipment (just in case the acupuncture had provided only a temporary relief against shock) home with me. Sadie was so impressed when I told her about the little terrier that she did not object when I brought the dog to bed with me while I read the newspaper. I had intended to let the dog sleep next to the bed when we turned the lights out. But, when I woke up the next morning, the newspaper was lying on the floor and Jessie was sleeping peacefully on my chest.

That night, the television carried a dramatic report on the way acupuncture had saved a dog's life. So dramatic was the story, that the national network picked it up and broadcast it around the country.

It was, I had to admit to myself, pretty heady stuff—until I got the rumbling call from the president of the Board of Examiners for Veterinary Medicine. Because the board could get apoplectic about anything that reeked of advertising or publicity seeking by a veterinarian, I suspected what the call was all about.

"Younker, if what I hear about these television things are true, you ought to be impeached."

"Impeached?" The Nixon business, I guess, was getting to everyone. I tried to laugh him off. "I don't hold any office."

"You know goddamned well what I mean, Younker. I think you had better drop by my office and we'd better have a word."

The following week I drove out to see him. I took along Andrea Cannon and Bill Garvey to attest to the fact that I was not looking for personal publicity in making the acupuncture program known to the public. And I took Sadie because she looks so sweet and Christian. I wanted to hedge all my bets.

I sat through a withering lecture on self-aggrandizement.

"How can you complain about my getting publicity when I am not getting paid for the thing I'm getting publicity for?" I asked when he finally stopped. "If I got ten thousand acupuncture cases as a result of those television programs, I wouldn't make a nickel. All the money we take in goes into the acupuncture program itself."

The president of the Board of Examiners sneered. "Younker, it's obvious you are getting it back under the table somehow."

I worked hard to control myself. "If you are going to make allegations like that," I answered evenly, "then you have an obligation to audit my books and those of the association we are working with. In fact, I have spent three thousand dollars of my own money getting Chinese literature translated and even paying the acupuncturists when there was not enough money coming in to pay them."

He was not to be shaken in the belief that I was out to become a millioniaire by telling people that I believed in acupuncture.

"I'm sorry, but I just don't believe that anyone will take one or two days off a week from his practice for a year without getting paid for it."

Andrea, who had been sitting quietly by, broke in. "Don, I've known you for ten or twelve years, right? Now, I'm involved in this acupuncture business. They've been doing it out at the ranch. Do you think I'm getting money under the table?"

"No, no, of course not."

"All right, then. You can believe me when I tell you that Younker isn't getting any money under the table either. That is foolish talk."

The president looked at her, almost disappointed in what she had told him. But he recouped. "If you say so, Andrea. Of course, I'll tell you this, Younker. If you *are* working one day a week for no pay, it's pretty unprofessional and demeaning."

Veterinary Catch-22.

The Board of Examiners was acting on the basis of complaints issued by veterinarians who were evidently jealous of the publicity the project was getting. But, when it became obvious that the acupuncture clinic would not be stopped by pinning a dubious publicity charge on me, other efforts were made to squash the research effort. The Board of Examiners ordered us to stop work unless we could: 1) set up a nonprofit organization controlled by veterinarians to substitute for our current organization which had loose connections to U.C.L.A.; 2) open a treatment facility that was independent of any offices where conventional veterinary medicine was being practiced; 3) find someone on the staff of the University of California at Davis Veterinary School, several hundred miles away, to serve on our staff in a supervisory capacity.

But we managed to beat them. Although it was expensive, we set up a nonprofit entity, largely with the help of my personal lawyer who volunteered time to do the necessary legal work. We scraped together enough money to lease Forrest's old clinic. (The lease on it had run out for him and rather than renew it, he had moved to Idaho to practice. The M.D. who owned it was sympathetic to our problems and gave us a very reasonable first-year lease.) And we managed to establish the right connections to the University of California at Davis to satisfy the requirement that we have some academic supervision.

Chapter Twenty-Four

As I looked around the dusty stable and corral and the hordes of flies, I thought to myself how nice it would be to have a nice sterile surgical suite for equine surgery. I was at the Fernwood place to castrate a three-year-old Arabian. But there was just no place where I could do the job without increasing the risk of an infection. Mrs. Fernwood, a tired woman who was struggling to keep her large and expensive house after her husband's death (he had left her with no insurance), watched as I scrutinized the area.

"Doc," she finally said, reading my thoughts. "How about the front lawn? The grass is in good shape."

I didn't particularly like the idea of operating in full view of passing pedestrian and vehicular traffic, but there didn't seem to be much choice. Somewhat unhappily, I went back to the truck to get my bag and the emasculator.

Mrs. Fernwood brought the horse to the front lawn and came over to the truck to watch me lay out and arrange my equipment. She was one of those people who takes a keen interest in everything the doctor does. "What are you going to use on him?"

"I'll give him a little tranquilizer first," I said, glancing over at the Arabian. The horse, aware that something was afoot, was starting to get excited. "Then I'll give him some Demerol and then a local anesthetic."

"A local? Are you kidding? You're not going to knock him out? I never have seen anyone castrate a horse that was standing up. Dr. Purvis does it by knocking them out first."

"A general makes it a lot easier on the veterinarian but there is always the risk the horse will injure himself when he falls down or is waking up. I'd rather do a castration with the horse in a standing position and avoid the possibility that he'll injure himself."

I filled a syringe with the tranquilizer and slowly approached the Arabian. But by now, the horse was in an uproar. He was pawing hard at the manicured lawn and dancing about on the end of the lead shank. As I walked toward him, he backed up, not heeding the soft assurances I was whispering.

Suddenly, he reared up, pawing at the air. Cold fear ran through me. Not because I was afraid that the horse would strike me, but because he was off balance. And, right behind him was the house's living room—and its vast picture window.

An eternity passed as the horse's momentum carried him backwards toward the plate glass. At the very last moment, he stopped, wavered and came back down. I grabbed for the lead rope that Mrs. Fernwood's daughter had dropped and managed to calm down the horse. I injected the tranquilizer and then the Demerol. After scrubbing the horse with surgical scrub soap, I injected the local anesthetic. After that initial scare, the rest of the castration procedure came off smoothly.

That night, at the Equine Veterinarian's meeting, I told my colleagues about the close call I had had with the Arabian colt.

"Having a horse go through a window would have been nothing," Dr. Gerbner said. "I had a horse wind up in a tree during a castration."

"In a tree?" the rest of us called out almost in unison.

"Yeah. It was when we first started to use succinylcholine."

Succinylcholine is a drug that stirs up considerable debate. Some veterinarians and horse people are very much in favor of the drug. They believe that succinylcholine, which acts like curare and paralyzes the horse, is the best drug for castration because it acts very quickly and because, unlike anesthetics, it is quite safe. Others do not like to use the drug because it does nothing to anesthetize the horse. It immobilizes him, but he can still feel everything that is being done to him.

"I was one of the first veterinarians to use it," Gerbner said, wiping his mouth and taking a drink of water in preparation for telling his story. "When word got around, some

244

of the other veterinarians asked me to do a demonstration so they could see how the drug works. I said, line me up a castration and I'll come do it for you.

"When I got to the place where the castration was to be done, I got a little nervous because there was this little crowd there, waiting for me to put on a show. Anyway, someone picked the horse out of the corral and led it to this little hill nearby. The corral was kind of small and it was right in the middle of an orange grove. The hill was grassy and gave us some space in which to work.

"The selling point of succinylcholine is that it is safe. And it is absolutely that—if you use the right dose. But if you give too much, you can paralyze the breathing muscles and suffocate the horse. I was a bit edgy about the whole thing and just to be on the safe side, I cut back on the dose a little bit.

"The horse dropped and I did one side. But just as I started to do the other testicle, the horse leaps to its feet, rears up, falls over backwards, rolls down the steep side of the hill, and lands right on top of an orange tree.

"I couldn't believe it! There I am, standing there, looking down on a half-castrated horse, lying in the tree. Jesus, was I humiliated."

"Did you climb into the tree to finish the job?" someone who was not a succinylcholine admirer asked, unwilling to let the opportunity for a dig go by.

Gerbner ignored the provocation. "Man, I don't even want to tell you what it takes to get a horse out of a tree."

Because Sadie and I were leaving for Mexico for a week's vacation early that evening, I had a very light afternoon scheduled. The most important thing on my agenda was a brief meeting with Denny Myers. Denny was coming in to pick up Glenda, her border collie.

I dreaded the meeting. The dog had been suffering vomiting attacks for almost five months now and, as hard as I tried, I had not been able to find the cause.

When Denny had brought the dog in, she said that Glenda might have swallowed a superball, one of those small, hard, rubber balls that has an exaggerated bounce to it. But conventional X rays, barium X rays, and a battery of other tests had not turned up traces of the ball in the gastrointestinal tract. Just to make sure I was not misreading the X rays, I had asked Denny to bring in a ball similar to the one she thought Glenda had swallowed. We put the ball between the dog and the X-ray table and took more pictures. On that series, the second ball showed up very clearly. I was convinced more than ever that Glenda had not swallowed a ball.

We kept an eye on her in the clinic for a couple of days and managed to stop the vomiting. Denny picked her up, full of hope that Glenda was cured. But a week later, the border collie was back. She had started vomiting again, this time worse than ever. Glenda had been brought in on a day when I was over at the acupuncture clinic and Dr. Mandel, who was covering my regular practice for me, called me to tell me that Glenda was back. He thought, he told me, that he could see something suspicious in Glenda's stomach in one of the barium X rays.

"Marty, if you think there is something in there, go ahead and do an exploratory," I had told him. "I thought I saw something on one view, too, but Dr. Chadwick and his associates felt there was nothing in the films."

Marty did the exploratory and found nothing. Since there had been some biochemical indications that Glenda might have kidney disease, he did a kidney biopsy as well. That test also proved to be negative and we were still without a villain in the piece. I had prescribed more drugs to control the vomiting and, because I thought that perhaps Glenda had developed an allergy to commercial foods, I had also recommended a special, scientifically prepared diet for Glenda.

Nothing helped. The dog would stop vomiting for a few days and then start once again. Desperate, I ran Glenda through test after test. I even began to believe that perhaps a piece of cellophane had entered the stomach and was acting like a valve between the stomach and the esophagus, sometimes allowing food to go through normally, sometimes blocking it and setting off the vomiting. I found nothing. I tested for—and ruled out—acute nephritis, acute pancreatitis, subacute pancreatitis, adrenal cortical insufficiency, gastroenteritis. After a while I began to feel so badly about Glenda that I stopped charging Denny and Bob (her husband) for my services and billed them only for the cost of the tests and the medicine. After a while I even stopped charging them for that.

I consulted other veterinarians who were specialists in different fields of medicine. They could not suggest anything I had not already done.

I was so desperate I had even consulted with an animal psychic. I had met the psychic at one of our acupuncture clinics. She was a nice lady who claimed that animals talked to her. I was highly skeptical, but could not dismiss her out of hand. She had earned a Master's degree and was well on her way to a Ph.D. Moreover, I often see people who do have a very special way with animals, who can go up to a wild, uncontrollable horse, for example, put a hand on its neck and turn it into a soft, gentle creature.

When the psychic had come to my clinic, I had stood to one side as the woman, her pale blue eyes straining with concentration, stared into Glenda's face for several long silent minutes.

"Glenda is very upset," the psychic had finally told me. "She tells me that she is very unhappy with her home life. She says that everybody worries so much about her, it is making her feel even worse. If she were in a new home, a new environment, she would not be under so much pressure and she would feel much better."

"Did she say anything about having swallowed a ball?" I asked.

"No, nothing. All she says is 'this whole thing is my fault, I'm sorry.' "

When Denny came in, she had that hurt look she wore now every time she came for Glenda. "We've controlled the vomiting again," I told her. "I'm going to Mexico for a week. If anything happens, call Dr. Mandel. He'll be covering for me while I'm gone."

The Mexican vacation was everything I needed to get my mind off my problems. We stayed in a lovely little fishing village, south of Brownsville, on the Gulf of Mexico. There were no paved roads and no telephone. The electricity was turned off at nine at night. I say "was" because our lonely village recently became the focal point of a Mexican government plan to turn the area into a major recreational and resort area for tourists.

The walks and rides in the countryside, the strolls along the long, white, sandy beach, and the good dinners at the

El Malecon, a little bar that serves excellent food, relaxed me very quickly.

After dinner one night, we went to the bar, where an American woman was complaining to the bartender about a toothache.

"I can relieve you of the pain," I volunteered, feeling benevolent.

"Oh great! A doctor . . ."

"I'm not a medical doctor," I explained. "I'm an animal doctor but I can still help you out."

The woman's face fell. "Oh, a vet. No, I need a doctor. God! Nothing has helped. Aspirin, codeine. Nothing."

"Acupuncture will work."

"Oh no! I hate needles. I'll take the toothache, thanks."

"I can do it without needles. I'll use acupressure. It will work almost as well."

With some hesitation, she agreed to let me try to do away with the toothache. I pressed one point on her hand—the point called Large Intestine Four—and one on her foot—called Stomach Forty-four. Her toothache vanished.

"Wow!" was all she managed to say for a moment.

"Don't get your hopes up too much," I told her. "The toothache will probably come back in three to four hours. But I'll show you where to press so you can control the pain until you get to your dentist."

Antonio, the owner of El Malecon, was standing off to one side, watching all of this. He was a tall, good-looking man. He was always well dressed. And he always wore expensive jewelry, jewelry I would have guessed should have been beyond the income this small bar in the countryside would generate.

"You are a doctor of animals, señor?" Antonio asked.

I confirmed the fact.

"Then, my friend, you are a gift from God. My poor cat needs help very badly. May I bring him to you?"

Antonio disappeared into his office. When he came back, he was leading a Margay, an exotic feline that looks like a miniature leopard. Not exactly a house cat. The cat, I saw, was limping slightly.

"I am told that if you take the sex organs of the cat, the cat stays nice and does not get mean. Is that right?"

"Yes. How old is he?"

"He is about seven months old."

"Well, I wouldn't wait much longer to do it."

"That is exactly why I spoke to you. I have asked our veterinarian here to do it, but he said I can do it myself. He said I should tie some rubber bands around its *cojones* and that they would fall off by themselves."

"That's one way, true. They do sheep that way sometimes. The rubber band cuts off the circulation to the testicles and then they shrivel up and fall off. But I wouldn't do it that way. It's cruel. Besides, the cat could get a serious infection. I'd have it done with an operation."

"Exactly. But our veterinarian has told me he is not able to do this operation. Are you able to castrate this *tigre?*"

"I could do it now, but I need anesthetic. I'll pick it up at the pharmacy tomorrow."

Antonio beamed.

Things, however, were not to be that simple. The pharmacist refused to sell me the anesthetic without a prescription.

"No problem, doctor," Antonio said when I told him the disappointing news. "I will get the anesthetic for you. You wait here and have a Coca-Cola."

Antonio put on his hat and left. A half hour later he was back with a scalpel, a hemostat, sterile gloves—and the anesthetic from the pharmacist. Unfortunately, he had gotten ten milligram per cc bottles.

"Those are too small," I told him. "I need fifty milligram per cc vials."

Antonio put on his hat again and left. Ten minutes later, fifty milligram per cc vials in hand, he was back.

"That's great, Antonio," I said. "But how did you get them without a prescription?"

Antonio's eyes twinkled. "I have my ways."

We cleared off a table next to the bar, put a fresh tablecloth on it, laid out the tools, knocked out and prepped the cat.

I reached for a scalpel, but Antonio coughed politely. "Doctor Lucas. The cat's eyes. They are still open."

"I know, Antonio. I know you love this cat very much. But don't worry. That is the way the anesthetic works. The cat is out cold. He can't see or feel anything."

Without further incident, I castrated the cat.

The anesthetic I had used was a potent one and animals

can take twelve to twenty-four hours to come out from under its influence. To boot, I had used a little more than usual because sometimes, under a light dose, the animal, even though it cannot feel anything, will make little noises. I didn't think Antonio was the kind of man who wanted to hear little noises coming from his beloved cat while he was under the scalpel.

As a result, the cat was taking longer than usual to return to normal. It had woken up all right, but after eighteen hours had come and gone, the cat was still groggy. It fell off chairs, bumped into tables, knocked over plants.

I was not too worried about all of this until, on the day after the surgery, Sadie and I ran into the local water delivery man. "Boy, Antonio is really worried about his cat," he said when I stopped to chat with him. "I hope it wakes up soon completely."

"It will," I assured him. "Don't worry."

"Oh, I am not worried if it does not come back to normal. It is you should worry, señor."

I didn't like the tone of his voice. "The *tigre* is fine. It just takes a long time to come out from under the drug completely."

He shrugged and grimaced. "Antonio loves that cat very much. And, Antonio is, how do you say it in America, a very important man in this area. They say that two weeks ago only he had a man killed in a town a few kilometers from here. . . ."

"Terrific!" Sadie whispered under her breath.

Luckily (I guess) the cat started to act normal again that evening. After that, I didn't pay for a meal or a drink at El Malecon.

When we got back to Los Angeles the following Sunday night, I called Ben Turley, my veterinary technician, to ask him what was going on. "Mrs. Myers brought Glenda in late last night," he told me. "She wants you to call her as soon as possible."

I hung up and dialed Denny's number. "She was okay most of the week," Denny told me. "But Friday morning she started vomiting again. I called your office yesterday, hoping you'd come back early. Your associate was there and said to bring her in right away. He put her on some medication and on IV feedings but he said it doesn't look good at all this time."

Immediately, I called Chadwick. "I think Glenda is in a lot of trouble," I told him. "Can I come over tomorrow and use your gastroscope? I want to look in her stomach again, just as a last resort."

The next morning, using the gastroscope, which we had placed into her stomach through her esophagus, we looked to see if we could find anything. The organ looked absolutely normal. I was besides myself with frustration.

"Chad," I said. "This dog is dying and I'm at a loss. I think we should do another exploratory, even though Marty already did one. What do you think?"

"We got her down already. Let's open her up."

Don Bates, Dr. Chadwick's technician, and I prepped Glenda for surgery. Chadwick and I started to make the incision as Don busied himself watching the anesthesia machine and the oscilloscope monitoring Glenda's heartbeat.

"She's gone into bradycardia," Don yelled, warning us that a potentially deadly heartbeat irregularity had set in. I tensed. But Don, an unflappable technician, gave Glenda atropine and sodium bicarbonate.

I held my breath as I watched the oscilloscope. The irregular, slow signal became normal again, indicating that a normal heartbeat had been restored.

As soon as the incision was completed and we were in the abdomen, I reached in. Almost immediately, I felt a mass in the small intestine. When I pulled a portion of the gut into the opening, it was obvious that there was a small ball inside the intestine.

We isolated the piece of intestine, packed it off and opened it up. Inside, discolored and slightly corroded by gastric juices, was the superball. I was tremendously relieved—and terribly depressed that I had not found the problem sooner.

"How do you figure we missed it the first time around?" I asked Chadwick.

"I guess it was in the stomach when Marty did his exploratory. But the table was probably tilted and I bet when he pulled on the stomach to palpate it, the ball may have gone well up into the esophagus where he could not feel it. It was a freak accident, that's all."

251

"She sure wouldn't have lived much longer with that ball completely obstructing her intestine."

"That's for sure. She would have died pretty quickly if we hadn't gotten it out."

"All that grief," I said as we stopped to shake hands before I left.

Chadwick put his hand around my shoulder. "It happens," he said.

It sure does, I said to myself as I walked on down the hall, bouncing the ball on the floor. It's the sort of thing that helps keep you humble.

ON SALE WHEREVER PAPERBACKS ARE SOLD
— or use this coupon to order directly from the publisher.

Books that mean better
Health & Nutrition

Diet & Diets

V4518	**CHOLESTEROL COUNTER $1.25** E. Weiss & R. Wolfson. A handy guide to a healthier heart, with a listing of the cholesterol content of most common foods.	
A3228	**THE GREENGROCER $1.50** Joe Carcione How to buy fresh produce at its money-saving best for taste and nutrition.	
V4219	**INTRODUCTION TO LECITHIN $1.25** Howard E. Hill The "miracle" substance that can help improve your circulation, strengthen your heart and control your weight.	
A2043	**THE POISONS IN YOUR FOOD $1.50** W. Longgood An explosive report on the deadly chemicals that have invaded your daily diet.	
P3301	**PROTEIN PLANNER $1.00** E. S. Weiss & R. P. Wolfson How to get the most protein for the least money, with a list of the protein values of the most common foods.	
A2570	**RAW VEGETABLE JUICES $1.50** Dr. N. W. Walker Help nature supply your body's needs and find your way to glowing good health.	
M3222	**STROKES AND THEIR PREVENTION $1.75** Arthur Ancowitz, M.D. A life-saving guide to causes, treatment and prevention of strokes.	
A3595	**THE USE OF HERBS IN WEIGHT REDUCTION $1.50** Richard Heffern A guide to Nature's mysterious herbs that help pare away unwanted pounds.	
A3234	**THE VEGETARIAN WAY OF LIFE $1.50** Hans Holzer How the truly natural foods may determine every aspect of your life.	

NT-15